MAKING
AMERICA'S
BUDGET
POLICY
From the 1980s to the 1990s

MAKING
AMERICA'S
BUDGET
POLICY

From the 1980s to the 1990s

Joseph J. Minarik

M. E. Sharpe, Inc.
Armonk, New York
London, England

Library of Congress Cataloging-in-Publication Data

Minarik, Joseph J., 1949–
    Making America's budget policy from the 1980s to the 1990s / by
Joseph J. Minarik.
      p.   cm.
    ISBN 0-87332-573-7—ISBN 0-87332-621-0 (pbk.)
    1. Budget—United States. 2. Taxation—United States. 3. Budget
deficits—United States. I. Title.
HJ2051.M56   1990
353.0072′2—dc20   89-27503
                                                 CIP

Printed in the United States of America

ED 10 9 8 7 6 5 4 3 2 1

To Bill
swish
buzz
roar

Contents

Foreword

Senator Bill Bradley

This book describes the last five years of what was a long journey for me.

In 1967, after I signed my first contract as a professional basketball player, an attorney asked me, "Do you want to take your pay as salary, as deferred compensation, as fringe benefits, or what?" I said, "I don't know. I just want to be paid well for doing something I love to do." He replied, "It's not that simple."

That was my first contact with the complexity of the federal income tax code.

Then in the mid-1970s, I read some articles by Stanley Surrey, a law professor at Harvard, who had been at the Treasury Department in the early 1960s when President Kennedy proposed his historic tax cuts—which (though no one remembers today) included a substantial broadening of the tax base along with a reduction of tax rates. I was shocked that the tax rates could go as low as President Kennedy proposed if we just closed some loopholes.

So, my personal involvement began with the introduction of the Bradley-Gephardt Fair Tax Act back in 1982. There followed the introduction of the so-called Kemp-Kasten bill in the House of Representatives; then "Treasury I," with President Reagan's strong commitment to tax reform; then "Treasury II," proposed by the president to the Congress; and then the Tax Reform Act of 1986, which so surprisingly became law.

There are, in my view, three basic rationales for tax reform. There is an economic rationale, there is a cultural rationale, and there is a political rationale.

The economic rationale is very simple. If you want long-term, stable, noninflationary economic growth, you need two things. The first is an awareness of the world trading and financial system. The second is the most efficient allocation of resources domestically.

The question is then posed: Which is the more efficient allocator of resources? Is it the Ways and Means Committee and the Finance Committee, or is it the free market? I believe it is the free market. In the past, the tax code was a barrier between the investor and the ultimate investment. Tax reform removes that barrier so that capital is deployed in the most economically efficient way, which will not only generate jobs and wealth, but also enhance our comparative advantage internationally.

That is the economic rationale for tax reform. Succinctly put, the rationale is to invest money to make money, not to lose it for tax purposes. But there is another rationale that I call the cultural rationale.

I think that any taxpayer in this country could express the cultural rationale for tax reform. It is a frustration and an anger with the tax law. I remember a few years ago when I appeared on a call-in show in New Jersey. A caller said, "You know, I really like that tax proposal you have made." I asked, "Why?" He said, "I pay an effective tax rate of 38 percent, and my next-door neighbor, who makes the same income I do, pays an effective tax rate of 6 percent. He thinks that I am stupid because I don't spend all my time trying to figure out how I can lose money to pay less taxes. But," he said, "I am a chemist. I like doing what I do best—working in the laboratory. And with this tax reform, I will be able to do that and my neighbor will have to pay his fair share."

The cultural rationale for tax reform is that people with equal incomes should pay equal tax. Just a few facts convey that meaning. The first fact: In the years just preceding tax reform, the effective tax rate paid by many people who made more than $1 million in this country was about 17 percent. This is what they actually paid. Many middle-income families paid more than that.

The second fact: In 1969, there were 10,000 tax shelter cases in some stage of audit or litigation. The Commissioner of the Internal Revenue Service told the Congress that, in 1985, there were 263,000 tax shelter cases in some stage of audit or litigation.

The third fact: In 1967, the value of all tax loopholes was about $36 billion. By 1986, the value of all loopholes had grown to over $400 billion.

I was on a dais in New Jersey in 1984, seated next to an executive of a major corporation, who said to me during the salad, "You know, Senator, I have a problem with my son." For a politician, that is what I call a threshold question: Do you follow up on it or do you leave it? I was up for reelection, so I followed up on it.

He said, "My son is twenty-seven years old and he works for a successful corporation, but all he can think about is how to avoid paying taxes. I tell him, 'Look, go to work, learn your profession, move up in the company, pay your taxes; don't try to avoid it.' But all he thinks about is trying to avoid paying taxes." Then he said, "Senator, you know my concern? I am afraid there is a whole generation of young people out there who will grow up believing they have no responsibility to pay for the functions of government, and I am worried."

He should be worried. We should all be worried because voluntary compliance, which has characterized the income tax system from the beginning, is eroding. That might be why the seventh largest economy in the world is the underground economy of the United States. That might also be why when, in 1981, a pollster named Dan Yankelovich asked a sample of the American people, "Do you think you will get ahead if you abide by the rules," 81 percent of the people answered "No."

I think the rules that they were thinking of were the tax rules, under which equal incomes did not pay equal tax. With tax reform, there will be a restoration of trust in the tax rules. So that is the cultural rationale.

Even though there is an economic rationale (let the market allocate the resources) and a cultural rationale (equal incomes should pay equal tax), laws are made in Washington, and so there must be a political rationale as well.

There is a slogan, in the political rationale, that Democrats argue for tax reform because it allows them to be for growth and equity simultaneously; and Republicans are for tax reform because it is a realignment issue. But those are just slogans. If we really want to find the political rationale for tax reform, we have to look at who the taxpayers are, and we have to remember that, in 1984, more people signed income tax returns than voted for president.

There are only two facts that we have to remember about who the taxpayers are. The first fact: The median income in the United States in 1986 was $23,450. About half the taxpayers earned more, about half earned less. The second fact: 85 percent of all taxpayers earned under $40,000.

Sometimes in Washington, politicians talk as if people making

$75,000, or $80,000, or $90,000, or $100,000 are middle-income people. People certainly have a tendency to spend up to their incomes, and therefore everybody feels pinched. But fully 97 percent of all taxpayers earned under $75,000. So keep in mind who these taxpayers are as you think about tax reform.

The key to understanding the political rationale, in addition to knowing who the taxpayers are, is in the figures on the value of loopholes. The loopholes in 1967 were worth $36 billion; the loopholes in 1986 were worth over $400 billion. In that period from 1967 to 1986, because of economic growth and inflation, the Federal Government had growing revenues, and had to decide what to do with them. One of the things it did was spend some more in certain program areas. But what it did most was increase the number and value of loopholes from $36 billion in 1967 to over $400 billion in 1986. The one thing the Congress did not do with the new revenues was to recycle them to middle-income taxpayers through lower tax rates, or to low-income taxpayers through increased exemptions and increased standard deductions. As a result, more and more low- and middle-income taxpayers paid a greater and greater proportion of their family budgets in taxes.

So when members of Congress argued against tax reform because they had not heard anyone clamoring to support it, that did not surprise me. They had heard from a number of special-interest groups who opposed it. When a politician mentions the word "taxes," people figure, "Whoops, here it comes, another grab for my hard-earned money."

Tax reform was one bill that was different, particularly for middle- and low-income taxpayers. The one thing that every member of Congress liked was that this bill took six million poor people off the tax rolls. This was a major accomplishment. Likewise, low- and middle-income taxpayers had their taxes reduced. For example, a single parent with three children making $12,000 now pays $1,200 less in income tax, an 83 percent tax cut. A couple with two children making $15,000 receives a tax cut of $826.

A bill that takes six million poor people off the tax rolls and that gives a sizable tax cut to low-income working families underlines and emphasizes the values we all share—values that say work instead of welfare, dignity instead of despair.

What about the middle class? Just a few facts and definitions. Let us define middle class as a household with an income of $19,000 to $47,000. In 1978, the middle class (defined as $19,000 to $47,000 in constant dollars) represented 52 percent of the American taxpayers. By 1984, that group included only 44 percent of the American taxpayers. So what happened to those Americans who left the middle class? Over two-thirds of them, or 70 percent, dropped down under the middle-class boundary of $19,000; their economic circumstances deteriorated.

We have an obligation to reverse that trend. I would argue that tax reform did reverse that trend. First of all, four out of five taxpayers now pay no more than a 15 percent marginal tax rate. Before bracket creep accelerated in the mid-1960s, four out of five taxpayers paid no more than the bottom tax rate (then 20 percent). Tax reform returned us to the time when four out of five taxpayers paid no more than the bottom rate.

Middle-income taxpayers also kept their biggest deductions in tax reform. They kept their mortgage interest deductions and their property tax deductions; they kept their $2,000 deductible IRA; they kept their charitable contributions deduction; they kept their credit for child-care expenses. Those middle-class persons, who represent the vast majority of taxpayers, not only got a 15 percent tax rate, but they also kept the deductions that they most use.

In the first year after passage of the bill, 69 million Americans earning under $50,000 in income got a tax cut, and only 12 million got a tax increase. But the value of tax reform to the middle-income taxpayer was not what happened in that snapshot, because tax reform was not a one-year tax cut, but a reform of the system. The middle-income family pays less of its additional income in taxes because it is still in the 15 percent bracket. In fact, some families that were in the 33 percent bracket moved to the 15 percent bracket. A family of four can earn over $40,000 before it is bumped into the higher bracket. And even then, it will pay only 28 percent.

So as a result of tax reform, no longer will people in poverty pay more tax than some millionaires. No longer will some middle-income taxpayers pay a higher tax rate than some multimillion-dollar corporations.

What about simplicity? For 13 to 14 million Americans who once itemized their deductions, the increased standard deduction gives both a tax cut and freedom from the record keeping required to fill out the long form.

So tax reform has an economic rationale, a cultural rationale, and a political rationale. Through tax reform, Democrats and Republicans have joined together to do something positive for America. This should give the American people greater confidence about our ability to deal with the other complex and controversial economic issues we face.

Ultimately tax reform is about a debate as old as the nation, and prominent in the Federalist Papers: Is a legislator's job to represent one or another narrow interest, or to represent the general interest? I believe the latter, and I believe that in tax reform, the Senate and the House acted in the general interest.

I thank Joe Minarik for all the rabbits he pulled out of the hat, and for his expertise, hard work, and generous commitment to tax reform—all of which are evident in this volume.

At least for a time, those of us who worked for tax reform have won. I am proud of what we did. If there is one lesson that I personally take away from this effort, it is this: If you work hard, if you think a problem through, if you think about how to communicate it and how it affects people's lives, if you recognize that it takes more than just one person, that it takes many people to succeed—then you can overcome even the most entrenched interests and the most difficult obstacles.

Acknowledgments

Many friends aided in the work presented in this volume through their ideas and support. Particular acknowledgments are attached to the individual chapters. Special mention is due to present and former colleagues: Benjamin A. Okner, Joseph A. Pechman, and Emil M. Sunley at The Brookings Institution; Valerie L. Amerkhail and James M. Verdier at the Congressional Budget Office; and John L. Palmer, Rudolph G. Penner, and Isabel V. Sawhill at The Urban Institute.

Charles R. Hulten and Charles F. Stone, former colleagues at The Urban Institute, provided countless insights that I struggle to remember over countless hamburgers that I struggle to forget. Marcia Aronoff and Gina Despres afforded equally valuable thoughts and feedback, though their taste in lunches was fortunately lighter.

Without Bill Bradley there would be no story to tell. His trust is a treasured memory for me, and his political courage and hard work are an invaluable model for anyone who aspires to public service.

After the work on this book was completed, Representative Lee H. Hamilton offered me the position of Executive Director of the Joint Economic Committee of the U.S. Congress. I would like to thank Representative Hamilton for his generous permission to "go on the record" with this volume. It should be understood that the opinions expressed here are my own, and should not be associated with the committee, Chairman Hamilton, or any other member.

Finally, I thank my wife, Eileen, my daughters, Mara and Sara, and my "Italian daughter," Paola Filippi, who have helped me in ways that they could never understand.

PART I
INTRODUCTION

1 • The Making of Tax and Fiscal Policy: An Overview

This volume is a collection of papers written during the 1980s—a decade with the most violent swings in federal fiscal policy in recent peacetime memory. These policy fluctuations affected not only the size of the nation's fiscal deficit, but how its revenue was collected. The papers themselves range from nonpartisan evaluations of our policies and prospects to advocacy of specific policy initiatives, but they are all written from a common perspective—specifically, one that was hostile to the 1981 tax cuts, but supportive of more fundamental income tax reform. Therefore, the papers tell a common story.

The fiscal challenges of the 1980s were twofold. The decade dawned with the emergence of the economy from the short but deep recession of 1979–80, and the consequent bulging deficit. The recession had been precipitated by the second oil shock of the 1970s, and with inflation and interest rates riding high, the public was dissatisfied with its economic leadership.

The author would like to express his appreciation to Marcia Aronoff, Livia Bardin, Peter L. Baumbusch, Bill Bradley, Gina Despres, Richard A. Gephardt, Jane G. Gravelle, Charles R. Hulten, Jim Jaffee, Bob Klayman, Lawrence F. O'Brien III, Joseph A. Pechman, Emil M. Sunley, Tom Troyer, James M. Verdier, Fred Wertheimer, and Mike Wessell for helpful comments and conversations. He would also like to thank Richard B. Booth, Timothy A. Cohn, Robin Mary Donaldson, Todd E. Easton, Nancy E. O'Hara, Arthur Morton, Katherine J. Newman, and Laurent R. Ross for research and programming assistance during his work on tax reform. None of the above should be implicated in any errors. This paper is a product of the *Changing Domestic Priorities* project which is funded by a consortium of foundations and corporations, principally the Ford Foundation and the John D. and Catherine T. MacArthur Foundation. Opinions expressed herein are the author's alone and should not be attributed to The Urban Institute, its officers, trustees, or funders.

In addition, however, the nation was unhappy with its method of collecting revenues. Over the preceding decade, hostility toward the income tax—the primary means of funding the federal government— had risen to a near-boil. Generic antitax sentiment had already taken its toll at the state and local level with the "tax revolt" of the late 1970s. Now the tax revolt was to reach the national level in a change of administration, and of the leadership of the Senate and the ideological balance of the House. In the wake of these changes, the nation's fiscal posture was to be altered radically.

The income tax was cut drastically, with both an across-the-board reduction of individual income tax rates of 23 percent, and an enormous expansion of a range of tax preferences, especially those for businesses. The effect was twofold. First, the income tax, the object of such dissatisfaction, was made less burdensome; and second, the federal budget deficit was increased substantially. The objective of this exercise, according to its proponents in the administration and the Congress, was to stimulate the supply side of the economy through additional incentives to work and invest, and to constrain the growth of federal spending. With the help of spending cuts on the domestic side of the budget, these influences were predicted to overcome the first-round revenue loss and a substantial increase in defense spending, and balance the budget in three years.

Reality was somewhat less kind. For one thing, by the best indicator, public esteem for the income tax was not improved by the large tax cuts—the annual poll of the Advisory Commission on Intergovernmental Relations showed no decline in popular hostility. The public was apparently as displeased by the explosion of tax preferences, especially those benefitting businesses, as it was relieved by the lifting of a substantial share of the individual income tax burden.

And even more seriously, the economy fell into another, even deeper, recession. The deficit mushroomed to record size, and even after the onset of economic recovery and the herculean efforts of the Congress, it continued well outside of historical bounds. The nation's debt, and therefore its long-term debt service costs, escalated inexorably. Further, our excessive demands for credit came to be filled by foreigners, raising the price of our currency and throwing the nation into a continuing trade deficit.

Thus begins our story. It is the story of a two-front war to improve both the nation's method of collecting revenues and its overall fiscal posture. On the former front, the story is left with apparent success but lingering vulnerabilities. On the latter, it ends with apparent failure reprieved by good economic fortune into a lingering near-crisis. Thus, on neither front is this war yet terminated.

Part II of this volume provides a more complete description of the policy environment of the early 1980s. Chapter 2 sets the budgetary stage by discussing federal revenues in the context of the deficit. It sets forth the history of the tax system as of the early 1980s, and examines closely the 1981 tax cuts and the Congress' first attempt to remedy the resulting budget deficit in 1982. It follows with an analysis of the policy options for dealing with the deficit.

One of the options discussed in chapter 2 is a radical restructuring of the income tax—the wholesale elimination of numerous preferences, coupled with the reduction of income tax rates to a level low enough to nearly compensate for the broadening of the income tax base, but high enough to retain a margin of the proceeds to reduce the deficit. Chapter 3 takes up that approach in more detail, from the tax policy perspective. It considers the pressures on the income tax from all directions—the public hostility, the mismeasurement of income in times of inflation, and the double taxation of corporate-source income—and the policy options for dealing with them. It concludes that tax reform in the traditional sense—the broadening of the income base and the reduction of marginal tax rates—could mitigate all of the problems, while making an additional contribution to the reduction of the deficit.

As the 1980s developed, it became apparent that the nation would attempt to "muddle through" on its budget deficit problem. The short-term threats to our economic well-being thankfully failed to material-ize, with the unfortunate side effect that all sense of urgency was lost and the long-term costs of the deficit proceeded to mount. At the same time, however, interest was piqued in the potential for fundamental tax reform. Part III deals with the economic and political issues surround-ing tax reform as they evolved during the 1980s, from the gestation of the issue through the legislative process.

In the judgment of the author as well as numerous other observers, the growth of tax reform from a decades-old "impossible dream" into a live political issue was largely the result of the efforts of Senator Bill Bradley, who along with Representative Richard A. Gephardt spon-sored the Fair Tax Acts of 1982 and 1983. These bills demonstrated the potential for a dramatic reduction of tax rates through the elimination of tax preferences. As chapter 4 argues, however, they also showed the way to improving the public trust in the revenue system and refocusing the energies of our economy onto productive activity.

The tax reform coalition was quite diverse. Some supporters of the 1981 law thought of the elimination of preferences and of rate graduation—thus, a single-rate or "flat-rate" tax—as the logical culmination of their efforts. This school of thought provided a counterpoint to the graduated-rate theme enunciated by Bradley. Chapter 5 is an attempt to reconcile these themes, and to argue for the primacy of tax preference repeal and the equity of the distribution of the tax burden in fulfilling the potential of tax reform.

Tax reform received a crucial boost when the Treasury submitted its own plan to the President in November of 1984. Chapter 6 lays out the major issues raised by the Treasury approach, and the choices faced by the President in taking his initiative to the Congress. Then, in the legislative process, the pain of tax reform often came to overwhelm the potential. Chapter 7 describes the economic and political issues that played major roles in the deliberations of the House and the Senate, plus the stories of the near-interment of tax reform on the floor of the House, and its second miraculous resuscitation in the Senate Finance Committee.

Part IV of this volume provides a retrospective of the outcome of the tax reform process. Chapter 8 weighs the final product against the potential. It underlines the areas of the new law that appear most short of the ideal and most vulnerable to revision, but it concludes that the realization could well fulfill the potential.

Chapter 9 is an account of the tax reform process. It begins with the historical background of the development of the tax law and the growth of its weaknesses, and the corresponding awakening of interest in tax reform. It explains the flaws in the 1981 law, and how they created the opportunity for an initiative toward tax reform. It shows how the Bradley-Gephardt effort capitalized on that opportunity, and how it framed the tax reform issue to maximize the probability of success in the debate. Finally, it provides an account of the legislative process itself, highlighting the key events and contributions.

Chapter 10 provides still further perspective with a view of the reactions of the taxpayers, and the development of some of the key issues cited in chapter 8. Chapter 10 concludes that the new law may well have weathered a painful start and reached a period of basic stability, despite the threats that unquestionably remain.

While the nation achieved tax reform, it did manage to muddle through on the budget deficit; short-term economic dislocations have been avoided, and a record of consistent, if modest, economic growth has been achieved. However, the risks of a deficit shock transmitted through the financial markets still remain; and the long-term burden of the deficit has accumulated in the form of an enormous national debt coupled with international imbalances. Chapter 11 closes the volume by bringing the deficit issue up to date. It explains the short-term risks caused by the nation's reliance on foreign credit, and how those risks could materialize in a fashion similar to Black Monday of 1987. It discusses how the overall budget deficit erodes our living standards over the long term, and negates the separate accumulation of a reserve for Social Security's obligations for the retirement of the baby boom generation early in the next century. It shows how the structure of the budget will make any initiative on the deficit difficult and painful. Finally, it identifies areas of the budget, including both outlays and taxes, where deficit savings might be achieved. This sobering accounting finds that even a long list of politically adventurous steps would leave the budget far from its ideal state of providing a long-term accumulation of capital. The deficit battle, therefore, is hardly begun.

What does this decade of fiscal policy change portend for the future?

Certainly, the biggest disappointment of tax reform was its failure to deal with the deficit. An important opportunity was lost when at least some small fraction of the proceeds of broadening the tax base was not retained to move the budget toward balance.

But this shortcoming was neither a conceptual flaw of tax reform nor a sign of some weakness of tax reformers. President Reagan declared emphatically that he would accept no tax increase as a part of tax reform. Those who wished to address the deficit in tax reform could do so only with the certainty that their efforts would be erased by a politically appealing veto. So deficit reduction was never on the menu of tax reform because of the President's preference, not because of any limitation of the concept.

Still, given this inability to deal with the deficit, some commentators and members of Congress argued that tax reform was irrelevant at best. Some went even further, and suggested that tax reform was a diversion to prevent action on the deficit. These claims, in retrospect, seem inaccurate. It is especially unreasonable to suppose that, absent the tax reform effort, the Congress would have undertaken a major deficit reduction initiative instead. President Reagan's stricture against a tax increase in tax reform would have held at least as strongly against a free-standing tax increase; and this restriction complicated any movement toward consensus on the spending side as well. In short, the notion that the resources of time and effort that the Congress expended on tax reform would otherwise have been devoted to deficit reduction is fanciful at best.

And as to the potential for future deficit reduction, tax reform was hardly irrelevant. If tax revenues are to be increased, as the vast majority of experts agree will be necessary, the new income tax can provide the revenue more fairly and at a lower economic cost. The potential remains for significant broadening of the tax base; with the new, lower statutory tax rates, the defense of any remaining tax preference will be less convincing. And if tax rates must be raised, with the new broader tax base, the number of percentage points of increase would be less than under the prior law. Starting from a base of tax rates so far below pre-1986 (and especially pre-1981) levels, even the worst case would leave economic incentives greatly enhanced.

There should be little doubt that deficit reduction is now the highest remaining economic priority for the United States. And sadly, the 1988 election campaign was a second missed opportunity. In fact, the dissembling from both camps, and especially the irresponsible pledge of "no new taxes" from one, has established an unfortunate new standard for candor (or the lack of it) that may limit future candidates.

At some point, with some good fortune and political courage, the deficit imperative will be addressed. But until that day and even beyond it, there remains the question of how we use our scarce budgetary resources to address our national needs. The 1986 tax reform can lead us toward more sound policies across a broad range of such issues.

Two key themes of tax reform were government neutrality toward the allocation of investment, and elimination and reduction of the tax burdens on poor and near-poor families. Each of these themes, and our experience in articulating them, has potentially useful applications in the making of other economic policy choices.

Where We Came From

The old tax law was the casualty of years of economic war—not in the marketplace, but in the halls of the Congress. Every interest group, convinced of its own importance to the nation, sought an "incentive"—in plain language, a subsidy—through the tax law. Those with political clout succeeded. And with every new subsidy came more petitioners, arguing that they needed comparable subsidies to compete. Equity was never sought through the removal of existing subsidies, only by the addition of new ones.

The examples over the years are legion. Rapid tax depreciation of buildings was enacted to encourage construction; then, because new construction was so attractive, building refurbishers pleaded simple justice in asking for a tax credit for rehabilitation. Oil deposit owners were given a special exclusion for the depletion of their reserves; there followed owners of every other imaginable mineral reserve, from clam shells to clay used for flower pots, asking for equal treatment. Immediate deduction of costs of research and development was allowed, in order to encourage innovation; so along came investors in machinery asking for faster depreciation of their costs. The list goes on and on.

This process made our very law a battleground for competing interests. It pitted one industry against another in a fight that had nothing to do with economic progress or prosperity. It forced even the most well-meaning legislators to promote their parochial interests in order to survive politically. With raw pork on the table, no Congressman could let a challenger argue that, "My incumbent opponent voted against a tax break for this district." This led to extremes of regional warfare, on the one hand, and temporary truces resulting in costly logrolling ("You vote for my tax break and I'll vote for yours"), on the other.

The resulting tax privileges were patently unfair; those with political influence got theirs, but others got less or nothing at all. Tax shelter operators pulled several tax loopholes together and often paid little or no tax on considerable incomes. And so unfairness was a key argument for tax reform.

But people came to understand that these tax preferences were bad economics as well. Tax breaks made favored businesses look better than they really were, and masked opportunities in other areas. Tax savings lured people into building shopping centers and office buildings rather than factories, for instance, even when retail and office vacancy rates were high. Meanwhile, the high tax rates that were needed to pay for big tax subsidies held back many profit-making businesses, and made borrowing at tax-deductible interest rates far too attractive.

The great majority of members of Congress came to understand that tax reform meant fairness *and* growth. The value of our gross national product is determined in the marketplace, not in the Congress. The multitude of public laws that attempted to measure the relative value of constructing a new building or restoring an old one, of drilling for oil or digging for clay, or of working in the lab or working on the shop floor, could not help but err. No committee is wise enough to pronounce economic value on such a large scale; the sectors of our economy that are either starved for capital or bloated to a state of sloth by such laws will be no match for fit competitors from abroad.

And just as tax reform conserves our economic resources, so does it conserve our political energies; just as the old tax law was divisive, so is the new one unifying. By aiming for a fairer law with fewer special favors, the Congress erected a barrier against the next petitioner swaggering toward the trough. So government can exert more of its effort on solving our common economic problems, and less at bickering over whose tax handout is bigger.

These lessons—the role of the market in economic growth, and the political costs of government intervention in the economy—became clearer as the tax reform debate wore on, and in the end, the new law passed overwhelmingly. But we must carry those lessons on to the new economic policy issues, including those that were prominent in the 1988 campaign.

Our Next Round of Choices: "Competitiveness"

For most of this decade, many prominent U.S. manufacturing firms have lost ground to their foreign competitors. As our trade deficit has risen, so has our concern over our industrial future. With this concern have come proposed remedies.

Some parts of these so-called "competitiveness" policies, within reasonable limits, may be constructive. Additional basic research in universities can generate valuable new ideas in many fields. Retraining of displaced workers is both compassionate and efficient if all of our human resources are to be utilized fully.

But other proposals under the competitiveness banner move in the wrong direction. Some are throwbacks to the "industrial policy" debate of a few years ago. The verdict of that debate, which was fought over the merits of tripartite boards (of business, labor, and government) and federal financing banks for industry, was to avoid such interference in the free market.

The resurrection of industrial policy has been fairly subtle. Some of the states have expanded their traditional menu of tax abatement subsidies used to lure businesses from other locations. New approaches include low-interest-rate loans as "seed money" for new businesses; grants to firms in favored, high-tech industries; subsidized rent in industrial parks; and so on. There followed proposed extensions in a federal competitiveness policy, to include market development assistance, employment subsidies, and other such devices.

Testimonials of successful firms that have benefitted from the state programs ("We couldn't have made it without that loan") are now exhibited as evidence that these policies work. They are no such thing. Subsidized businesses are certainly more likely to succeed than unsubsidized ones (at least in the short run); their success is no proof of the wisdom of the subsidy. The testimonials no one will ever see are from other firms in the same line of business that fail because of the subsidized competition; and from firms in other lines of business that fail because a subsidized business, with the help of a government, has elbowed in front of them in the queue for credit.

At bottom, all industrial policies are equivalent to cash subsidies, just like the tax loopholes repealed in last year's tax reform bill. A cut-rate loan is the same as a cash subsidy used to pay interest; subsidized rent is the same as a cash subsidy used to pay for office space. A federal market development program is the same as a cash grant used to buy advertising. Such proposals ignore the valuable lessons of the tax reform debate, and run in precisely the opposite direction.

Just like the old tax law, most proposed competitiveness policies are unavoidably divisive. We do not have enough cash to subsidize everyone; so who gets the money? It is unrealistic to assume that anyone or any group knows enough to place that money better than our financial markets. And it is naive to assume that the Congress or any executive agency will distribute the funds on purely economic grounds. The political price that we will pay will come in the Congressional infighting among members with seniority and power, in the pursuit of local advantage, and in the mutual backscratching. The economic cost will come in the higher taxes that all businesses will have to pay (implicitly or explicitly) to raise the funds for the programs, and in the higher interest rates that unsubsidized firms will be charged for their seed money.

Such competitiveness policies are a clear echo of the broken-down tax policies that we rejected in 1986. A different set of firms (maybe) would get the subsidies, but the results, political and economic, would be the same.

Our Next Round of Choices: Trade

While competitiveness advocates seek to improve the performance of U.S. firms, some others want to alter the terms of trade with other nations. These analysts contend that our firms are handicapped by restrictive trade practices abroad, and that the U.S. should retaliate in kind.

The case that trade restrictions by other countries have caused the recent deterioration of our trade balance is weak. The trade practices of our competitors have hardly changed in the past six years, and so the precipitate drop in our trade balance over the same period cannot be assigned to unfair practices abroad. This is not to deny that unfair practices exist, but only to put them in perspective.

Even if foreign barriers are not the cause of our trade deficit, we might still try to make protection a part of the cure. Certainly, there are domestic producers under pressure from imports who argue that they could prosper with some temporary relief. But again, any quota or tariff for a specific industry is no different from a cash subsidy; a firm can use the freedom from competition to increase sales or prices, and can invest the added profits or just pass them on to the shareholders. Protection for one sector is no less costly to the rest of the economy than is a tax used to finance a cash subsidy: businesses and consumers have to pay more for imports subject to a quota or tariff, or use more expensive or less efficient substitutes. So just like some competitiveness policies, protectionism is a U-turn from the principles we learned and understood in the debate over tax reform.

Like any policy of handing out subsidies, protectionism would be profoundly divisive. Thinking only of its own profit, any firm with foreign competitors (unless it depended on imported goods as inputs to its production) would like to have protection. So if we all must pay to protect an industry, how many industries should we protect? And which ones? Again, our political system is forced to play referee in a divisive dispute among industries and regions. And other nations could choose to retaliate with new barriers against U.S. exports. Our farmers, our successful manufacturers, and our high technology sectors would be prominent targets. U.S. banks and indebted developing nations would join in the fray, fearing that a trade war would trigger numerous national defaults. So we would have a debate not only among industries seeking the head of the line for protection, but also between those and successful firms who would fear that new foreign barriers would rob them of their success. Many firms who buy and sell in international markets are not sure where their interest lies; can the Congress do better in these circumstances?

The Risks of Government Intervention

To see how protectionism and industrial policy can backfire, consider an admittedly extreme example.

Suppose the U.S. slide-rule industry is hit hard by a flood of cheap pocket calculators. To save the jobs of the slide-rule workers, the federal government provides a subsidy to cover the industry's losses. But as calculators become cheaper and cheaper, the losses grow; and so does the subsidy, becoming a progressively heavier burden on the rest of the economy. Suppose the calculators are imported. The only way to shore up the still-failing slide-rule industry is to add a calculator quota to the subsidy. That keeps the slide-rule makers going, all right; but it also forces U.S. scientists and engineers to saw away on slide rules while their foreign counterparts are punching calculators. U.S. costs rise and technology remains stagnant while other nations leap ahead. Before long, still more U.S. firms are asking for subsidies and protection; in time, the economy becomes a museum of industrial archaeology.

This example is extreme, but the point is correct. A U.S. firm seeking a cash subsidy or protection may not have its sales falling to zero, as would our hypothetical slide-rule maker after the introduction of the calculator; but a firm at a technological disadvantage could easily need growing protection or subsidization over time just to stay above water. A quota on competing imports might not force U.S. producers to use technological relics in their production; but it could force them to pay more for their inputs, and thereby put them at a significant disadvantage against *their* competitors abroad.

But perhaps the key objection to such an example would be that the nation would not subsidize or protect such clearly obsolete industries; it would pick only those that could recover to profitability. But how do we know that? If a firm in trouble has a clear route to recovery, then it can turn itself around. If it needs outside capital and its prospects are good, then the market will provide the funds. But if outside lenders and investors will not take a chance on a firm, based on their knowledge from direct participation in those markets, why should we presume that the federal government's judgment would be any better—especially with the enormous political pressures to "do something for my district"? And with each such government subsidy taking resources from some other sector of the economy, do we really believe that such government-mandated transfers of capital will leave the economy better off on balance?

Our Economic Policy Goals and Strategy

The U.S. achieved rapid economic growth after World War II, when much of the rest of the world was still rebuilding. Then, our competitors were weak. Now, our margin for error is much smaller. We cannot afford to waste our resources on new businesses and investments that are less than the best. That means that we cannot substitute government edicts for the verdict of the marketplace. Further, the adjustment to living in a more competitive world will strain our political institutions. That means that we cannot waste our political energies on disputes among petitioners for public subsidies.

On both economic and political grounds, industrial policies and trade protection push in the wrong direction. They allow arbitrary judgments to take the place of the market in moving our resources among industries; and they pit industries and regions against one another in bidding for public subsidies and protection. This process could only reduce our economic well-being and distract our political institutions from our real needs.

The 1986 Tax Reform Act follows fundamentally different principles. Because only real economic success—determined in the marketplace—contributes to growth and prosperity, the new tax law rewards that success with lower tax rates—and removes costly subsidies that prop up unsuccessful firms and provide windfalls to successful firms. To insure fairness, the law cuts taxes directly and substantially for low- and moderate-income persons. And extra relief is directed to low-income working parents through the earned income tax credit—in a fashion that (unlike an increase in the minimum wage) would not add to business costs. These twin principles—letting the market provide the rewards, while channeling relief directly to persons who need it—apply to all economic policy issues, not just taxation.

Letting the market render its verdict and eliminating business subsidies—tax and otherwise—means that only firms that produce will prosper. But that is what competitiveness is all about. As a political theme, real competitiveness—with losers as well as winners—is unattractive. American compassion and concern for the underdog lead us to rally around those who are under pressure. We don't want to see workers lose their jobs. But our public commitment—and our public policy relief—should go to *people*, not to their *jobs*. Applying the "law of the jungle" to people is heartless; applying it to businesses is essential. Not all business failures can be reversed, and it can be counterproductive to try.

Is this abandoning the American worker? Not if we stick to principle and put the policy relief on the worker, where it belongs. We can, as a society, make a commitment of assistance in retraining, relocation, and temporary income support to workers who are displaced by technological change or foreign competition. This commitment must be a fair bargain; in return, a worker must be willing to retrain and relocate. Such a commitment could not eliminate the risks of competition in a world of technological change, but no one—not even the federal government—can guarantee that any worker can keep the same job, in the same location, at the same real wage, forever. Consider how few of today's jobs existed ten, or twenty, or thirty years ago, and the inevitability of industrial change becomes quite clear. But a commitment to the worker would ease the pain of unavoidable change. And it would allow the market to render its verdict, leaving our economy free to use the latest technology to compete and grow.

The correct policy response to slow growth and unbalanced trade is not yet clear; but we do know that it should be defined in human, not industrial, terms. We must educate our youth to understand the technology around them. We must help today's workers to adapt to change. They, not some benevolent bureaucracy, or committee, or board, will find the opportunities ahead.

So industrial policies and protectionism are doomed to fail. Their focus is misplaced. They substitute imperfect government edicts for the ultimate authority in world economic competition, the free market; and they distract and degrade our governmental institutions by making them referees in contests over pork. The next task of economic policy is not to hand out subsidies and protection to the highest legislative bidder. Instead, we should follow the lead already set by the 1986 tax reform law: get the government out of the business of handing out subsidies; reward real success in the marketplace; and recognize that a competitive society will have losers as well as winners, and that a compassionate society will act accordingly.

PART II
THE POLICY ENVIRONMENT
OF THE 1980s

2 • Tax Policy in Historical Perspective

By now, there is almost unanimous agreement that the federal budget will be in substantial deficit for the foreseeable future, notwithstanding the prospect of sustained recovery from our recent deep recession, unless government policies change. This paper explains the recent changes in the federal tax system and discusses several tax increase options designed to narrow the budget gap. The search for more revenue can open the entire federal tax system to wholesome scrutiny. The effects of the tax system on overall economic efficiency, through reduced incentives for productive activity and distortions of resource allocation, are now widely discussed. And at the same time, as opinion polls show, the public increasingly believes that the federal tax system is unfair. So even people who want only an alternative way to collect the current level of revenues may welcome an airing of tax policy issues.

The first section of this paper shows how economic and tax policy developments led to the watershed legislation of 1981 and 1982, while the second section explains those major tax bills. Section three explores the current policy dilemma and potential strategies for dealing with it, and a closing section weighs the merits of the available options.

The Federal Tax System Since World War II

At the end of World War II, the United States inherited its first peacetime mass tax system. The pressures of war finance had required new

Reprinted with permission from *Federal Budget Policy in the 1980s*, The Urban Institute, Washington, D.C., 1984, pp. 209–242. © The Urban Institute.

levels of government revenues, and so federal tax collections, which had grown from only 3.8 percent of the gross national product (GNP) in 1929 and 5.5 percent in 1939, leaped to 19.5 percent in 1946. Federal tax receipts as a percentage of GNP since 1946 have changed little, at least in relation to the leap in the World War II years (see Table 2.1); the peak tax share of GNP in 1981 exceeded the 1946 figure by less than two percentage points.

Total federal tax revenues have by no means been a constant share of GNP, however. For one thing, two of the most important federal taxes—the individual and the corporate income taxes—are highly sensitive to the state of the economy. The individual income tax is the highest yielding of all federal taxes, supplying at least 40 percent of total revenues in every year since 1950. Individual income tax liabilities increase more than in proportion when income increases, either from real growth or inflation, because the additional income is taxed in each taxpayer's highest marginal rate bracket. And in a recession, individual income tax revenues fall more than in proportion to the decline in incomes. The substantial increases in such revenues in the late 1960s and 1970s and the equally sharp declines in the early 1960s and mid-1970s demonstrated the sensitivity of income tax revenues to the state of the economy (see Table 2.2). Magnifying this sensitivity has been the frequent use of the income tax as a countercyclical economic policy tool; taxes have been cut in economic downturns (when revenues are already reduced) to add purchasing power in the private sector, and taxes have been raised at times of excessively fast growth. The discretionary tax cuts of 1964 and 1974–1975 and the Vietnam war surtax of 1968–1970 are examples.

The corporate income tax is also highly sensitive to economic conditions. Corporate net income is a residual—gross revenues less a number of costs that are generally fixed in the short run. When business turns down, the bills still have to be paid, so most of the reduction in sales is compensated for from profits. When business rebounds, profits jump sharply. Corporate tax liabilities move with the economy just as sharply as profits do, as the jump with economic recovery in 1977 and the drop with the recession in 1983 exemplify.

The federal tax take has changed for more than cyclical reasons, however; there have been structural changes in the tax system as well. Corporate income tax revenues, beyond fluctuating with the economy, have tended to drop because of the discretionary tax cuts targeted on investment and capital formation—particularly accelerated depreci-

Table 2.1

**Federal Revenues and State and Local Tax Revenues,
Fiscal Years 1946–1982**
Percentage of GNP

	Federal revenues	State and local tax revenues[a]	Total
1946	19.5	5.2[b]	24.7
1947	17.3	5.4	22.7
1948	17.0	5.6	22.6
1949	15.1	5.8	20.9
1950	14.9	6.3	21.2
1951	16.5	6.0	22.5
1952	19.5	6.0	25.5
1953	19.3	6.1	25.4
1954	19.1	6.4	25.6
1955	17.2	6.6	23.8
1956	18.1	6.8	24.9
1957	18.4	7.1	25.5
1958	18.0	7.3	25.3
1959	16.7	7.4	24.1
1960	18.6	7.8	26.4
1961	18.5	8.2	26.8
1962	18.2	8.3	26.4
1963	18.4	8.4	26.8
1964	18.2	8.5	26.7
1965	17.7	8.6	26.3
1966	18.1	8.5	26.6
1967	19.2	8.7	27.9
1968	18.4	9.2	27.6
1969	20.5	9.4	29.9
1970	19.9	10.0	29.9
1971	18.1	10.2	28.3
1972	18.4	11.1	29.5
1973	18.4	10.7	29.1
1974	19.1	10.5	29.6
1975	18.9	10.6	29.5
1976	18.2	10.7	28.9
1977	19.1	10.8	29.9
1978	19.1	10.6	29.7
1979	19.7	10.0	29.6
1980	20.1	9.9	30.0
1981	20.9	9.7	30.6
1982	20.4	9.9	30.3

Source: Office of Management and Budget, "Total Government Finances," February 1984, p. 2.

Notes: Percentage shares for individual years may not add to totals because of rounding.

[a]State and local tax revenues equal state and local receipts less grants-in-aid from the federal government.

[b]Author's estimate.

Table 2.2

Federal Government Revenues by Source, Fiscal Years 1946–1986

Percentage of Total Receipts

	Individual income tax	Corporate income tax	Social insurance taxes	Excise taxes	Estate and gift tax	All other receipts	Total
1946	41.0	31.1	7.8	16.9	1.7	1.4	100.0
1947	46.7	22.4	8.7	18.7	2.0	1.5	100.0
1948	46.2	23.2	9.5	17.6	2.1	1.4	100.0
1949	39.4	28.4	9.7	19.0	2.0	1.5	100.0
1950	39.9	26.5	11.1	19.1	1.8	1.7	100.0
1951	41.8	27.3	11.1	16.7	1.4	1.7	100.0
1952	42.2	32.1	9.8	13.4	1.2	1.4	100.0
1953	42.8	30.5	9.8	14.2	1.3	1.4	100.0
1954	42.4	30.3	10.3	14.3	1.3	1.4	100.0
1955	43.9	27.3	12.0	13.9	1.4	1.4	100.0
1956	43.2	28.0	12.5	13.3	1.6	1.4	100.0
1957	44.5	26.5	12.5	13.2	1.7	1.6	100.0
1958	43.6	25.2	14.1	13.4	1.7	2.0	100.0
1959	46.4	21.8	14.8	13.3	1.7	1.9	100.0
1960	44.0	23.2	15.9	12.6	1.7	2.5	100.0
1961	43.8	22.2	17.4	12.6	2.0	2.0	100.0
1962	45.7	20.6	17.1	12.6	2.0	2.0	100.0
1963	44.7	20.3	18.6	12.4	2.0	2.1	100.0
1964	43.2	20.9	19.5	12.2	2.1	2.1	100.0
1965	41.8	21.8	19.1	12.5	2.3	2.6	100.0
1966	42.4	23.0	19.5	10.0	2.3	2.8	100.0
1967	41.3	22.8	22.0	9.2	2.0	2.7	100.0
1968	44.9	18.7	22.2	9.2	2.0	3.0	100.0
1969	46.7	19.6	20.9	8.1	1.9	2.8	100.0
1970	46.9	17.0	23.0	8.1	1.9	3.0	100.0
1971	46.1	14.3	25.3	8.9	2.0	3.4	100.0
1972	45.7	15.5	25.4	7.5	2.6	3.3	100.0
1973	44.7	15.7	27.3	7.0	2.1	3.1	100.0
1974	45.2	14.7	28.5	6.4	1.9	3.3	100.0
1975	43.9	14.6	30.3	5.9	1.7	3.7	100.0
1976	44.2	13.9	30.5	5.7	1.7	4.1	100.0
1977	44.3	15.4	29.9	4.9	2.1	3.3	100.0
1978	45.3	15.0	30.3	4.6	1.3	3.5	100.0
1979	47.0	14.2	30.0	4.0	1.2	3.6	100.0
1980	47.2	12.5	30.5	4.7	1.2	3.9	100.0
1981	47.7	10.2	30.5	6.8	1.1	3.6	100.0
1982	48.2	8.0	32.6	5.9	1.3	4.0	100.0
1983[a]	48.0	6.0	35.2	5.8	1.0	4.0	100.0
1984[b]	44.1	9.0	36.5	5.6	0.9	3.9	100.0
1985[b]	44.2	9.3	37.1	5.1	0.8	3.6	100.0
1986[b]	44.4	9.8	37.6	4.2	0.6	3.3	100.0

Sources: Office of Management and Budget; 1983–1986 estimates and projections, Congressional Budget Office.

Notes: Percentage shares for individual years may not add to 100 percent because of rounding.
[a]Estimate.
[b]Projections, assuming no change in current law.

ation and investment tax credit. Revenues have declined still further because rapid inflation has encouraged firms to finance their investment through debt rather than equity. Inflation depreciates the value of outstanding debt principal, thus benefiting debtor corporations; the interest outlays to service this inflation-motivated debt are tax deductible, thus reducing corporate tax liabilities.

While the trend in corporate tax liabilities has been downward, Social Security payroll tax liabilities have been zooming up. Increasing real benefits, unfavorable demographics, above-average inflation in medical care costs, a stagnant economy, and a period of overcompensating indexing for inflation have combined to swell the system's revenue needs. The decline of the corporate tax was more than offset by the increase in the payroll tax share of total revenues, which more than tripled between 1946 and 1981.

By the early 1980s, the cyclical fluctuations in the economy and changes in the tax system combined to drive federal tax revenues to a post-World War II peak. While Social Security payroll tax revenues continued to climb, rapid inflation pushed individual income taxpayers into higher tax brackets. In fiscal 1981 federal taxes hit 20.9 percent of GNP, well above the highest peacetime value then on record. At the same time, taxpayers were hard-hit by state and local taxes, which had more than doubled as a share of GNP since 1946. Despite some relief as a result of a tax-cutting drive in the late 1970s, state and local taxes had retreated little from their record levels of 1976 and 1977. The federal revenue peak in fiscal 1981 coincided with a record tax take of 30.6 percent for the entire government sector.

It is not surprising that this confluence of factors and the highest total tax take in postwar history led to irresistible pressure for tax cuts.

Tax Policy Changes between 1981 and 1983 and the New Outlook for Revenues

The Economic Recovery Tax Act of 1981 (ERTA) was the response to the cyclical peak in federal tax revenues reached in that year. ERTA was an especially far-reaching piece of tax legislation, with provisions affecting individual and corporate income taxes, the estate and gift tax, and other taxes.

ERTA aimed to increase economic efficiency and incentives, much as the Kennedy-Johnson tax cuts of 1962 and 1964 had done. Like those tax bills, the "supply side" emphasis of ERTA was embodied primarily in cuts in individual income tax rates and more favorable tax treatment of fixed investment for business.

Also like the legislation of the early 1960s, ERTA was universally recognized to cause a substantial loss of revenue, abstracting from any possible changes in taxpayer behavior. The most hotly debated issue was whether taxpayer behavior would change under the influence of the act, and if so, to what degree.

The supply-side case for ERTA never really came to trial. The economy fell into a deep recession in mid-1981, and substantial unemployment and idle capacity turned the work and investment incentives into moot issues.

As the economy languished in the recession of 1982, the new risk was the federal deficit. ERTA had drastically reduced federal revenues; congressional estimates at the time of enactment showed the six-year revenue loss at $700 billion (see Table 2.3). Enacted spending cuts were far short of this magnitude. With the economy operating well below the capacity expected just a year or two before, an extraordinary deficit loomed. The deficit forecast was all the more disturbing because it showed a continuing budget gap even as the economy grew toward full utilization over several years. The tax cuts were simply too large, given the amount of spending reductions that were forthcoming, to yield budget deficits anywhere near the historical range even with rapid economic growth.

The will of Congress was galvanized by the danger that these continuing deficits would collide with business and consumer credit demands as the economy grew, driving up interest rates and choking off the recovery. In response to the mandate of the budget resolution for FY 1983, Congress passed the Tax Equity and Fiscal Responsibility Act of 1982 (TEFRA). Like ERTA, TEFRA was a broad-ranging piece of legislation. Unlike ERTA, TEFRA was intended to increase tax burdens.

ERTA had emphasized the reduction of tax rates and the increase in economic incentives. TEFRA trod lightly over or avoided the incentive issues, achieving its revenue gain through structural changes relating to leakages in the tax base (see Table 2.4). Because these changes offset only a small part of the revenues lost as a result of ERTA, TEFRA's net effect in company with ERTA should not be exaggerated. With respect to both incentives and fiscal policy, TEFRA was only a retreat, not a change of direction.

Table 2.3

Estimated Revenue Effects of Selected Provisions of the Economic Recovery Tax Act of 1981, Fiscal Years 1982-1986
Billions of Dollars

Provision	1982	1983	1984	1985	1986
Individual income tax provisions					
Rate cuts	−25.8	−65.7	−104.5	−122.7	−143.8
Deduction for two-earner couples	−0.4	−4.4	−9.1	−11.0	−12.6
Indexing	—	—	—	−12.9	−35.8
Other	−0.9	−2.8	−5.3	−7.3	−12.5
Total	−27.1	−72.9	−118.9	−153.9	−204.7
1983 Reestimate[a]	−28.9	−68.0	−105.2	−126.5	−155.3
Business incentive provisions					
Accelerated cost recovery	−9.6	−16.8	−26.3	−37.3	−52.8
R & D Credit	−0.4	−0.7	−0.9	−0.8	−0.5
Other	−0.7	−1.2	−1.2	−1.3	−1.4
Total	−10.7	−18.7	−28.4	−39.4	−54.7
1983 Reestimate[a]	−9.2	−17.2	−25.7	−34.5	−42.5
Estate and gift tax provisions					
Unified credit	b	−1.1	−2.0	−2.8	−3.8
Reduction in rates	b	−0.2	−0.4	−0.6	−0.9
Other	−0.2	−0.8	−0.8	−0.8	−0.9
Total	−0.2	−2.1	−3.2	−4.2	−5.6
All other	0.3	1.0	0.5	−1.7	−2.7
Total	*−37.7*	*−92.7*	*−150.0*	*−199.2*	*−267.7*
1983 Reestimate[a]	*−38.4*	*−87.8*	*−134.8*	*−166.6*	*−205.2*

Sources: Joint Committee on Taxation, *General Explanation of the Economic Recovery Tax Act of 1981*, table V-3, pp. 382-91; Congressional Budget Office, *Reducing the Deficit: Spending and Revenue Options*, table X-2, p. 230.

Notes: Revenue effects shown were estimated at time of passage of legislation. Estimates at time of this writing, if available, would differ because of changes in actual and forecast economic conditions. Columns may not add to totals because of rounding.

[a]The 1983 reestimates account for changes in economic assumptions. The reestimates do not allow allocation of miscellaneous provisions to estate and gift tax category. Only Accelerated Cost Recovery System (ACRS) revenue losses applicable to corporations are included in the business category, which is therefore a slight underestimate.
[b]Loss of less than $5 million.

Provisions Primarily Affecting Individual Taxpayers

The individual income tax provisions of ERTA received the most public attention because they represented a significant departure from the provisions of previous legislation.

Table 2.4

Estimated Revenue Effects of Selected Provisions of the Tax Equity and Fiscal Responsibility Act of 1982, Fiscal Years 1983–1987
Billions of Dollars

Provision	1983	1984	1985	1986	1987
Individual income tax provisions					
Alternative minimum tax	a	0.7	0.7	0.7	0.7
Medical expense deduction	0.3	1.8	1.7	1.8	1.9
Casualty loss deduction	—	0.7	0.7	0.8	0.9
Total	0.3	3.1	3.1	3.3	3.6
1983 Reestimate[b]	4.9	12.7	12.5	14.8	17.8
Provisions primarily affecting business					
Tax preferences	0.5	0.9	0.9	0.9	1.0
ITC basis adjustment	0.4	1.4	2.7	4.1	5.6
Repeal 1985 and 1986 accelerations of cost recovery	—	—	1.5	9.9	18.4
Leasing	1.0	2.6	4.3	5.5	7.0
Other	3.5	8.4	7.1	7.6	8.1
Total	5.4	13.3	16.5	28.0	40.1
1983 Reestimate[b]	7.4	16.3	19.2	26.2	31.6
Compliance provisions					
Withholding on interest and dividends[c]	1.3	5.2	4.0	4.6	5.2
Other	2.0	3.6	4.7	5.6	6.0
Total	3.4	8.9	8.7	10.2	11.2
Additional IRS enforcement	2.1	2.4	2.4	1.3	0.6
Other	4.0	6.0	7.3	6.9	6.9
Total	*18.0*	*37.7*	*42.7*	*51.8*	*63.9*
1983 Reestimate	*17.9*	*37.7*	*41.7*	*46.9*	*54.2*

Sources: Joint Committee on Taxation, *General Explanation of the Revenue Provisions of the Tax Equity and Fiscal Responsibility Act of 1982*, table V–3, pp. 457–59; Congressional Budget Office, *Reducing the Deficit: Spending and Revenue Options*, table X–2, p. 230.

Notes: Revenue effects shown were estimated at the time of passage of legislation. Estimates at time of this writing, if available, would differ because of changes in actual and forecast economic conditions. Items may not add to totals because of rounding.

[a]Less than $50 million.

[b]The 1983 reestimates account for changes in economic assumptions. Reestimates do not allow allocation among all categories. Individual income tax category includes compliance and enforcement revenue gains. Business category includes only revenue changes attributable to corporations, and is therefore a slight underestimate.

[c]Repealed before taking effect.

Rate Reductions

ERTA reduced marginal tax rates under the individual income tax by a total of approximately 23 percent over three years. Tax rates for calendar year 1982 were cut about 10 percent below those under prior law; rates for 1983 were cut about 19 percent; and in 1984 and later years, rates would be the full 23 percent lower. (Of course, most taxpayers actually felt the reductions in tax rates through changes in withholding on wages and salaries, which took effect on October 1, 1981, July 1, 1982, and July 1, 1983. Withholding affects only wage and salary income, however, and does not determine total tax liabilities. The withholding changes are thus irrelevant to the incentive aspects of the tax cut.)

Effective January 1, 1982, all tax rates that would have exceeded 50 percent, given the 10 percent rate reduction then in effect, were immediately reduced to 50 percent. This reduction in the highest tax rates carried with it an equivalent reduction in the maximum tax rate on capital gains, from 28 percent (that is, the 40 percent of long-term gains subject to tax times the 70 percent maximum statutory rate) to 20 percent (40 percent times the new 50 percent top statutory rate). In fact, through a special legal provision, the capital gains rate reduction was even further accelerated, applying to all asset transactions after June 9, 1981. So two of the major incentive provisions of ERTA, reductions in the highest capital gains tax rate and in the highest tax rate on other forms of income from capital, took effect on June 9, 1981, and January 1, 1982, respectively, earlier than many people perceived.

Indexing of Tax Rates

ERTA provided that tax rate brackets, personal exemptions, and zero bracket amounts be indexed for inflation beginning in 1985. The purpose of indexation is to prevent bracket creep—inflation combining with the progressive income tax—from increasing real tax liabilities.

Social Security Amendments of 1983

These provisions were enacted to shore up the system against expected short-term and long-term trust fund deficits. The legislation did increase revenues, but its near-term budgetary implications were limited for two reasons. First, some of the revenue gain for the Social Security trust funds was implicitly achieved through transfers of general revenues that would have been collected in any event; and second, some of the balance of the revenue pickup came through accelerated increases in tax rates that were already scheduled for later years, thus adding to revenues temporarily rather than permanently. All in all, the legislation will raise a significant amount of revenue over the seventy-five-year planning period commonly used for Social Security, but its effect on the more immediate budget projection period is far more limited.

Surface Transportation Assistance Act of 1982

This bill raised the federal gasoline excise tax from 4 to 9 cents per gallon. Although it increased federal revenues by about $5 billion per year, this increase had no net budgetary impact, because the additional revenues were dedicated to transportation improvements.

Provisions Primarily Affecting Business

While ERTA's business tax provisions received less public attention, at least at first, they were if anything a more radical departure from prior law than the provisions affecting individuals. The departure proved so great that TEFRA staged a significant retreat the next year.

Accelerated Cost Recovery

Through its new Accelerated Cost Recovery System (ACRS), ERTA provided businesses with a substantially simplified depreciation code. Under the prior law's complex asset depreciation range system, assets had been categorized according to their expected useful lives. ACRS divided equipment into only three categories, with virtually all equipment assigned a useful life of five years; very short-lived equipment (including vehicles) is assigned a three-year life, and some public utility property a ten-year life. Over these lifetimes ERTA prescribed a declining-balance cost recovery allowance of 150 percent, with acceleration to 175 percent in 1985 and 200 percent in later years. Buildings were assigned useful lives of fifteen years and 175 percent declining-balance allowances.

ACRS also allowed a 6 percent credit for investments in equipment in the three-year-life class and a full 10 percent credit for investments in longer-lived equipment. This was substantially more generous than prior law, which gave a 3⅓ percent credit for three- and four-year assets, a 6⅔ percent credit for five- and six-year assets, and the full 10 percent credit only for seven-year and still longer-lived assets. Under these terms, ACRS substantially liberalized capital cost recovery. ERTA left some potential tax policy problems, however. Cost recovery was not uniform from one type of asset to another.[1] Such a distortive government policy makes businesses reject investment options that provide more value in the marketplace in favor of other options that provide less value. The result was a reduction of total output. Furthermore, the schedule of future accelerations of capital cost recovery, to a declining-balance of 175 percent, and ultimately to a declining-balance of 200 percent in 1986 and thereafter, was an incentive to postpone investment and thereby take advantage of the more generous provisions in the future.

Finally, the new fifteen-year depreciable life for buildings was a substantial acceleration from prior depreciation and could easily lead to overinvestment in apartment and office buildings. Industry reports indicate that investments in tax shelters in 1983 could increase by as much as 50 percent over 1982, and the greatly liberalized cost recovery provisions for buildings could be a major reason.[2] Despite these apparent flaws, ACRS did reduce the tax burden on business capital investment in general, potentially increasing such investment.

TEFRA sought to tie up some of the loose ends in ERTA with respect to capital cost recovery. The largest single step was unquestionably the repeal of the scheduled 1985 and 1986 accelerations of capital cost recovery allowances for equipment, making the current 150 percent declining-balance system permanent. This slowdown of future cost recovery allowances unquestionably made investment somewhat less attractive, but it also eliminated the incentive to defer investment until the more favorable rules took effect. Furthermore, it made the tax system more neutral among investors and reduced (but did not eliminate) the opportunities for outright tax sheltering.

Also in TEFRA, Congress established a basis adjustment for the investment tax credit. In so doing, it eliminated a double benefit in which firms were allowed to depreciate the portion of an investment that was, in effect, paid for by the federal government through the investment tax credit. Congress determined that a basis adjustment for one-half of the amount of the tax credit, rather than the full credit, would provide sufficient additional revenue and bring effective tax rates on equipment investments to an acceptable level (taking into account TEFRA's other changes in ACRS). Although the one-half basis adjustment might well satisfy those criteria, it left tax policy in a highly unstable position. Tax policy theorists will probably criticize the one-half basis adjustment because only a full-basis adjustment accurately accounts for the government's contribution to the purchase of an asset through the investment tax credit. Advocates of capital formation will argue that the one-half basis adjustment reduces the investment tax credit's incentive for investment. No one will defend the one-half basis adjustment on principle. Thus, the investment tax credit and its basis adjustment will probably be debated further whenever tax policy issues come to the fore.

Leasing

As has already been noted, ACRS substantially liberalized cost recovery and investment tax credits. In fact, the liberalization was so great that many firms could not take full advantage of it. This situation would especially afflict not only new firms, which make large "set-up" investments and are thus unprofitable in their early years, but also older, recently unprofitable firms with large net operating losses that make them nontaxable. In contrast, a large, highly profitable firm might find that the ACRS deductions and credits from a particular new investment would wipe out its tax liability on the income generated by that investment, sheltering income from other sources besides. This divergence in the cost of capital investments could force disadvantaged firms to forgo profitable investments, while strong firms consolidated their hold on markets. Even worse, profitable firms could buy firms in related or unrelated lines of business with large reserves of net operating losses, simply to use up the tax benefits.

To release these pressures of built-up unusable tax deductions and credits, ERTA eliminated or eased the prior law's restrictions against leasing as a means of transferring tax benefits.[3] Under the new "safe harbor" leasing, a profitable firm could nominally buy an asset, claim the tax benefit, and lease it back to the actual user at a favorable rate. The result was a much simpler transfer of tax benefits, and probably a greater share of those benefits for the equipment user, than in the leasing practiced under pre-ERTA law. In the first months after the passage of ERTA, the leasing market was highly active, aided at least in part by a retroactivity provision allowing the leasing of equipment purchased as early as January 1, 1981—well before the enactment of ERTA.

In response to a public outcry over conspicuous use of the safe harbor leasing provision and in search of revenue, TEFRA repealed this liberalized means of transferring tax benefits. In its place Congress established a new mechanism known as "finance" leasing, which was more liberal than pre-ERTA leasing but more restrictive than safe harbor leasing. TEFRA cut back on the worst of the dangers of unusable tax benefits by reducing the deductions and credits under ACRS, as already described. The potential imbalances that motivated safe harbor leasing remain, though to a reduced degree, and the issue could easily arise again through new legislative proposals or economic or legal pressures in mergers, antitrust actions, or other areas.[4]

Corporate Tax Preferences

TEFRA provides for a 15 percent cutback in a list of tax preferences. The cutback applies only to corporations; small-business (Subchapter S) corporations are not affected. The existing corporate minimum tax is adjusted to prevent interactions with the new provisions. The cutback works by reducing each deduction by 15 percent.

Other Provisions

There were many ERTA provisions beyond those specifically discussed in this paper. Most notable were a tax exclusion for two-earner couples, to encourage labor supply; an expansion of the individual retirement account (IRA) provisions, and a net interest exclusion to encourage savings effective for taxable years beginning in 1985; a tax credit for increases in research and development activities; a reduction in corporate tax rates applying to the first $50,000 of profits; and substantial reductions in the estate and gift tax.[5]

TEFRA was projected to raise substantial revenues from a number of provisions designed to improve taxpayer compliance. One of those provisions—withholding of tax on interest and dividend income by banks and other financial institutions—was subsequently repealed on the grounds that it would pose an administrative and financial burden on interest and dividend payers and recipients, and that it would discourage saving. Federal excise taxes on air travel, telephone services, and cigarettes were temporarily increased. Taxation of unemployment insurance benefits under the individual income tax was made more stringent.[6] The alternative minimum tax for individuals was strengthened, and the system for itemizing deductions for medical expenses and casualty losses was simplified and rules tightened.

Revenue Implications

As has already been noted, ERTA indisputably caused substantial revenue losses abstracting from any changes it induced in economic behavior. Cuts in individual income tax rates accounted for well over one-half of the projected six-year loss of $700 billion in revenues; ACRS and related provisions accounted for another $100+ billion (see Table 2.3). Advocates of ERTA had claimed that it would stimulate enough additional work, saving, and investment to yield more revenue than the static estimates, but the 1981 recession eliminated that possibility for virtually the entire forecast period. Real incomes and inflation declined enough to reduce the ERTA revenue losses significantly below the original estimates, as Table 2.3 shows.

The business tax provisions of TEFRA provided for almost one-half of the bill's revenue pickup through FY 1985 and more than one-half thereafter (see Table 2.4). The compliance provisions, including the since-repealed withholding on interest and dividends, were the second-largest contributor. TEFRA proved to be a retreat rather than a reversal in the drive toward greater economic incentives. The individual income tax provisions of TEFRA had extremely small revenue implications and did not touch the ERTA tax rate reductions. The compliance provisions were nearly as modest in terms of expected revenue pickup and can be identified with economic incentives only through tortuous and questionable logic. In the business provisions the picture is much more mixed; TEFRA provided for less than one-half of the original projected revenue loss in ERTA to be recaptured between 1984 and 1986, but more than one-half in later years.[7] TEFRA did raise revenue, but the deficit problem and the need for additional revenue remain.

Revenue Strategies to Deal with the Deficit

In TEFRA, Congress acknowledged that tax increases are needed to move the budget toward balance, but it did not move far enough. The current policy budget deficit still exceeds $200 billion, 5 percent of GNP, in FY 1988. Even with substantial spending cuts, between $50 billion and $100 billion per year in revenues over and above TEFRA would be needed in FY 1988 to cut the structural deficit to manageable proportions.

The Problem

Raising so much additional revenue is a daunting challenge; to add some perspective, TEFRA will raise just about $50 billion in 1988 under current economic assumptions. So the difficulty of this task should be obvious—considering that TEFRA itself came under such heavy criticism, including the subsequent repeal of one of its most important provisions. And as logic suggests that TEFRA included the most palatable revenue options, we can only expect that the remaining alternatives will be even harder to swallow.

Before going into specifics, we must discuss principles. Economic recovery has apparently taken hold, but a large and immediate tax increase could reduce demand and slow or even stop real growth. Tax increases ideally should be relatively small in the initial years and should grow as the economy moves toward full employment. A tax increase that is properly timed to shrink federal credit demands as private demands for investment financing grow could keep credit needs and available funds in balance, facilitating capital formation and long-term growth.

But a tax increase that grows over time may lack credibility. A pledge to raise $50 billion in 1988 could be greeted with the same lack of respect as a resolution to quit smoking at the same date. Unless deficit reduction policies are considered reliable, they will not calm the credit markets. The contingency tax plan proposed in the administration's FY 1984 budget, consisting of a 5 percent income tax surcharge and a $5 per barrel excise tax on oil to take effect in 1986, is a case in point. The new taxes were made contingent on several factors, including congressional compliance with other administration proposals, the rate of growth of the economy, and the level of the deficit. Although an administration proposal for a tax increase might have been expected to impress the credit markets, the many contingencies apparently convinced most observers that the proposal was not serious, and so its effect has been nil.

The prescribed tax increase, then, must equal or perhaps double the revenue yield of TEFRA in a credible form. Political and economic criteria for such a revenue initiative are numerous and often conflicting. A few large revenue-raising provisions might be enacted more easily than many smaller items, but raising tens of billions of dollars at a single stroke is not easy. Some promising initiatives simply will not yield that much revenue; others would involve serious costs if stretched that far, either in perceived fairness (such as a national sales tax or value-added tax) or in economic efficiency and incentives (such as increases in income tax rates). Thus, no one or two provisions will fill the revenue gap. In all likelihood, only a package at least as complex as TEFRA will do.

Any such package must balance competing economic objectives. Collecting more revenues can mean heavier burdens on the taxpayers who must struggle to bear them, along with stifled incentives for all. Thus, sparing low- and moderate-income taxpayers would seem to require making the individual income tax more progressive; such measures would maintain consumer demand as the economy climbs toward full employment. But if substantial revenues were drained from the people who do most of the saving in our economy in a way that also dampened their incentive to save, the investment needed for growth of output and productivity would not be forthcoming. So just as consumption and investment must be balanced over the course of the recovery, tax fairness and efficiency must be balanced in any revenue-raising legislation.

Strategies to Deal with It

Several revenue strategies could reduce the budget deficit, some to a larger extent than others. Each strategy has its own advantages and disadvantages, and it appears likely that several of the strategies must be pursued together to raise sufficient revenue.

Some approaches would build on existing taxes; examples are increases in individual income tax or excise tax rates. Other approaches would involve entirely new taxes, such as taxes on energy or on consumption in general. New taxes tend to involve greater uncertainty and costs of transition, including long start-up periods, but existing taxes have some well-known flaws. Choosing among these strategies ultimately requires balancing conflicting values.

The strategies discussed in this section include increasing the rates under the current individual income tax, either directly or by repealing indexing; eliminating income tax preferences, either selectively or almost completely to create a new broad-based income tax; broadening the base of the corporate tax; taxing consumption; taxing energy; and increasing existing excise taxes.

Increasing Tax Rates

One strategy would be to run ERTA in reverse, taking back some of the revenue that ERTA lost. The most obvious target for a weary revenue hunter is surely ERTA's reductions of marginal tax rates under the individual income tax. The rate reductions were the largest single revenue item in ERTA, and TEFRA left them untouched. As an example of this strategy, the administration's 5 percent surtax (part of the contingency tax proposals), in effect a rate increase, was estimated by the Congressional Budget Office (CBO) to raise $20 billion per year by FY 1988. The revenue potential of this strategy is obviously substantial.

Nonetheless, the revenue hunter can approach this enticing target only with trepidation. Marginal rate reductions are an imposing adversary, not just because people viscerally favor them, but also on the merits. Between the tax cuts of 1964 and 1981, substantial inflation made the federal income tax more progressive, because taxable incomes of middle- and upper-income households were disproportionately pushed into higher tax brackets. Changes in the tax law returned almost all the resulting revenue increase to the taxpayers but in ways (increased exemptions and zero bracket amounts, per capita tax credits) that gave disproportionate relief to low-income taxpayers. As a result, the income tax became still more progressive (see Table 2.5). Thus, it can be argued that by 1981 the income tax had become *too* progressive by historical standards, and such complaints cannot be dismissed out of hand.[8]

Beyond these issues is the problem of implementation. ERTA broke a psychological barrier when it reduced the maximum tax rate on any form of income from 70 percent to 50 percent. With this reduction, the federal government moved from the role of senior partner to equal partner in many investments and enterprises. Should that step be reversed? While an increase of a small number of percentage points might be expected to have only modest effects from a strictly dispassionate viewpoint, it could have powerful symbolic connotations.

Further questions arise. Under pre-ERTA law, the maximum marginal tax rate on income from labor was limited to approximately 50 percent by the maximum tax provision of the Tax Reform Act of 1969.[9]

Table 2.5

**Average and Marginal Individual Income Tax Rates
at Multiples of Median Income, Selected Years**

Year	25% of median income	50% of median income	Median income	Twice the median income	5 Times the median income	10 Times the median income
			Average Rates			
1965	0.0	2.8	7.4	12.2	20.5	36.5
1978	−7.3	3.4	11.6	17.3	30.9	41.0
1981	−8.4	5.7	13.3	18.5	31.7	40.6
			Marginal Rates			
1965	0.0	14.0	17.0	22.0	39.0	55.0
1978	10.0	16.0	22.0	36.0	55.0	66.0
1981	12.5	18.0	24.0	43.0	59.0	68.0

Source: Computed by author.

Notes: Computed for families of four with typical standard or itemized deductions for the particular income level in the particular year. The median income is for tax-filing families: in 1965, that figure was $7,500; in 1978, $18,500; and in 1981, $23,700. The 50 percent maximum rate on income from labor is assumed not to apply. The 1981 tax rates do not include the influence of ERTA.

If the top rate were increased from 50 percent to perhaps 52 or 55 percent (the administration's contingency tax would make it 52.5 percent), would we accept an increase in the tax rate on labor incomes? Or would we reintroduce the complicated tax forms that the maximum tax provision required to reduce the highest tax rate on labor income by just two or five percentage points? Thus, the apparently simple decision about the top tax rate is seen upon examination to be rather involved.

Suppose it is decided to raise marginal tax rates but to leave the highest rate at the landmark 50 percent level. Then a whole new set of problems arises, most of them related to perceptions of fairness. If the tax rates below the top bracket are increased to 50 percent or less, but the top rate remains at 50 percent, the amount of the tax increase in dollars reaches a plateau at the bottom of the highest tax bracket and does not further increase no matter how much income increases. This is precisely the problem that arose in, and drew considerable criticism to, the proposal to cap the July 1983 tax cut at $700.

Table 2.6 illustrates this problem using the July 1983 tax cap as an example. Because tax rates below the top bracket are increased, the impact is first felt (though in very small dollar amounts) at comparatively modest income levels. The tax increase reaches a peak at what might be called the upper-middle income level, when the tax rate hits 50 percent. The tax increase in dollars then remains constant as income increases (because the 50 percent top rate does not increase), which means that, in percentage terms, the tax increase falls. Critics of such an increase in tax rates argue that the burden on middle- and upper-middle income taxpayers, in comparison with the small percentage increase for the highest-income taxpayers, is unfair.

A final issue also relates to fairness. A major complaint about the existing income tax is that some taxpayers can avoid paying tax, but a rate increase would hit only the people who already pay taxes. As Senator Robert Dole said in dismissing a 10 percent surtax as part of TEFRA, "Ten percent of nothing is nothing."

So recapturing the revenue cost of the ERTA tax rate cuts is not a simple matter. The magnitude of the incentive benefits of the rate cuts is debatable, but their existence is not. The symbolic 50 percent top bracket rate poses problems of complexity and perceived unfairness whether it is pierced or not. Increases in marginal tax rates should not be ruled out if the need for additional revenue is pressing, but policymakers should understand the problems associated with their choices.

Repealing Indexation

Like increases in marginal tax rates, the repeal of indexing has a certain appeal as a revenue-raising step. It would raise no revenues until FY 1985, so there would be no fiscal drag on the recovery while it is still getting off the ground. However, the drag comes on strong in later years, with a likely revenue pickup of $65 billion in FY 1989. The repeal of indexation would spread the tax increase over all taxpayers, making the burden on any one fairly modest. The burden would nevertheless increase with income, up to a dollar ceiling. Repeal of indexing also would raise a substantial amount of revenue in a single policy step, making the political process somewhat more manageable. And an unindexed progressive income tax is a built-in stabilizer against too-rapid economic growth and inflation.

As with tax rate increases, however, the repeal of indexing has drawbacks. The perception that the government profits from inflation would be troublesome, as would increases in individual taxpayers' real tax burdens because of inflation. It can be argued that repeal of indexa-

Table 2.6

Comparison of Federal Individual Income Tax Burdens
Under 1984 Law and $700 Cap (Rate Increase) Proposal

Income	Single taxpayers				Joint returns, two dependents			
	Present law tax	Proposed tax	Change (dollars)	Change (percentage)	Present law tax	Proposed tax	Change (dollars)	Change (percentage)
30,000	4,385	4,385	0	0.0	3,003	3,003	0	0.0
35,000	5,540	5,540	0	0.0	3,903	3,903	0	0.0
40,000	6,827	6,959	132	1.9	4,874	4,874	0	0.0
45,000	8,210	8,496	286	3.5	5,952	5,952	0	0.0
50,000	9,673	10,113	440	4.5	7,165	7,273	108	1.5
55,000	11,222	11,838	616	5.5	8,436	8,698	262	3.1
65,000	14,456	15,457	1,001	6.9	11,159	11,729	570	5.1
75,000	17,915	19,188	1,273	7.1	14,085	14,963	878	6.2
85,000	21,611	23,038	1,427	6.6	17,205	18,391	1,186	6.9
95,000	25,307	26,888	1,581	6.2	20,439	21,933	1,494	7.3
100,000	27,155	28,813	1,658	6.1	22,056	23,704	1,648	7.5
200,000	65,585	67,313	1,728	2.6	58,190	61,836	3,646	6.3
300,000	104,085	105,813	1,728	1.7	96,600	100,336	3,736	3.9
500,000	181,085	182,813	1,728	1.0	173,600	177,336	3,736	2.2
1,000,000	373,585	375,313	1,728	0.5	366,100	369,836	3,736	1.0

Source: Joint Committee on Taxation.

Notes: Assumes itemized deductions are 23 percent of adjusted gross income. Computed without reference to tax tables.

Table 2.7

Three Measures of the Tax Increase for Typical Four-Person Families in 1985 Due to Repeal of Indexation

1983 Income (dollars)	1985 Income (dollars)	1985 Tax with indexation (dollars)	1985 Tax without indexation (dollars)	Tax increase (dollars)	Tax increase (percentage)	Decrease in after-tax income (percentage)
5,000	5,496	0	0	0	0.0	0.0
10,000	10,993	365	410	45	12.3	0.4
15,000	16,489	1,079	1,117	38	3.5	0.2
20,000	21,986	1,748	1,800	52	3.0	0.3
30,000	32,979	3,404	3,513	109	3.3	0.4
50,000	54,965	8,148	8,427	279	3.4	0.6
100,000	109,930	24,751	25,267	516	2.1	0.6
500,000	549,648	191,765	192,715	950	0.5	0.3

Source: Congressional Budget Office.

Notes: Assumes all income is from wages and salaries earned by one spouse; deductions are the greater of the zero bracket amount or 23 percent of income; and income increases equal the rate of inflation. Earned income tax credit is omitted. Inflation projections are from the CBO economic projections.

tion is an underhanded way to increase revenues and expand the federal government. And indexing certainly could not be defended as a deficit solution over the long term; continuously increasing revenues through bracket creep could soon force compensating rate cuts. Without indexation, Congress has traditionally cut taxes periodically in response to inflation. In all likelihood such discretionary tax cuts would continue if indexing were repealed.

Another problem with the repeal of indexing is the possible perception of unfairness. Changes in tax liabilities at different income levels with and without indexation can be interpreted in several different ways. Under likely rates of inflation, repeal of indexation would increase low-income taxpayers' liabilities most when measured in percentage terms, although the increase would be very slight in dollar terms (see Table 2.7). This result might suggest that repeal of indexation would be unfair. But in dollar terms repeal of indexing most increases upper-income taxpayers' liabilities, and in percentage terms, most reduces middle-income taxpayers' disposable income. Thus, who would be the primary victims of repeal of indexation is essentially a matter of interpretation. What is certain is that, confronted with the prospect, almost everybody would complain. Low-income taxpayers have suffered considerably from the absence of indexing since 1978; the personal exemption and zero bracket amounts have been substantially eroded. But future indexing is not a remedy for past bracket creep; it merely keeps the process from going further. A discretionary increase in the personal exemption and zero bracket amounts is the proper, belated, remedy for the inflation of the early 1980s.

So, like marginal tax rate increases, repeal of indexation has potential to reduce the deficit and has obvious real or perceived drawbacks as tax or distributional policy. As with just about every other option in this imperfect world, we must weigh the benefits against the costs and compare the alternatives. There are several options other than outright repeal of indexation; among them are postponement of the effective date of indexation, indexation for only part of inflation (such as indexation for inflation in excess of 2 percent or for one-half of actual inflation), or indexation of only the personal exemption and zero bracket amounts (to protect low-income taxpayers, but make others bear some of the costs of inflation).

Repealing Selected Individual Income Tax Preferences

Another approach to increasing individual income tax revenues is to broaden the tax base, rather than increasing tax rates. TEFRA trimmed a small number of tax preferences in what came to be known as a "cats and dogs" approach. The stray animals caught by TEFRA were probably the slowest; although the next roundup will be more difficult, there are many more strays around. If only a small number of preferences are to be repealed, then each candidate can be considered on its own merits. In contrast, repealing most or all preferences would change the basic character of the income tax and raise an entirely different set of tax policy questions. That option will be discussed later.

The preferential income tax provisions discussed in this section include savings incentives, wage supplements, and miscellaneous individual provisions. Repeal of any of these preferences would have both a strong economic rationale and significant revenue implications. A longer list could be made under less stringent restrictions.[10] (Revenue effects are shown in Table 2.8.)

The individual retirement account (IRA) provision included in ERTA has some definite weaknesses as a savings incentive. Because the maximum tax-deductible contribution for each worker is limited to

Table 2.8

Revenue Effects of Tax Increase Options, Fiscal Years 1985–1989

Billions of dollars

	1985	1986	1987	1988	1989
Reduce R & D credit to 10 percent	0.3	0.4	a	a	a
Repeal percentage depletion for oil and gas	0.6	1.4	1.2	1.3	1.3
Repeal expensing of intangible drilling costs	3.1	5.4	5.1	5.0	4.9
Repeal capital gains treatment of timber	0.3	0.7	0.8	0.8	0.8
Eliminate tax exemption for pollution control bonds	a	0.1	0.3	0.4	0.5
Limit nonbusiness, noninvestment interest deductions to $10,000	0.3	2.0	2.2	2.4	2.6
Lengthen the building depreciation period to 20 years	0.3	1.3	2.5	3.6	4.9
Tax accrued interest on life insurance reserves	2.1	5.7	6.2	6.8	7.5
Repeal the net interest exclusion	1.0	2.9	3.1	3.4	3.6
Eliminate tax exemption for small-issue industrial revenue bonds	0.1	0.6	0.9	1.0	1.1
Require full-basis adjustment for the investment tax credit	0.4	1.5	2.8	4.1	5.5
Tax employer-paid health insurance premiums over $80 per month ($200 for families)	1.8	3.5	4.7	6.1	7.8
Eliminate tax exemption for private hospital bonds	0.1	0.3	0.6	1.0	1.4
Eliminate deductibility of state and local sales taxes	0.8	5.6	6.3	7.2	8.1
Increase IRS audit coverage	0.8	1.7	3.0	4.7	6.7

Source: Congressional Budget Office.

Notes: Assumes January 1, 1984 starting date for all changes.

aLess than $50 million.

$2,000 under most circumstances, the IRA provides no marginal incentive, only a windfall, to taxpayers who would save more than $2,000 even without the subsidy. The value of the deduction is greatest for those who need it least—taxpayers with the most income and therefore the highest tax rates. Finally, the deduction can be claimed by taxpayers who do no new saving at all, but rather borrow money (or withdraw it from prior savings) and deposit it in an IRA. The net interest exclusion to take effect in 1985 under ERTA avoids this last tax-gaming flaw, but has all the other failings of the IRA. Repealing the net interest exclusion and the broadened IRA would save about $6 billion per year.

Among other savings incentives, the exclusion from tax of interest earned on life insurance reserves provides a questionable subsidy to this form of saving relative to others. Repeal of this exclusion would raise revenues by more than $5 billion per year. Perhaps even more suspect, the deductibility of interest on consumer loans (credit card balances, auto loans, etc.) acts as a negative savings incentive; it encourages and subsidizes borrowing. Repeal of these deductions would make saving more attractive and encourage capital formation, while raising significant amounts of revenue. Even limiting annual interest deductions (including the deduction on mortgages) to $10,000 plus the amount of investment income would raise about $2 billion per year.

Employees may receive income in several noncash forms free of tax. Employer contributions toward life and health insurance premiums and pensions are the largest of these wage supplements, but others include legal insurance, employer discounts, and subsidized meals and parking. This tax exemption encourages compensation in these forms, which narrows the tax base and forces tax rates up. This exemption also favors taxpayers who receive income in these forms over those who do not. The exemption for health insurance premiums encourages the purchase of first-dollar coverage that may add to inflation in health care costs in the long run. Taxing only employer-paid health insurance premiums over $200 per month ($80 per month for single people) would raise almost $8 billion by FY 1989.

Among the remaining major tax preferences, the itemized deduction for state and local sales taxes has questionable merit. It is a highly inaccurate compensation for such expenses, which are generally small and uniformly spread across most of the population in any event. Eliminating this deduction would increase revenues by almost $5 billion per year.[11]

Repealing or restricting preferential tax provisions like these would require some taxpayers to make painful adjustments. But raising any taxes would cause some pain, and targeting on tax preferences has the virtue in placing the burden where there was once an extraordinary benefit. Another targeted step to effectively broaden the tax base would be to increase IRS audit coverage to see that taxable incomes are accurately reported and that taxes due are actually paid. Almost $7 billion per year could be raised by 1989, net of additional outlays, if the number of returns audited were increased from 1.3 percent to 1.9 percent of the total.

Repealing Business Tax Preferences

Another strategy would be to broaden the base of the corporate income tax. Such a step would be controversial because increases in corporate taxes would tend to reduce investment. But again, raising taxes requires imposing burdens somewhere in the economy, and the business sector was treated relatively generously in ERTA, even after TEFRA. Further, such changes could make the taxation of business income more neutral and improve the allocation of investment. This strategy could include retrenchments of cost recovery under the Accelerated Cost Recovery System (ACRS) and repeal of various tax preferences for corporations.

TEFRA has already reclaimed some of the revenues lost through ACRS in ERTA, but there may be a case for still further paring back the ACRS tax cuts. The basis adjustment for one-half of the investment tax credit under TEFRA is unjustifiable on tax policy grounds. A basis adjustment would eliminate the double benefit of the investment tax credit and cost recovery deductions and would thus take some of the shine off many tax shelter schemes that are based partly on the investment tax credit.

Tax shelter concerns also arise in the depreciation of buildings. Some economists believe that the nation is overinvesting in residential and office buildings; as evidence they cite the boom in tax shelter investments that are made through real estate. The rapid growth of sale-leaseback arrangements involving governments and other nonprofit entities is cited as evidence of possible excessive depreciation of buildings (and some equipment). Building depreciation could be trimmed either by increasing the assumed useful life of fifteen years, or by slowing the 175 percent declining-balance rate of cost recovery, or by a combination of these. Legislation has already been introduced to cut back on sale-leasebacks by nontaxable institutions through targeted denial of ACRS benefits.

A final potential area for increasing tax revenues is ACRS itself. As was noted earlier, ACRS tends to favor some investments over others, distorting economic decisions and reducing output. It is possible to improve the system so that it distorts less and is simpler. At the cost of somewhat reduced investment incentives, revised depreciation rules could also raise revenue. (Of course, if investment were allocated more efficiently, the economy need not be worse off.) Legislation has been introduced to streamline ACRS and make it more efficient; it would raise no revenue, however. [12]

Simple tightening of the ITC and cost recovery provisions of ERTA would obviously reduce incentives for investment to some degree. In a period when capital formation is badly needed, this consideration should not be ignored. Yet it must be weighed against the need for revenue and the efficiency gains that could be reaped through greater tax neutrality and reduced tax sheltering. Carefully planned corporate tax increases as part of a deficit reduction program could leave both the tax system and the economy better off.

Turning to other corporate tax preferences, ERTA's tax credit for increases in qualifying research and development (R & D) expenditures (effective only through calendar 1985) is complex and arguably inefficient. "Qualifying expenditures" can be difficult to interpret, and restricting the credit to increases in research and development expenditures eliminates the incentive to continue programs in progress. The credit also may be used as a tax shelter. Despite the benefits of additional R & D expenditures, it may be better to allow firms to undertake projects on their own initiative, rather than attempting to influence their judgments through tax incentives.

The selective tax benefits for oil production—the expensing of intangible drilling costs and the use of percentage depletion—were originally intended to maintain a sound domestic industry in the face of cheap imports. That situation no longer obtains. Moreover, these provisions can distort the operation of the market by attracting capital from other activities into petroleum production, by changing the way individual firms explore for and extract oil, and (because percentage depletion is now available only to independent firms) by altering the allocation of resources among firms. Finally, these provisions are used in arranging tax shelters. Repeal of these tax preferences would surely be controversial at a time when the domestic industry is in some distress. However, the problems of the oil industry may be caused not by the tax system, but rather by fluctuations in the world market, conservation, and the slow domestic and world economy. Another consideration is that ACRS treatment of comparable investments is almost as generous as the expensing of intangible drilling costs.

Income from cutting timber is now treated as long-term capital gain and thus receives the 60 percent capital gains exclusion, even though timber is produced for sale in the same way as any other product. Repeal of capital gains treatment of timber would increase tax revenues and reduce distortions in the allocation of capital. Administrative complexities would result, however, and tightening of this provision would hit the timber industry after it had suffered disproportionately through the recent recession. Again, in assessing this decline, policymakers must weigh carefully the role of tax factors as opposed to market forces.

Use of tax-exempt state and municipal securities to finance private-purpose activities has been growing rapidly. (Examples include small-issue industrial revenue bonds, private hospital bonds, and mortgage subsidy bonds. See Ladd [1984] for further discussion.) Such financing can crowd the market for state and local securities and convey competitive advantage to private users. Cutback or repeal of these financing opportunities would help public-purpose state and local financing and reduce the deficit. (Mortgage subsidy bonds were scheduled to expire December 31, 1983, although legislation has been introduced to renew them.)

Revising the Income Tax

An alternative strategy is to repeal most or all individual and corporate tax preferences, rather than a selected few. The tax base would be so broadened that tax rates could be reduced in partial compensation, still leaving an increase in revenue.

Repealing income tax preferences is seldom easy, as has been noted, so the wholesale broadening of the income tax base might be judged extremely difficult. In this case, however, the whole could be less than the sum of its parts. Repealing one tax preference appears to single out its beneficiaries, and the gains for other taxpayers and the budget deficit tend to be relatively small. A wholesale approach that touches most or all preferences could appear fairer, and everyone can benefit at least to some degree from a general rate reduction.

Proposals for a "flat-rate tax" gained great prominence in 1982, and many bills were submitted in Congress. Although some bills were quite general, those that proposed a single rate structure were criticized as sharply redistributing the tax burden from upper-income taxpayers to middle- and lower-income taxpayers. Perhaps for this reason, there are fewer genuine flat-rate proposals in the current Congress. With a broadened base and graduated rates, however, such redistribution can be avoided, and some proposals have followed that line. Maximum tax rates of 28 to 30 percent, in contrast to the current law's 50 percent, have been proposed to Congress.[13] Substantially reducing marginal income tax rates would increase capital formation and the incentive to work. And if the tax base had fewer (or no) preferential provisions, the allocation of resources would be more efficient. If the tax stayed within the conceptual confines of the current law, the transition could be much simpler than any transition to a new and different tax.

The individual and corporate income taxes together yield more than one-half of total federal revenues. These taxes are thus not only likely sources of further revenues but also essential elements in the current revenue system. By all accounts, however, the public at large highly distrusts the income tax; because these taxes rely heavily on voluntary taxpayer compliance, some remedy is essential. The perceived unfairness, complexity, economic distortions, and inefficiency of the current tax system can all be traced to the array of special tax preferences that narrow the tax base and force the imposition of high marginal rates. Eliminating or cutting back tax preferences is always painful, because individual taxpayers are reluctant to yield the particular preferences from which they benefit, and there is no excess revenue for a general tax cut to ease the transition. But barring an end run around the income taxes through an entirely new tax, some restructuring may be unavoidable.

Taxing Consumption

Another strategy to narrow the deficit would be a broad-based tax on consumption, either in place of or in addition to the income tax. There are basically two ways to tax consumption: through a value-added tax or a personal expenditure tax. The value-added tax (VAT) is intended to shift the burden of taxation away from income and toward consumption. A VAT would be the economic (though not the administrative) equivalent of a national sales tax and thus would fall directly on consumers.

A VAT could be added to our current tax system to yield whatever additional revenues were desired to narrow the deficit, thereby shifting the relative balance of federal taxation away from income and toward consumption. A VAT with a higher rate could substitute in full or in part for the existing income tax, increasing the shift toward taxing consumption.

The revenue potential of the VAT is considerable. The tax base theoretically would be all of personal consumption; at 1983 levels of roughly $2.2 trillion, a 10 percent VAT would raise $220 billion, or more than enough to wipe out the deficit. In practice, however, some classes of expenditures almost certainly would be excluded from the tax, for administrative or hardship reasons (although such exclusions would make the tax less neutral). Food, housing, and medical care taken together constituted about $900 billion of total consumption in 1983; so the revenue of a 10 percent VAT excluding those items would be cut to $130 billion. Of course, draining that much purchasing power from the economy would significantly alter the federal government's fiscal policy stance and would require some compensating adjustments. A VAT could completely replace the corporate income tax, which will yield about $60 billion in FY 1984, or it could significantly reduce the individual income tax, which will yield about $300 billion in FY 1984.

The objective of such a shift of taxation from income to consumption is to increase capital formation. If saving is tax deductible, it will tend to increase, and consumption will tend to fall. More output will thus be channeled into investment; the capital stock will grow and output will increase in the future. The degree to which capital formation increases, of course, depends on the responsiveness of savings and consumption to these tax rates. The evidence suggests that this responsiveness is small.[14] Furthermore, there is the problem of stimulating more investment when demand is reduced for the consumer goods that this investment would produce.

The VAT is sometimes criticized for its treatment of taxpayers at different income levels. The VAT allows no exemption or deduction. Each taxpayer, regardless of means, pays tax on the first dollar of consumption of taxable goods. As a result, the tax would bear more heavily on people with the lowest incomes than does the income tax, which exempts the poorest outright and has rates that are graduated by income. The VAT would also be regressive over the entire income range, because low-income taxpayers spend a larger fraction of their incomes than do taxpayers with higher incomes. Low-income households could be provided relief through a refundable income tax credit, but such a mechanism would be extremely complex. To claim the credit, many persons now exempt from filing returns would have to file, adding a heavy administrative burden on the IRS.

A VAT as an additional tax would add substantially to the workloads of business and the federal government. Retail firms in states with sales taxes are prepared generally to deal with the kind of accounting a VAT requires, so there is a strong argument on administrative grounds for a national sales tax rather than a VAT. Even so, where state sales tax bases differ from the federal, confusion would result. For the federal government, either tax would be an entirely new and heavy burden. The United Kingdom has found that the collection cost per dollar of revenue for its VAT is as great as for its income taxes.[15]

Similarly, exempting certain kinds of products to reduce the burden of the tax has administrative consequences. Presumably, if food were to be exempted from the VAT, food producers should be exempted from the VAT on the food containers they purchase. But the manufacturer of the food containers might also make containers for nonfood products. That manufacturer would have to keep separate records for food and nonfood container sales, and the IRS would have to verify them. Similarly, we might not want the American Cancer Society to pay VAT on a typewriter, but we would want to collect from American Motors. Some nations with VATs have gone so far as to charge different rates on different kinds of commodities. For all the reasons suggested here, such differentiation adds tremendous complexity.

Both the administrative load and the perceived fairness of a VAT would depend heavily on the features of the tax. The reporting and collection burdens of any VAT are the same regardless of the tax rate charged, so it might not be worth imposing at any rate less than about 10 percent. The higher the rate, however, the greater the burden on low-income taxpayers, and the greater the likelihood that a complex and cumbersome refund scheme will be deemed necessary. In addition, imposition of a VAT or national sales tax would cause a one-time increase in inflation, and the higher the tax rate, the greater the inflation.

In the final analysis, however, the key points about the VAT are what it would do to the economy and who would have to pay. Collecting additional revenue through a VAT instead of a tax on income might result in greater capital formation, but the extent of the beneficial effect is uncertain, and the best evidence suggests that it would be quite small. The VAT would least affect people with the greatest ability to pay, and would most heavily affect people who need to spend all their modest incomes to maintain an adequate standard of living. Compensating for the effects on low-income taxpayers might require complicated programs. The weighing of benefits and costs depends on each person's perception of the need for capital formation and concern about the distributional consequences.

Unlike the value-added tax, which is collected by sellers on each transaction, the expenditure tax (or consumption tax) is collected from individuals or families on an annual basis, like our current income tax. But like the VAT, the expenditure tax moves the basis of taxation from income to consumption.

Most simply put, the expenditure tax is like our income tax, but with two changes: Any income that is saved would be tax deductible, whereas any money that is borrowed, or any prior saving that is spent, would be taxable. In practice, taxpayers would report their income on annual tax returns, just as they do now, but they would add to income all money borrowed and all withdrawals from savings, and would deduct from income all deposits in savings. The result, called taxable receipts, would be the basis for computing the expenditure tax liability. The expenditure tax so computed would replace the current income tax, in whole or in part.

The main reason for choosing an expenditure tax rather than a VAT would be the ability to control the distribution of the burden. An expenditure tax could include substantial personal exemptions or some form of standard deduction to make low-income persons nontaxable. To increase the liability more rapidly as expenditure increased, the expenditure tax could have graduated rates.

The objective of the expenditure tax, like the VAT, is greater capital formation. With savings tax deductible, taxpayers might save more and consume less. That action would lead to more investment and a larger capital stock. As with the VAT, the size of the beneficial effect is unknown but likely to be small. The definition of savings for tax purposes is likely to be contentious. Speculative purchases of precious metals and collectibles could be defined as savings but would not advance capital formation. However, the expenditure tax would surely be a more efficient savings incentive than provisions like the IRA under our current income tax. Because savings would be deductible without limit, taxpayers would always have a marginal incentive to save. Furthermore, because borrowed money would be taxable, the expenditure tax could not be gamed by the borrowing-and-lending schemes that are used on the IRA provision.

The impact of an expenditure tax on different taxpayers is hard to assess. Theoretically, the tax rate schedule could be chosen to duplicate the current distribution of taxes by income group, but the data needed to determine such a tax rate schedule do not exist. Because the tax base of the expenditure tax is smaller than that of the income tax by the amount of savings, the expenditure tax rates must be higher. (Some people assert that the many "loopholes" that exist under the income tax would be repealed under an expenditure tax, but there is no way to know if that would occur.) What evidence there is suggests that people with higher incomes save greater proportions of their income, so the tax rate schedule will have to be steeper as well. Those higher rates will discourage extra work for purposes of consumption.

Perhaps the greatest distinction among taxpayers would be based on wealth. People who had already accumulated wealth could reinvest and accumulate the proceeds without tax. The taxation of gifts and bequests therefore would be crucial; unless such transfers were treated as taxable receipts to the donor or the recipient, wealth could pass from generation to generation while bearing little tax. Some economists have argued for a strengthened gift and estate tax or even a periodic wealth tax to supplement an expenditure tax. Others have argued that either practice would be inconsistent with the purpose of greater capital formation.

Another question about the burden of the expenditure tax relates to the timing of payment. People tend to borrow in the early years of forming a household, save over the more prosperous middle age, and spend their savings in retirement. The expenditure tax would increase the tax burden in youth, in old age, and in years of below-average income due to illness or unemployment, while it would decrease the tax burden in the peak earning years.

Patterns of wealth-holding and timing raise an important administrative question as well. To simplify, if people work today and retire on their earnings tomorrow, they pay tax today under the income tax but tomorrow under the expenditure tax. It follows that people who save in taxable forms under an income tax and retire at the time of transition to an expenditure tax could be badly hurt by double taxation; they would pay income tax when their income was earned and expenditure tax when it was spent. These people would need some form of basis adjustment so that their consumption out of fully taxed income would not be taxed again. At the same time, people who retire on untaxed income (such as withdrawals from IRAs, benefits from qualified pensions, and unrealized capital gains) should be taxed on their expenditures. Distinguishing between taxed and untaxed wealth at the time of transition to an expenditure tax could be a major administrative problem. To prevent concealment of wealth, balance sheets would be needed at the time of transition; this could be a major burden for the taxpayer and the IRS. In addition, a large-scale education program would be needed to acquaint taxpayers with the concepts involved in the expenditure tax.

In sum, the case for the expenditure tax is much like the case for the VAT. Capital formation might increase under the expenditure tax, but the available evidence cannot suggest the size of that effect with any certainty. The effects on taxpayers at different levels of income or consumption could raise perceptions of unfairness, and the changeover to an entirely new tax system cannot be easy. And so, again, the conclusion depends on the individual observer's subjective weighing of the pluses and minuses of the alternatives.

Increasing Existing Excise Taxes

Yet another deficit-narrowing strategy would be to increase existing federal excise taxes. Although excise taxes are currently a small part of the federal revenue system and could not reduce the deficit sufficiently without other action, these taxes could play a significant role in a larger package.

TEFRA increased several excise taxes, but it passed over the excise taxes on alcoholic beverages. These taxes have not been increased since the early 1950s, and because they are defined as a certain number of dollars for a particular volume of beverage, they have been substantially eroded by inflation. The federal excise tax is only about 3.4 cents on a 750-ml bottle of wine, 12 cents on a six-pack of beer, and $1.68 on a fifth of 80-proof liquor. Obviously there is room for an increase. Furthermore, alcohol consumption imposes many public costs and a higher excise tax may be seen to compensate for those costs. There might be less resistance on fairness grounds to increased excise taxes on alcoholic beverages than to a more general consumption tax. However, the beverage and restaurant industries opposed increases in these taxes during deliberations on TEFRA, and their continued opposition can be expected. Doubling excise taxes on alcohol would raise about $4 billion per year.

TEFRA temporarily increased excise taxes on cigarettes and airline and telephone services. The telephone tax was increased from 1 to 3 percent, and its scheduled expiration was postponed from the end of 1984 to the end of 1985. The cigarette tax, which had not been increased since 1951, was doubled through October 1, 1985. Both tax increases raised revenue, but the cigarette tax increase was also motivated by the public costs of smoking. The air passenger ticket tax was increased from 5 to 8 percent; the air freight waybill tax was reimposed (having expired in 1980) at 5 percent; and the international departure ticket tax was reimposed (also having expired in 1980) at $3. These increases are to expire in 1985 and 1987 (air transportation only). Extending these tax increases would narrow the deficits projected for fiscal 1985 and beyond by more than $4 billion per year.

Imposing an Excise Tax on Energy

A final strategy for reducing the deficit would be to impose an excise tax on energy. Among the best news for the economy in recent years has been the softening of oil prices. To some people, taxing energy in this period of relief has all the appeal of shooting oneself in the foot. To others, however, the weakness of oil prices today simply portends renewed tightness tomorrow, and the growing complacency, as evidenced in the greater demand for large automobiles, is extremely disturbing.

People who believe that oil prices will rebound find some appeal in an oil import fee. A fee of $4 per barrel would leave prices below their recent peak. In fact, given the softness of the market, foreign producers might have to cut their prices and thereby absorb part of the tax. Such a fee would encourage domestic conservation and the production of coal and gas as well as oil. If the international market should later tighten, the fee could be reduced or eliminated to cushion the blow to consumers and the economy.

The oil import fee does have some drawbacks: (1) Beyond raising energy prices and thereby boosting inflation, it would initially burden disproportionately the areas of the country (primarily the Northeast) that burn imported oil. In the longer run, however, energy prices should equalize around the country. (2) A more general energy tax, on either all oil or all energy, could have a more uniform burden initially; but a general oil tax would not have the same incentive effect on domestic production as the oil import fee, and the general energy tax would not even encourage production of domestic coal and natural gas. Furthermore, the oil import fee would be simpler to administer. The revenue gain from an oil import fee would be between $1.5 billion and $2.0 billion per year for every $1 per barrel.

Sorting Out the Options

Additional revenues of $50 billion to $100 billion per year by 1988 seem essential to hold the deficit to manageable proportions. The foregoing discussion suggests that only a substantial undoing of ERTA will hit the upper end of that range in one easy stroke, and that option would be costly in political and economic policy terms.

Some smaller steps can probably be taken first. The excise taxes were called on early for contributions in TEFRA, and they will probably be called on again. Extension of the cigarette, telephone, and air travel taxes imposes no new pain, and so is a live option. The alcohol taxes escaped in TEFRA but might be caught in a more careful policy search this time. Then, despite the pain, some energy tax could emerge; the political costs of dependence on foreign oil could impel action. Despite the interest and dividend withholding debacle, further steps on compliance could be implemented. Together these steps would raise between $20 billion and $25 billion per year by 1988.

At this point, distinct alternative pathways begin to emerge. The simplest way to complete a deficit reduction package would be to raise tax rates by a small amount. Either a belated rollback of the third year of the ERTA tax cuts or a repeal of indexation would raise about $40 billion in 1988, and the president's proposed 5 percent surtax (part of the contingency tax package in the FY 1984 budget) would yield about $20 billion. Because Congress has already rejected a $700 cap on the third-year tax cut worth less than $10 billion, action on this front would require a change of heart. On the merits, a tax rate increase is not the best solution, but inaction may prove to be worse.

A second path involves a limited closing of loopholes, à la TEFRA. The options described in this paper show that closing more loopholes causes more pain, but the perceived unfairness and economic distortions associated with tax preferences also cause problems. At current tax rates, the options described here could raise more than $30 billion.

Fiscal policy and economic efficiency would benefit, but the burden of narrowing the deficit would rest heavily on the taxpayers whose preferences were chosen for the sacrificial altar.

A third path, more radical than the first two, is the wholesale repeal of income tax preferences, coupled with a lower rate schedule as partial compensation. Under this option everyone's ox is gored and everyone gets the benefit, either psychological or financial, of sharply reduced marginal tax rates. (As already noted, a 30 percent maximum rate with deficit reduction is feasible.) Perceived fairness and economic efficiency could substantially improve; however, it would be difficult for policymakers to reach a collective decision to forgo the many tax preferences now in the law, and for the users of those preferences (potentially including the homeowner deductions) to endure a possible painful transition.

A fourth option is the value-added tax or a national sales tax to supplement the excise taxes discussed earlier. This approach might be characterized as more adventurous than the more broadly based income tax because it requires the establishment of an entirely new tax (even though the sales tax has been a fixture at the state level for many years). Especially if the national sales tax is chosen, this approach can boast relative simplicity for individual taxpayers, but it would add substantially to the workloads of businesses and the federal government. The one-time inflationary shock upon enactment would be a serious cost. Another disadvantage would be the burden on taxpayers with modest incomes; for political reasons, a complicated refund mechanism might be necessary.

The final option would be a personal consumption tax to back up the excise taxes. This option is clearly the farthest from the terra firma of our current tax system, involving as it does an entirely new tax in use nowhere else in the world. The personal consumption tax has distinct theoretical advantages, but the uncertainty about its practical operation and the certainty of transition problems make it a questionable choice.

Beyond a rerun of the short list of cats and dogs from TEFRA, the simplest and probably least controversial revenue-raising strategy would be increases in the income tax rates, or a cutback or repeal of indexation. Compared with no action at all such an approach might be welcome for fiscal policy, but from the tax policy perspective it would be a disappointment. A better, more politically ambitious, approach would be a restaging of TEFRA, with a new cast of preferential tax provisions cleared from the tax code. Better still would be a complete restructuring of the income tax law, reducing distortions and perhaps even reducing marginal tax rates. This course would answer long-term and widely held concerns about the fairness and complexity of the tax code. Clearly, however, under the pressures of time and politics that the deficit dilemma imposes, restructuring the law would be a giant step indeed.

Notes

1. Jane G. Gravelle, "Effects of the 1981 Depreciation Revisions on the Taxation of Income from Business Capital," *National Tax Journal,* vol. 35, March 1982, pp. 1–20.

2. "Real-Estate Tax Shelters Booming, But Critics Move to Trim Benefits," *Wall Street Journal,* July 5, 1983, p. 25.

3. Among the relevant requirements were (1) the leased equipment must have been usable by firms other than the actual user (thus, highly specialized equipment could not be leased); (2) the owner must have maintained at least a 20 percent interest in the equipment; (3) the owner must have shown a profit from the lease without reference to the tax benefit; (4) the user of the equipment could not have a right in the lease to purchase the equipment at the end of the lease term at less than its fair market value; and (5) the user must not have had an investment in the lease and could not lend any of the purchase price of the asset to the owner.

4. Indeed, a proposal that firms be enabled to borrow against unused investment tax credits (H.R. 3434, the Work Opportunities and Renewed Competition Act of 1983) has already been cosponsored by Representatives James R. Jones and Barber B. Conable, Jr. Furthermore, perhaps because of heightened awareness of the potential of leasing after ERTA, a rash of leasing by nonprofit institutions and governments has broken out.

5. These and all other provisions of ERTA are described in Joint Committee on Taxation, *General Explanation of the Economic Recovery Tax Act of 1981* (Washington, D.C.: Government Printing Office, 1981).

6. These and all other provisions of TEFRA are described in more detail in Joint Committee on Taxation, *General Explanation of the Revenue Provisions of the Tax Equity and Fiscal Responsibility Act of 1982* (Washington, D.C.: Government Printing Office, 1982).

7. There is some inconsistency between the economic forecasts underlying the revenue loss estimates of the two laws.

8. In fact, the situation is even more complex. While the federal individual income tax was becoming more progressive, regressive taxes such as the payroll tax and state sales taxes were growing in their share of total revenues, leaving the progressivity of the overall tax system little changed. It is highly debatable whether the individual income tax should compensate for shifts in the progressivity of other taxes, including state and local taxes.

9. Emil M. Sunley, Jr., "The Maximum Tax on Earned Income," *National Tax Journal,* vol. 27, December 1974, pp. 543–52, explains how the marginal tax rate could be higher than 50 percent in some cases.

10. For longer lists of options and more detailed discussion, see Congressional Budget Office, *Reducing the Deficit: Spending and Revenue Options* (Washington, D.C.: Government Printing Office, 1983), and Joint Committee on Taxation, *Descrip-*

tion of Possible Options to Increase Revenues (Washington, D.C.: Government Printing Office, 1982).

11. For further discussion of this option, see Ladd, "Federal Aid to State and Local Governments," in Gregory B. Mills and John L. Palmer, eds., *Federal Budget Policy in the 1980s* (Washington, D.C.: The Urban Institute, 1984), pp.191–96.

12. S. 1758, the Accounting Cost Recovery Simplification Act of 1983, introduced by Senator Lloyd Bentsen.

13. A broad-based income tax that merely equaled the revenue yield of the current law in one year might raise more revenue later. In recent years, untaxed noncash employer compensation (described earlier) has grown faster than the economy as a whole, moving an increasing share of national income outside the tax base. Taxing such compensation, and any other growing tax-preferred income source or deduction, would thus increase the expected rate of growth of the tax base, apart from raising the level of revenue. If noncash forms of compensation are made taxable, they surely will become less attractive to employees, who may ask to be compensated in cash instead. Even with this change in behavior, however, the currently untaxed noncash compensation will be moved into the tax base, raising its growth rate over time.

14. Assuming a 30 percent increase in the real after-tax rate of return because of the changeover to consumption taxation, and further assuming a 0.2 percent elasticity of savings to that rate of return, personal savings would increase by 6 percent. At 1982 levels, the savings would mean an increase from $125.4 billion to $132.9 billion. However, that $7.5 billion increase would add only 1.4 percent to the actual $521.6 billion of total private savings.

15. Richard Hemming and John A. Kay, "The United Kingdom," in Henry J. Aaron, ed., *The Value-Added Tax: Lessons from Europe* (Washington, D.C.: The Brookings Institution, 1981), pp. 75–89.

3 • What's in Store for the Income Tax?

The first thing we realize as we look toward the future of the individual income tax is that we stand at a most unusual vantage point.[1] The Economic Recovery Tax Act of 1981 (ERTA) was unprecedented. It was the largest tax cut in the history of the Republic, perhaps the largest since the fall of the Roman empire. Nobody seems to know for sure.

The size of the ERTA cuts convinced many tax analysts that there would be no further income tax legislation for some time. The reasoning was that no further tax cut would even be considered, and that no other tax change would be politically feasible without an accompanying tax cut to sweeten the deal. This sense of immutability evaporated as the long-term implications of ERTA became clear. The fear of ever increasing budget deficits, even with the administration's proposed 1983 budget cuts, has galvanized the will of the Congress to do something that it has always hesitated to do: raise taxes.

Will the individual income tax be changed in a long-run budget realignment? The size of the looming budget deficits (exceeding $200 billion per year by fiscal 1985 on a current policy basis) strongly suggests that there must be substantial changes in both outlays and revenues. On the revenue side, the individual income tax seems to be a prime target for at least two reasons: first, it is the largest current source of revenue, and thus would require the smallest proportional increase of any existing tax to yield a given additional revenue; and

Reprinted from *Challenge*, 25:5, 14–24. This article was a paper delivered at the Annual Symposium of the National Tax Association/Tax Institute of America in May 1982. Reprinted, with some minor revisions, from the September 1982 issue of the *National Tax Journal*, with permission.

second, it was just cut substantially, and so some partial backtracking might not be too painful. To these two reasons some tax experts might add the shortcomings of the current individual income tax, and the chance that a revenue raising bill might improve the tax system.

Though our individual income tax is generally acknowledged to be the most successful tax in the world by any criteria, complaints (perhaps caused in part by our high standards) would surprise no one. The complaints can be summarized as follows: the tax system is too complicated; inflation distorts the intended effects of the system, particularly with respect to income from capital; and the mass of special features in the code diverts resources from productive activity toward tax gamesmanship, provides windfalls to those who can manipulate their affairs to take advantage, and requires high marginal tax rates that choke off work, saving, and investment. It may be fairly easy for us to agree on such an indictment of the income tax, but agreeing on a solution would be far more difficult. Therein lies the heart of the following discussion: How might we increase federal revenues and come closer to our goals of efficiency, simplicity, and fairness for the individual income tax?

An Expenditure Tax?

One alternative to the current individual income tax is a progressive expenditure tax. The expenditure tax has roots extending back to Kaldor and beyond.[2] The case for the expenditure tax is well developed and well understood, at least among tax economists. Controversy over its merits continues because value judgments, the bane of the social scientist, influence or perhaps dominate the debate.

Some discussion of the expenditure tax is essential to the evaluation of the future of the income tax. To reassure the uninitiated, while an expenditure tax would require us to pay a year-end tax on our spendings at the grocery and the five and dime, it would not require that we save all of those cash register tapes under penalty of the stockade. Rather, the expenditure tax would work superficially much like the current income tax.[3] The tax would be withheld out of workers' paychecks, just as it is now. When the expenditure tax return was filed, the same income computation as is made now would be the first step in finding the final tax liability. However, from income would be deducted all saving: the increase in checking and savings account balances, purchases of stocks and bonds, and so on (saving could obviously be negative rather than positive). The tax base would thus be all of income that was not saved (or all of income plus further spending out of prior saving): hence, expenditure.

Fairness

A tax on expenditure as so defined has numerous properties with respect to fairness that are very attractive to some economists.[4] Some tax experts argue that expenditure is a better measure of what a taxpayer takes out of the economic system than is income, and thus is a more appropriate tax base. Further, the expenditure tax, unlike the income tax, has a coherent interpretation in the context of the taxpayer's entire lifetime. Two taxpayers with equal discounted lifetime incomes and no prior wealth or saving at death will pay equal discounted lifetime taxes under a proportional expenditure tax. This equal treatment over the lifetime ex ante is an attractive property. Another aspect of the same attribute is the close association of consumption and expected lifetime income, which is an implication of the permanent income hypothesis. Thus taxation of consumption in any given year is likely to be a closer approximation of taxation of lifetime income (which some would argue is the correct tax base) than is taxation of current income.

Against these attractive properties of expenditure taxation must be weighed counterarguments and qualifications.[5] Other tax experts argue that income measures the taxpayer's power to consume, and that income is thus the better tax base. One could question the importance of equal present discounted tax liabilities of equally endowed individuals in a world of rapidly changing fortunes and economic conditions, as well as widely diverging endowments. Further, the assumptions required for this ex ante lifetime equivalence will surely not be borne out in practice, because bequests diverge quite far from zero, and an expenditure tax would certainly not be proportional. (In fact, if upper-income households saved more of their income, as is thought to be the case, the expenditure tax would need a steeper rate schedule than the income tax to achieve the same progressivity with respect to income.) One might further question the wisdom of a tax on consumption as a proxy for permanent income. Such a tax would increase liabilities relative to an otherwise equivalent income tax for the taxpayer's years of lower than trend income, such as youth, old age, and (most significantly) involuntary and unexpected unemployment. Finally, a tax on the more stable tax base of consumption would be nearly procyclical, compared to the automatic stabilizer effect of the income tax which cushions macroeconomic fluctuations.

A final possible fairness problem is the accumulation of wealth. Wealth accumulated tax-free under the expenditure tax could be more easily passed on to succeeding generations (even considering our current estate tax, which was designed to deal with accumulations from income that was already taxed). Concerned economists have advocated periodic wealth taxes, more stringent estate taxation, or taxation of gifts and bequests to the donor as his consumption. The fear is that if such taxation were absent, wealth would be saved without tax, accumulate without tax, and then be given to an heir without tax (as a gift, or lightly taxed as a bequest) to accumulate further without tax. Others have argued that taxation of gifts and bequests to the donor, and then again to the donee when consumed, would be double taxation; or that heavier wealth taxation would be a significant disincentive to saving. Of course, the Congress has been extremely tentative in its handling of the taxation of wealth: it sharply cut back estate taxation last year. Virtually nothing definitive can be said in this area. I can only note that the treatment of wealth, gifts, and bequests in an expenditure tax will be extremely controversial; that we know virtually nothing about the effect of wealth taxation on taxpayer behavior in the current context, much less under an expenditure tax; that the choices made could have enormously significant implications for the distribution of wealth; and that the legislative outcome in this area would be highly unpredictable.

Simplicity

A second criterion for comparison of the income and expenditure taxes would be simplicity and ease of administration.[6] Theoretically, the expenditure tax does not require many of the special provisions (or "loopholes" if you prefer) of the income tax. Thus, the expenditure tax might have a cleaner base and be simpler for taxpayers and administrators. Of course, the income tax has no theoretical need for those special provisions either, but they exist nonetheless.

Would the expenditure tax in fact have a cleaner base? Perhaps an expenditure tax could be passed while the lobbying interests were caught with their conceptual pants down, not understanding the expenditure tax and thus not prepared to argue their cases effectively. Perhaps starting from a clean slate would encourage the Congress to resist the special pleaders. On the other hand, the forces behind the complexity of the current tax code might seize the opportunity, and convince the Congress to give them more than they already have. One could imagine any number of socially admirable forms of expenditure—housing, education, medical care, charitable giving, etc. (automobiles?)—that might be exempted from expenditure taxation by a sympathetic Congress. We could easily exchange a leaky and inefficiency-inducing income tax base for an equally leaky and inefficiency-inducing expenditure tax base.

One special attempt to simplify the expenditure tax is the prepayment concept, pioneered by the Treasury under David Bradford.[7] Under the expenditure tax as previously conceived, taxpayers would be required to report each purchase of an asset (in order to claim the deduction for saving) as well as each sale (in order to report the receipt of the proceeds). Thus, in comparison to the current income tax, under which only sales need to be reported, the expenditure tax would require twice as much paperwork. Advocates of the prepayment approach reason that investment outcomes are essentially random, and so the Treasury should be indifferent as to whether taxpayers deduct their investments when they make them and pay tax on the proceeds upon sale; or forgo the deduction upon making the investment and then omit paying tax on the proceeds when the asset is sold. If all taxpayers declined the deductions for the purchases of investment assets in any given year, and then omitted the sales proceeds from taxable receipts the next year, the Treasury would collect $N of additional taxes in the first year and $N $(1 + r)$ less in the second (where r is the average rate of growth in the economy). There would thus be no revenue consequences for the Treasury in present value terms, neither sales nor purchases of prepaid assets would be taxable events, and the compliance load would be decreased rather than increased relative to the income tax.

The prepayment option is an intriguing approach to simplifying tax administration and compliance. Unfortunately, it has some possibly serious problems.[8] For one thing, tax returns are filed several months after the tax year ends. An investor could make an investment, observe its performance for a year or more, and then file his return electing prepayment or postpayment to his own advantage (and the detriment of the Treasury). This problem could be solved by requiring the taxpayer to make an immediate election, but that would send millions of pieces of paper floating to the IRS each year, totally negating the simplification attributed to prepayment. (Mandatory prepayment would not work either, because many taxpayers of modest means would need the immediate deduction for their saving.) Even with immediate elections, the system could still be successfully gamed. Investments could be partitioned into low and high return portions, or common and preferred stock could be issued, allowing investors to make informed choices in their tax elections. In short, the Treasury would not get a random draw under prepayment. And one might just imagine the public reaction to the first highly successful prepaid investment, in light of our recent experience with safe harbor leasing (under which corporations were legally enabled to exchange their tax advantages).

The expenditure tax is not simple. A transition to it would involve considerable difficulty in appropriately forgiving tax on consumption out of income already taxed under the income tax. At the same time, fairness requires taxing consumption out of income untaxed under the prior income tax regime (such as accrued but unrealized capital gains). Hoarding of cash and tax evasion over the transition period would have to be detected. The administrative burden under such a transition would be immense. All of our tax treaties with other nations would have to be renegotiated, puzzling conceptual problems would be raised, and our bargaining positions would probably be weak. Finally, the routine administration of the expenditure tax would have to be developed at considerable cost. It has been argued that the administrative problems of the expenditure tax are no more formidable than those of the income tax. However, administration of the income tax has been learned by doing, over sixty years, in part while the public sector and the yield of the income tax were both small. Leaping into the expenditure tax cold turkey with a much larger fiscal and administrative load would be costly, even though those costs might be paid in full once we accumulate an equivalent stock of expenditure tax experience.

A final complication of the expenditure tax is that borrowed money must be taxed just like wages or interest income. Without this feature, taxpayers would be able to borrow money without tax consequences, put it in the bank, and claim a tax deduction for saving; if such maneuvering were permitted, the expenditure tax would be essentially optional. Needless to say, many taxpayers might be confused if such a provision were to appear in the tax law.

Economic Efficiency

This brings us to the final (and to some observers, the crucial) criterion for judging the two tax systems: economic efficiency. The expenditure tax would reduce the tax burden on income from capital by exempting saving from tax. In so doing, it would equate the before- and after-tax rates of return on saving; under the income tax, the after-tax return is lower because income is taxed when earned and its subsequent investment return is also taxed. This leads to two advantages for the expenditure tax: first, the incentive to save is probably increased; and second, the allocation of saving and consumption over time is made more efficient. Of the two advantages, the second seems to attract less interest from noneconomists, and so we might pay more attention to the effect of the expenditure tax on saving.

Despite the theoretical ambiguity, it seems likely that the expenditure tax would increase saving relative to an otherwise equivalent income tax: that is to say, saving would probably increase due to an increase in the after-tax rate of return.[9] However, the magnitude of the increase in saving is likely to be small, and given the relatively limited role of personal cash saving in total U.S. capital formation, the effect on the size of the capital stock is likely to be quite small.[10] There may also be offsetting efficiency losses. To the extent that the tax burden on income from capital is decreased, the tax burden on income from labor must increase if an equal or greater revenue yield is to be achieved. This would lead to possible reductions in labor supply. The manifestation of this shift in tax burdens would be the higher marginal tax rates under an expenditure tax. For the same degree of leakage from the tax base, the expenditure tax, with its deduction for saving, would require higher marginal rates. Thus, income that is received and consumed currently, typically income from labor, would be taxed at higher rates.

Not only is the effect of the expenditure tax on saving highly uncertain, but saving behavior under the current tax law is not well understood. Data are extremely sparse and inexact.[11] Thus, the proper tax rate schedule for a new expenditure tax would be difficult to determine, with error likely on both the distribution and the yield of the tax relative to what was intended. Some income groups are likely to receive unintended tax cuts or face unintended tax increases, and the federal government could easily impose a "fiscal surprise" shock on the economy by miscalculating the revenue yield of the tax.

Finally, the expenditure tax has a theoretical advantage in its handling of inflation. Because consumption is a current concept, the expenditure tax base would need no adjustment for inflation. If the expenditure tax had graduated rates and relief for low expenditure taxpayers, it would still require bracket and exemption indexing to be fully inflation-proof; but that would be much simpler than indexing the tax base. The inherently current expenditure tax base also eliminates the need for measurement of depreciation, a complication under the income tax.

To summarize, the choice between the expenditure tax and the income tax on efficiency grounds is probably a close call. The expenditure tax has benefits in its treatment of income from capital, but its concomitant increase in taxes on labor income must be considered in determining the overall welfare gain or loss. Likewise, with respect to fairness, the expenditure tax has the attractive quality of equal taxes on equal lifetime expenditure streams; but there are reasons to question the importance of that attribute, and other questions might be asked about accumulations of wealth. Policy makers who have to choose between the two tax systems might be swayed by the imponderables of transition to and administration of a totally different tax system.

So before we either snap up the expenditure tax or reject it out of hand, we should consider other options for the income tax itself.

Indexing?

The rapid inflation of the past decade has significantly distorted the operation of the tax system. Real tax liabilities have increased through years of slow growth and high unemployment, because inflation eroded the value of the personal exemption and zero bracket amount (formerly the standard deduction) and pushed taxpayers into higher marginal rate brackets. ERTA solved this problem by indexing the exemptions and the tax brackets (including the zero bracket), but indexing does not begin until 1985 (after the scheduled tax rate cuts are completed).

However, a potentially more serious problem remains. The amounts of income to be taxed are themselves distorted by inflation, in that dollar-denominated assets and liabilities depreciate in real terms when the price level rises. Thus, a 10 percent bond yields only 2 percent real interest during 8 percent inflation; with a 50 percent nominal tax rate, the real rate of tax is a confiscatory 250 percent. Mere tax rate indexing barely makes a dent in this problem. The solution is indexing the tax base: allowing the depreciation of assets due to inflation to be deducted from taxable income, and including the depreciation of liabilities in taxable income. Realized capital gains on assets with variable nominal values would also be indexed. These steps would eliminate the taxation of income that represented only compensation for inflation, and would initiate the taxation of inflation's improvement of the real net worth of debtors. We might expect real interest rates to become more stable, because the risk of confiscatory real tax rates would be eliminated. The incentive to save might be increased for the same reason.

Of course, indexing's beneficial effects are not free. Indexing the tax base would require some extraordinarily complex changes in the tax code.[12] (For example: What would be the correct inflation adjustment on the sale of a home that had been financed with a mortgage loan? Only the seller's equity in the home should be indexed, but that equity changed continuously as the mortgage loan was amortized.) There would be further compliance and cash management problems for taxpayers. Until the inflation statistics were compiled, taxpayers would be uncertain of the tax liabilities on the income from their investments. Debtors would have to pay tax on the depreciation of their liabilities without a corresponding cash receipt from which to pay the tax. Leveraged investors might seek indexed incomes to assure themselves of cash to pay the tax on the depreciation of their liabilities if inflation accelerated. Thus, indexing the tax code might lead to further indexation of a broad range of financial transactions, causing a rapid transmission of inflationary shocks throughout the economy. Such a development would make inflation harder to stop.[13] Finally, the nominal and real revenue impact of tax base indexing would be extremely difficult to predict, because ostensibly offsetting inflation adjustments to borrowers and lenders might in fact move taxable income from high to low tax rate brackets or vice versa. Thus, the government's finances would be less predictable. The distribution of the tax burden could be drastically reshuffled, leaving many taxpayers with quite different liabilities from those they had expected and upon which they had planned.

The current budget outlook raises other questions about ERTA's tax rate indexing. With burgeoning deficits predicted for 1985 and beyond, some tax experts have called for the repeal of indexing to help narrow the gap. Others who value indexing highly have proposed retaining indexing, or even starting it sooner, while repealing some of the scheduled rate cuts or raising taxes in other ways.

Both tax rate and tax base indexing are controversial, and are likely to remain so. Continued progress in reducing inflation might set back the drive for indexing, while more rapid inflation will surely give it even greater impetus.

A Flat Rate Income Tax?

Probably the most frequently mentioned alternative to the current income tax is a flat rate system—the use of a single marginal tax rate. Obviously, one could institute a flat rate while doing nothing else whatsoever to the tax system, but most flat rate proposals include some broadening of the tax base to allow a lower marginal rate.

The rationale for the flat rate tax can spring from the most fundamental notions of fairness. The progressive income tax is based on the concept of ability to pay, according to which taxpayers with higher incomes should contribute greater shares of their incomes in taxes. However, some tax analysts as well as interested laymen argue that taxing everyone's income at the same rate is fairer than favoring some taxpayers with lower rates than others. Blum and Kalven in the classic, *The Uneasy Case for Progressive Taxation*, argue against progressive rates on a number of grounds and seem to view a flat rate tax with more favor.[14]

One could find more pragmatic advantages for a flat rate, especially in the current context. With virtually all taxpayers facing the same marginal rate, there would be no incentive to shelter income by artificially moving it from high- to low-bracket taxpayers. Taxpayers who are consistently taxable could not profit by timing their realizations of income to years when they are in the low tax rate brackets. The marriage penalty could be eliminated. And finally, the flat rate tax would have no "bracket creep" as such, and so it would be less sensitive to inflation than a tax with progressive rates.

Two distinct types of flat rate taxes have been proposed. The first is a gross income tax—that is, a flat rate tax on gross income of individuals[15] without exemptions or deductions of any kind. The reasoning behind the gross tax on income is that the marginal tax rate can be made so low with a broad tax base that no low-income relief is needed. System 1 in Table 3.1 shows the effect on tax liabilities by income class of a tax on annual gross income (including capital gains in full) yielding the equivalent of 1984 law tax revenues at 1981 income levels. The marginal (and average) tax rate needed is 11.8 percent. As is obvious from the table, the gross tax on income is starkly redistributive, increasing taxes for every income class below $30,000 and decreasing taxes for every class above. The tax reduction for the income class above $200,000 is 53.2 percent, while the tax increase at the $15,000–$20,000 level is 28.8 percent or over $450 per return. If these low-income taxpayers were to be held harmless by a mechanism outside of the tax system, a sizable increase in the present income support system of means tests and caseworkers would be required. If the tax system itself is to be used to reduce this added burden on the lowest income groups, then some form of relief for those groups must be introduced.

The other three flat rate tax systems in the table show how the introduction of low-income relief would alter the outcomes. System 2 demonstrates a change to a flat rate with the remainder of the 1984 tax law unaltered. The results suggest why most flat rate proposals specify a broadening of the tax base: the tax rate required, at 18.5 percent, is much higher than that of the gross tax on income using the broader base. Because the flat rate in this context is a straightforward rate

increase for low-income taxpayers and rate cut for upper-income taxpayers, the distributional result is not in doubt; taxes are increased by
30.0 percent at the $15,000–$20,000 income level, and cut by 56.5
percent at over $200,000 of income. Nonetheless, the introduction of
low-income relief does make the system progressive, in contrast to the
gross tax on income.

One approach to reducing both the required marginal tax rate and the
redistributional effect of the flat rate tax is to broaden the tax base.
Pulling some of the well-to-do's tax-exempt income into the tax base
raises their liabilities and reduces the required marginal rate, thereby
lightening the load of those with lower incomes. System 3 illustrates the
effect of broadening the tax base by taxing long-term capital gains in
full and prohibiting itemized deductions. The tax rate required to reach
1984 law revenues is reduced to 15.7 percent, but the redistributive
effect of System 2 is only partially offset. The tax increase in the
$15,000–$20,000 income class is 19.0 percent, or over $300 per re-
turn; the tax cut over $200,000 of income remains substantial at 38.7
percent, or almost $39,000 per return. It would be possible to broaden
the tax base still further, but System 3 probably encompasses the bulk
of the potential base broadening. Thus, any further neutralizing of the
redistributive effects of the flat rate tax would have to come from
expanding the low-income relief.

System 4 uses the same broadened tax base as System 3, but increases low-income relief significantly: the personal exemption is increased from $1,000 to $1,500, and the zero bracket amounts are
increased from $2,300 to $3,000 for single taxpayers, and from $3,400
to $6,000 for joint returns. The added low-income relief further miti-
gates but does not solve the redistribution problem. The expanded
exemptions and zero bracket amounts do reduce tax liabilities for low-
income taxpayers, but they also require a higher marginal tax rate, in
this case 18.7 percent. Taxpayers above $50,000 of expanded income
still receive tax cuts on average, with those over $200,000 saving 27.7
percent or almost $28,000 per return. Tax increases on average are
faced by taxpayers with expanded incomes from $10,000 to $50,000.
At the comparatively modest $15,000–$20,000 income level, tax increases average about $125, or 7.7 percent of 1984 law tax liability,
while in the $20,000–$30,000 income class the tax increases are 9.3
percent, or almost $250 per return.

This redistributive effect of increasing low-income relief under a flat
rate tax has a simple intuitive explanation. Increasing the amount of

Table 3.1

Distribution of Tax Liabilities under Alternative Flat Rate Tax Systems Compared to 1984 Tax Law[a] at 1981 Income Levels

Expanded income (thousands)	Number of taxable returns (thousands)	Tax liability 1984 law (millions)	System 1			System 2		
			Tax liability (millions)	Change (percent)	Change (dollars per return)	Tax liability (millions)	Change (percent)	Change (dollars per return)
<5	6,482	403	5,479b	1,259.5	783.07	1,574b	290.7	180.71
5–10	15,057	5,772	14,280	147.4	565.04	8,752	51.6	197.91
10–15	13,092	12,526	19,700	57.3	547.99	17,610	40.6	388.31
15–20	10,737	17,462	22,496	28.8	468.88	22,665	30.0	484.54
20–30	16,800	44,080	49,701	12.8	334.58	52,871	19.9	523.28
30–50	13,568	63,833	60,579	−5.1	−239.82	66,419	4.1	190.61
50–100	3,580	38,687	27,389	−29.2	−3,155.74	30,486	−21.2	−2,290.90
100–200	631	18,656	9,872	−47.1	−13,920.58	10,743	−42.4	−12,540.20
200<	164	16,385	7,675	−53.2	−53,107.15	7,129	−56.5	−56,438.05
Total	80,110	217,803	217,172	−0.3	−7.87	218,249	0.2	5.57

	System 3			System 4		
	Tax liability (millions)	Change (percent)	Change (dollars per return)	Tax liability (millions)	Change (percent)	Change (dollars per return)
	2,232b	453.7	282.10	1,996b	395.2	245.71
	7,854	36.1	138.26	5,345	-7.4	-28.33
	15,720	25.5	243.97	12,698	1.4	13.11
	20,778	19.0	308.88	18,802	7.7	124.76
	49,978	13.4	351.06	48,170	9.3	243.45
	66,466	4.1	194.08	68,804	7.8	366.41
	32,658	-15.6	-1,684.20	36,104	-6.7	-721.60
	12,459	-33.2	-9,821.59	14,344	-23.1	-6,833.56
	10,050	-38.7	-38,630.67	11,843	-27.7	-27,692.33
	218,194	0.2	4.88	218,106	0.1	3.78

Source: Joint Committee on Taxation.

System 1: 11.8 percent tax on adjusted gross income with long-term capital gains included in full.
System 2: 18.5 percent tax on 1984 law taxable income less zero bracket amount.
System 3: 15.7 percent tax on 1984 law taxable income less zero bracket amount, with long-term capital gains included in full, and no itemized deductions.
System 4: 18.7 percent tax on taxable income as in system 3 with increased exemption and zero bracket amount.

Notes:

ª To facilitate comparison, 1984 law does not include the earned income credit, the two-earner couple deduction, or the IRA or Keogh provisions. The flat rate tax systems similarly do not include those provisions.

b Outcomes under the flat rate tax for tax returns of under $5,000 of income would be highly uncertain. Some taxpayers at that income level currently make use of tax preferences that would be terminated under the flat rate tax, and those taxpayers would thus face substantial tax increases. A particular problem would arise under System 1, in which all income would be subject to tax without exemption or deduction; many households with very low incomes who are excused from filing tax returns under the 1984 law are therefore not represented in the table, but would have to file returns and pay taxes under System 1. The impact of this factor on the table would probably be small, though it would significantly change administrative burdens under the tax system.

income that can be received without tax reduces the tax burden on the lowest-income taxpayers. At the same time, the flat tax rate is still lower than the current average effective tax rate of the highest-income taxpayers, and so they get tax cuts too. With tax cuts for the top and the bottom, it is the middle that is left holding the bag. In comparing System 4 with System 3, the more generous low-income relief in System 4 exempts a family of four with incomes up to $12,000 from taxation, compared to $7,400 under System 3. However, the higher tax rate wipes out this advantage for the family of four at about $36,000 of income, and families with that comparatively modest income were already facing tax increases under System 3. Above the $50,000 income level, the flat rate tax still allows tax cuts compared to the 1984 tax law. There is no way to fine-tune these effects out of the system, because there are only two dials to turn—the flat rate and the amount of low-income relief—and they afford little flexibility, especially when a revenue constraint is imposed.

Perspectives on Redistribution

How much of a problem is this inherent redistributive effect of the flat rate tax? There are probably as many opinions on the proper degree of progressivity of the tax system as there are taxpayers. As was noted above, some people believe that the flat rate is a fair, equal proportional sharing of the tax burden, and let the liabilities fall where they may. Others might want more progressivity than any flat rate system could give. But there is one benchmark that the uncommitted would probably want to consider, and that is how tax liabilities are distributed now.

The table suggests that a flat rate income tax, however it is constructed and with no more than 1984 law yield, would impose a larger share of the tax burden on middle-income taxpayers. If (as was suggested at the outset) a revision of the individual income tax at this time would be likely to raise additional revenues, middle-income taxpayers would not only bear the entire tax increase, but would also make up the difference for the substantial tax cut for those with higher incomes. Further, the figures in the table show the average tax increases for the middle-income groups, but obviously some taxpayers would face larger tax increases than others. Taxpayers who lose their itemized deductions (including mortgage and auto loan interest and property taxes) in the base-broadening process would have the largest tax increases, and that group would include many homeowners who have much of their household budget contractually committed to mortgage and automobile payments. Such households would probably find the adjustment to higher tax liabilities difficult.

Another perspective on the redistribution of the tax liabilities in System 4 can be seen by combining its tax changes with those of the Economic Recovery Tax Act of 1981 (ERTA). It has been argued that ERTA's tax cuts were equitable because they averaged the same percentage (about 23 percent) in all income groups. If System 4 is combined with ERTA, however, the tax cuts relative to pre-ERTA law are between 18 and 20 percent for the $15,000–$50,000 groups, but about 30 percent for the $50,000–$100,000 group, 40 percent for the $100,000–$200,000 category, and almost 44 percent for those with over $200,000 of income.

This redistributive effect could be moderated by increasing the low-income relief still further, and raising the tax rate to make up for the revenue loss. However, such a change might make the flat rate less attractive. If all taxpayers faced a flat rate of perhaps 20 percent, the combined marginal tax rate on labor (including the Social Security payroll tax and state and local income taxes) might exceed 30 percent for most taxpayers. This would be an increase for many low-wage workers.

Of course, Congress would not necessarily veto a change in tax policy on the basis of its distributional effects alone; the benefits of the flat rate tax in terms of greater simplicity are significant. How many of these benefits would we have to give up to reduce the redistributional effects?

Old-fashioned Tax Reform?

We have examined several alternative futures for the individual income tax. The purposes of these alternatives have been to simplify the tax system, reduce or eliminate the sensitivity of the tax rates or base to inflation, reduce disincentives to work, saving, and investment, broaden the tax base, reduce horizontal inequities, and discourage manipulation of the tax system. Each of the options discussed requires a leap of faith: the expenditure tax would raise significant, and to some extent still unknown, administrative and distributional issues; indexing the income tax base would drastically reshuffle tax liabilities and alter borrower-creditor relationships; and the flat rate tax would systematically shift a greater share of the tax burden to the median voter. The traditional inertia of our taxwriting process would suggest that these options are longshots, although the recent rather adventurous adoption of the 5–10–10 tax cut, and the current dire budgetary situation, might lead us to reconsider the odds.

We might also throw into the hopper a least common denominator solution: good old-fashioned tax reform. If the Congress will broaden the tax base for the expenditure tax or the flat rate income tax, perhaps it will do so for the progressive income tax. The Congressional Budget Office (CBO) enumerated 40 possible base-broadening steps in *Reducing the Federal Deficit: Strategies and Options* earlier this year [1982], and there are surely many more base-broadeners waiting in the wings. Advocates of flat rate or expenditure taxation suggest that their strategy of surprise, in which a totally new and different tax system is sprung on the nation's tax lobbyists, is the best shot at cleansing the tax base. They may be right. But then again, they may be wrong.

Base-broadening under the progressive income tax would split the difference between the status quo and the conceptually more ambitious options on many of the tax policy goals. With base broadeners such as those suggested by CBO and others, the tax rate schedule could be lowered and flattened. To suggest orders of magnitude, a 14 percent first bracket rate with low-income relief would closely mirror the distribution of the 1984 tax law up to about the $40,000 income level. That would, in effect, give about 75 percent of all taxpayers a flat rate tax without redistributing income. Above that income level, a small number of additional tax brackets, perhaps three, would be needed to keep the distribution of tax liabilities approximately constant, with the highest tax rate under 30 percent. Such a tax system would approach the flat rate in simplicity, though some of the multi-bracket problems would remain. It would have a lower marginal tax rate for most taxpayers, but would require a slightly higher maximum rate. Bracket creep would not be eliminated as in the flat rate tax, but it would be significantly reduced. There would be a marriage penalty, but it would probably be less than half of that under current law, even without a special deduction. Finally, it would be possible to achieve the marginal rates stated above without elimination of the basic homeowner deductions (mortgage interest and property taxes); this would leave some of the complication in the tax code but would cause fewer taxpayers to face tax increases than would eliminating itemized deductions entirely.

In terms of economic efficiency, the broad-based progressive income tax would be comparable to the expenditure tax. The marginal tax rate on income consumed currently would be lower under the broad-based income tax than under the expenditure tax. Income from capital would continue to be double-taxed under the broad-based income tax, but at lower marginal rates than under the expenditure tax, and so the ultimate incentives to save might not be very different. The lower marginal tax rates would reduce (but not eliminate) the overtaxation of income from capital due to inflation, and the lower and flatter rate schedule would make market interest rate adjustments more effective in offsetting the rest of inflation's redistributive effects.[16]

What the broad-based progressive income tax lacks is conceptual purity: it does not offer a single tax rate, total inflation neutrality, or complete optimality in the treatment of saving. On the other hand, it is simple, operationally close to the system we already know and understand, would not drastically redistribute tax liabilities compared to current law, and moves in the right direction according to virtually every criterion.

In a legislative atmosphere of frantic activity and unbounded uncertainty, improving the tax system has as good a shot as anything else. It would be a shame if the advocates of simplicity, efficiency, and fairness came away empty-handed for lack of trying.

Notes

1. Valerie Amerkhail, James Nason, Kathleen O'Connell, Nancy O'Hara, Joseph Pechman, Pearl Richardson, Hy Sanders, Martha Smith, Emil Sunley, and James Verdier provided helpful comments on drafts of this paper. William Sutton and Xe Nguyen kindly advised on and executed the simulations in Table 1. Shirley Hornbuckle typed the manuscript. Responsibility for opinions and any errors is the author's alone and should not be attributed to the Congressional Budget Office or any of the above named individuals.

2. Nicholas Kaldor (1955). Kaldor quotes Fisher, Pigou, and Hobbes as supporters of the expenditure tax concept.

3. William D. Andrews (1974) originated the cash flow approach to expenditure taxation discussed here.

4. This discussion relies on U.S. Department of Treasury (1977) and David F. Bradford (1980).

5. This discussion follows Richard Goode (1980).

6. A highly detailed discussion is provided by Michael J. Graetz (1980); see also Sven-Olof Lodin (1980) and Paul R. McDaniel (1980).

7. U.S. Department of the Treasury (1977).

8. As explained by Graetz (1980) and Alvin C. Warren, Jr. (1980).

9. The research of E. Philip Howrey and Saul H. Hymans (1980), and comments by Michael J. Boskin (1980) and John A. Brittain (1980), indicate considerable uncertainty as to the exact elasticity of saving to the real after-tax rate of return, but suggest that it is probably positive and small.

10. Assuming a 30 percent increase in the real after-tax rate of return due to the changeover to an expenditure tax, and further assuming a 0.2 elasticity of saving to that rate of return, personal saving would increase by 6 percent, or at 1981 levels from $106.6 billion to $113.0 billion. However, that $6.4 billion increase would add only 1.3 percent to the actual $477.6 billion of total private saving.

11. Recent data are presented in U.S. Department of Labor (1978a) and (1978b). However, these data are from a relatively small random sampling of the population, and

thus include relatively few of the upper income households who are thought to do most of the saving. Total saving in these surveys seems to be roughly consistent with national accounts data, but conceptual differences prevent any definitive comparison.

12. This discussion relies on research presented in Henry J. Aaron (1976).

13. Arthur M. Okun (1981), chapter 7.

14. Walter J. Blum and Harry Kalven, Jr. (1953).

15. By "gross income" is meant a concept approximating adjusted gross income in the current income tax, which is the sum of numerous income components, some of which are "net"—e.g., net partnership income, net rental income, etc. It is not meant to suggest some measure of gross receipts, in which total business receipts would be included with no deduction for business expenses such as wages, cost of goods sold, etc.

16. If all taxpayers were subject to the same marginal tax rate during inflation, market interest rates could increase so as to hold constant both the real after-tax interest incomes of lenders and the real after-tax interest expenses of borrowers. See Tanzi (1980), chapters 10 and 11. While a system with more than one marginal tax rate (not to mention some nontaxable borrowers and lenders) prevents such a precise market adjustment, the broad-based income tax system with a flatter rate schedule would allow a more precise adjustment than the current income tax.

References

Aaron, Henry J., ed. 1976. *Inflation and the Income Tax*. Washington, D.C.: The Brookings Institution.

Andrews, William D. 1974. "A Consumption-type of Cash Flow Personal Income Tax." *Harvard Law Review* 87, 1113–88.

Blum, Walter J., and Harry Kalven, Jr. 1953. *The Uneasy Case for Progressive Taxation*. Chicago: University of Chicago Press.

Boskin, Michael, J. 1980. "Comments," in Pechman (1980), pp. 34–41.

Bradford, David F. 1980. "The Case for a Personal Consumption Tax," in Pechman (1980), pp. 75–113.

Brittain, John A. 1980. "Comments," in Pechman (1980), pp. 41–48.

Goode, Richard. 1980. "The Superiority of the Income Tax," in Pechman (1980), pp. 49–73.

Graetz, Michael J. 1980. "Expenditure Tax Design," in Pechman (1980), pp. 161–276.

Howrey, E. Philip, and Saul H. Hymans. 1980. "The Measurement and Determination of Loanable Funds Saving," in Pechman (1980), pp. 1–31.

Kaldor, Nicholas. 1955. *An Expenditure Tax*. Westport, Conn.: Greenwood Press.

Lodin, Sven-Olof. 1980. "Comments," in Pechman (1980), pp. 276–282.

McDaniel, Paul R. 1980. "Comments," in Pechman (1980), pp. 282–295.

Okun, Arthur M. 1981. *Prices and Quantities: A Macroeconomic Analysis*. Washington, D.C.: The Brookings Institution.

Pechman, Joseph A., ed. 1980. *What Should Be Taxed: Income or Expenditure?* Washington D.C.: The Brookings Institution.

Tanzi, Vito. 1980. *Inflation and the Personal Income Tax: An International Perspective*. Cambridge: Cambridge University Press.

U.S. Department of Labor. 1978a. *Consumer Expenditure Survey: Integrated Diary and Interview Survey Data, 1972-73*. Bulletin 1992. Washington D.C.: U.S. Government Printing Office.

U.S. Department of Labor. 1978b. *Consumer Expenditure Survey: Interview Survey 1972-73*. Bulletin 1997. Washington D.C.: U.S. Government Printing Office.

U.S. Department of the Treasury. 1977. *Blueprints for Basic Tax Reform*. Washington D.C.: U.S. Government Printing Office.

Warren, Alvin C. Jr. 1980. "Comments," in Pechman (1980), pp. 120–125.

PART III
ECONOMIC AND
POLITICAL ISSUES

4 • Why Bradley-Gephardt?

I am grateful for the opportunity to testify before this Subcommittee on the Fair Tax Act of 1983, known as the Bradley-Gephardt bill. Let me emphasize that opinions expressed in this statement are my own, and should not be attributed to the Urban Institute, its officers, trustees, or funders.

My mandate from the Subcommittee is to discuss Bradley-Gephardt primarily from the perspective of fairness. Because the bill is called the "Fair Tax," this must be a good place to start. But what sets Bradley-Gephardt apart from all of the other tax restructuring proposals to date is its *balance*—its ability simultaneously to get closer to *all* tax policy goals (economic efficiency, simplicity, and a smaller deficit, as well as fairness). Such balance requires a careful trade-off among these objectives, and so each provision of the bill affects every goal. Thus, even a targeted discussion of fairness in Bradley-Gephardt will necessarily be fairly general.

What Is Wrong with the Income Tax?

There is a growing consensus that the tax system must be restructured in 1985. We must understand the very serious problems that have motivated this consensus before we can solve them.

The symptoms of these problems are rapidly declining public esteem for, and deteriorating compliance with, the tax law. In a 1972 poll, a plurality of the American people (36 percent) identified the federal income tax as the most fair tax in the United States. (This is in comparison to 33 percent who named state sales taxes. Only 19 percent said that the individual income tax was the least fair tax.) But only 11 years later, a poll using identical language and sampling methodology showed that a plurality of the population (35 percent) now believes that the income tax is the *least* fair tax. A majority of respondents to a more detailed 1978 poll said, above all, that the income tax isn't fair; middle-income persons pay too much, while the wealthy and big corporations pay too little.

A similar message comes from tax-filing behavior. The Internal Revenue Service (IRS) estimates that revenue lost owing to taxpayer noncompliance more than tripled from 1973 to 1981. Indications are that taxpayers are increasingly reluctant to report their own incomes and pay their taxes.

At the same time, businessmen and economists complain that the tax system is stifling enterprise and growth. They blame high tax rates and complex legal provisions that intrude upon private decision-making.

What causes these problems? Popular perceptions of tax unfairness do not arise from any lack of progressivity in the conventional sense. Internal Revenue Service statistics show that tax liabilities as a percentage of income increase smoothly as income increases, so the wealthy do pay a larger share of their incomes in tax on average. Nor is the falling popularity of the income tax caused by more high-income persons avoiding tax entirely; the number of nontaxable upper-income persons has remained small and roughly constant over the past ten years. If we want to find the root of the problems with our tax system, we have to look in a somewhat different direction.

There is a common thread to all of our tax policy problems. It is the attitude that all of us—individual taxpayers, businesses, and tax policy-makers and administrators—have come to have toward the tax system.

The market economy in the United States is sometimes called an economic "game." This may seem a fairly casual reference for the economic system in which millions of Americans earn their livelihood; but that is how a market economy works, and that is the way we want it. The game has winners and losers, and it is the winner's prize that motivates people to work hard and come up with the new ideas that make everyone more prosperous.

Not too long ago, the income tax was just a means of raising revenue. People played the economic game, and then the winners gave a share of their prizes to the federal government. But now things are different.

The problem is that the income tax has become a part of the game.

The income tax is no longer just a share of the winnings determined by fixed, fair rules. Now it is a measure of success, subject to the control of the taxpayer, like a firm's costs or a household's expenses. Businesses compete with one another to cut their taxes—even by lobbying for favorable targeted tax legislation—just as they fight over customers. And "keeping up with the Joneses" means getting a better tax shelter to help pay for the longer vacation.

With the income tax thrown in, the game has become destructive. There is no longer an agreement on the rules. Some people still play the old way, with taxes a civic duty not to be manipulated. But others jump into the contest head first, using every technique—mostly legal, sometimes illegal—to cut their taxes. Those who still play by the old rules are being eaten alive by others who are not so restrained.

There are still others with a different problem. The average taxpayer, who works for a modest wage or salary to support a family, cannot play the tax game whether he is willing to or not. He cannot afford expert help, and most tax manipulation strategies are only profitable in the higher brackets anyway. Even if the average taxpayer were resigned to his share of the winnings under the old economic game, he is angry because he can't even compete in the tax game. To him, the tax system is unfair because of the advantages others have, and it is too complex because he can't understand how it works.

This limbo between the old and new rules of the game is breaking down our traditional standards. It is hard to resist the appeal of tax reduction strategies, so more and more people decide to play; that is why tax shelter investments have increased so spectacularly. People who are just beginning to climb up the ladder resolve that when they have the wherewithal, *they* won't be chumps for the tax collector. Each tax advisor—a member of a new profession—has to come up with the raciest deals for his clients; if he doesn't, someone else will. Everybody in the field knows that the IRS does not have the resources to examine even 2 percent of all returns, and so the tax planner can do anything short of the outrageous. And what is "outrageous"? Our standards are changing—some would say deteriorating—every day.

So everyone loses. The federal government loses revenue. Taxpayers lose their trust in the "system"—the income tax system and their government in general. Perhaps worst of all, everyday people view each other with distrust and suspicion. But it doesn't stop there.

The income tax game makes us all poorer. Income tax manipulation enriches the clever but stagnates the society. It is a distortion and a diversion. When people earn income in the traditional market economy, they add to our nation's wealth. In the long run, we all share in this wealth through a larger capital stock and higher wages. When people play in the income tax game, however, they add nothing to our national wealth; they merely transfer wealth from one sector to another. They contribute to their own prosperity, but not to the nation's.

And in the long run, even the selfish products of tax manipulation are illusory. While one taxpayer cuts his tax burden, others are doing the same. Ultimately, the federal government has to collect some given revenue, and so what taxpayers save by manipulating the tax law must be made up by general tax rate increases (or forgone tax rate cuts). It is what has been called "the fool's golden rule"; while one taxpayer is shifting his tax burden to others, those others are shifting it back.

How Can We Fix the Income Tax?

We have to take the income tax out of the economic game. We cannot continue with the income tax as an important strategic and tactical part of our economic life. Inaction will continue to drain the government's revenues, destroy our national morale, and erode our prosperity.

Such substantial reform is easier said than done. There has been growing sentiment for action, but little agreement on what should be done, with serious discussion of such radical steps as new taxes on consumption. For the last two years, however, the Bradley-Gephardt bill has attracted growing attention as a far-reaching but realistic approach. These hearings confirm this interest.

Bradley-Gephardt would reduce the incentives for tax manipulation by cutting tax rates, and would repeal tax provisions that permit manipulation and distort economic decisions. With these two steps, it would reduce the intrusion of the income tax into our economic life.

Reducing Tax Rates

With the onset of supply-side economics, tax rate cuts have become fashionable. Without question, cutting tax rates helps to get the income tax out of the economic game; zero tax rates certainly would accomplish this end, and otherwise, the lower the better. But we have to raise a certain amount of revenue to keep the deficit in bounds, and eventually to eliminate it. So tax rates cannot be cut casually.

The Bradley-Gephardt approach has some unique features. It starts with a basic tax of 14 percent that is the only tax for about 80 percent of the population (couples with incomes under $40,000, and single people with incomes under $25,000). The single rate will help to demystify the tax system for this group, which includes those who need the most help to understand it.

Above that level, tax rates increase in two steps. There is a 12 percent surtax on adjusted gross income (that is, *total* income) from $40,000 to $65,000 for couples ($25,000 to $37,500 for single people); this makes the combined tax rate in that range 26 percent (that is, the 14 percent basic tax plus the 12 percent surtax). The surtax rate increases to 16 percent on income above $65,000 for couples ($37,500 for single persons), making the combined maximum rate 30 percent.

The reduced maximum rate also helps to reduce the intrusiveness of the tax system. High-income taxpayers have the most to gain or lose from tax-related decisions; the higher the tax rate, the greater the incentive to shelter an extra dollar of income, and the less the incentive to earn another dollar. The lower the tax rates, the less these considerations intrude upon the dictates of the market.

Personal exemptions and standard deductions also are part of the tax rate structure. Bradley-Gephardt increases the taxpayer exemptions (for taxpayer and spouse only) to $1,600; other exemptions remain at $1,000. The standard deduction for married couples increases to $6,000; for single persons, to $3,000. With these changes, families of four can earn $11,200 before paying any tax, compared to $7,400 under the current law. This brings the tax-free income level, which has been eroded by inflation, up to the poverty line. Further, the flatter rate schedule and new standard deductions eliminate the marriage penalty for couples with incomes under $40,000, and reduce it substantially at higher income levels.

Cutting tax rates helps the tax system and the economy, but it will not work miracles. The 1981 tax law ignored this important fact; it cut tax rates with no other changes to the law, and assumed that all of our other tax and economic problems would just vaporize. It didn't happen.

The 1981 law was passed in anticipation of rapidly growing federal revenues. Instead we have the monster deficits that in part motivate this reexamination of tax policy.

The 1981 law was expected to enhance voluntary compliance and reduce the use of tax shelters. The Administration even recommended a cut in fiscal 1982 IRS examination funds on these grounds. In fact, however, all signs are that compliance continues to deteriorate. And not only has tax shelter usage boomed, but the supply-side rhetoric apparently carried very little water within the Administration.

So tax rate cuts are only one part of a package to deal the income tax out of the economic game. The 1981 tax law missed this reality, but Bradley-Gephardt does not.

Repeal of Tax Law Provisions

Legal provisions that reduce taxes under narrow conditions cause trouble. They encourage taxpayers to squeeze what they would do anyway into the tax-favored categories, reducing the government's revenue and the public's respect for the law. And they distort taxpayers' behavior, leading them into activities that are economically inferior to others in the marketplace.

There are three general categories of legal provisions repealed or cut back by Bradley-Gephardt: saving and investment incentives; targeted sectoral incentives; and itemized deductions.

Saving and Investment Incentives

Our nation may well need more saving and investment, but the tax incentives used thus far have been inefficient or counterproductive. Some of these provisions technically apply more to businesses than individuals, but individuals can and do form businesses for the express purpose of using these provisions to create tax shelters. This obviously reduces public respect for the income tax.

The accelerated cost recovery system (ACRS) and the investment tax credit (ITC) were intended to increase investment by reducing its tax burden. ACRS gives cost recovery deductions for investment in plant and equipment significantly faster than these assets actually wear out. The ITC reduces tax by a fraction of the cost of investment in equipment, thereby in effect paying for part of the investment.

The problem is that in a high tax-rate system, the cash value of these tax incentives can exceed the tax on the income generated by the investments; in other words, there can be a net subsidy rather than a net tax. Armed with these subsidies, tax planners can reap after-tax profits from relatively or totally unprofitable investments. Further, the federal government loses revenue even on investments that would take place without the subsidy. So rather than increasing productive investment, these incentives may divert funds into unproductive investment, and leave the federal government with less revenue to use in productive ways.

Bradley-Gephardt takes a better route. It repeals the ITC, and replaces ACRS with a simpler depreciation system that mirrors the actual wearing out of plant and equipment. The revenue so gained allows substantial cuts in marginal tax rates. The result is a low tax on investment income rather than a subsidy. It is unlikely that the low tax would discourage much productive investment. In fact, it might encourage *more* investment if firms make their investments in the expectation of earning large profits that would be taxed at the high marginal rates of the current law. What the Bradley-Gephardt approach certainly does is cut way back on purely tax-motivated investments that would generate little or no true income. With the tax subsidy gone, investments will have to generate income in the marketplace to be attractive.

Deductions for interest expense are another trouble spot in the current law, because a major element of the classic tax shelter is leverage. Taxpayers borrow to finance tax-favored investments, and deduct all of the interest. Bradley-Gephardt restricts this practice by limiting interest deductions to the amount of the taxpayer's investment income. (There is an exception only for mortgage interest under Bradley-Gephardt's basic 14 percent tax rate.) This interest deduction limit makes the tax system fairer by reducing tax manipulation, and more efficient by directing investment into profitable rather than tax-favored activities.

The exclusion for 60 percent of long-term capital gains is another savings and investment incentive that has gone astray. The exclusion makes some investments more attractive by cutting the tax on their returns more than in half. But it biases investment toward assets that throw off their returns as capital gains—for example, speculative real estate and unproductive collectibles. Conversion of ordinary income into capital gain is a major underpinning of most tax shelters, including the totally unproductive "tax straddles" so prominent of late. Finally, the exclusion for long-term gains discourages taxpayers from realizing short-term gains when it would be economically productive to do so.

Bradley-Gephardt repeals the capital gains exclusion. The tax rate cuts leave the maximum rate on capital gains just above that of the much-heralded tax cut of 1978. There is no relative disadvantage to realizing short-term gains, so taxpayers can realign their portfolios as often as they like. Income in different forms is taxed the same way, and so opportunities for tax sheltering are eliminated.

Other general savings and investment incentives are cut back or eliminated. The net interest exclusion, scheduled to take effect next year, is repealed. The contribution limits on top-heavy pension plans are reduced by one-third. For taxpayers without very large pensions, however, pension treatment will not change, nor will the rules for IRA and Keogh accounts.

There have been allegations that Bradley-Gephardt does not address the nation's capital formation problem, and that it is not an incentive for saving. This allegation misses the point. Bradley-Gephardt provides the strongest and most efficient incentive for saving: low tax rates on all income from capital, however derived. To illustrate: Compare Bradley-Gephardt to the net interest exclusion, a widely heralded saving incentive. The net interest exclusion (if and when it takes effect) will allow couples to exclude from tax 15 percent of their interest income, but not capital income in any other form, and not beyond $6,000 of income. For the top bracket taxpayer, this reduces the tax rate on some interest income from 50 percent to 42.5 percent. In contrast, Bradley-Gephardt reduces the top rate on *all* income from capital, not just interest and not just up to some ceiling, all the way to 30 percent. So Bradley-Gephardt is clearly superior to the net interest exclusion as an incentive to save.

The fatal mathematics of such saving gimmicks is fairly simple. While such provisions might induce a small amount of new saving, they inevitably also lose revenue for some past saving and for some current saving that would have taken place even without the incentive. So, for example, wealthy couples will receive $450 tax cuts under the net interest exclusion even though they would collect over $6,000 of interest income with no incentive. If the government is short of revenue, this unproductive revenue loss must be made up somehow, and in the final analysis it will happen through tax rates higher than they otherwise need be. But these higher tax rates will discourage *all* saving—not just some particular form of saving, and not just saving up to some particular ceiling. Worse still, the higher tax rates also will discourage work and investment.

So these saving gimmicks are like drilling holes in the bottom of a leaky boat to let the water out. Bradley-Gephardt takes a better path with a gimmick-free law and low tax rates for all income from capital and labor.

Targeted Tax Incentives

Today's tax law includes numerous targeted investment subsidies. These provisions are designed to provide relative advantages to particular industries or sectors of the economy. They are perhaps the worst intrusions of the tax system on the economic game.

Such targeted incentives distort investment decisions dictated by the market. They reduce taxes on investments that would have been made without the subsidy. When combined with general incentives such as ACRS and the ITC, they can create the most lucrative and unproductive tax shelters. Firms in unfavored but equally deserving industries ask for their own tax breaks to compete for investment capital, further complicating and eroding respect for the tax law. And as the targeted subsidies proliferate in number they tend to neutralize one another, defeating their original purposes.

Bradley-Gephardt repeals or cuts back more than a score of such provisions, including incentives for oil and gas, timber, building rehabilitation, life insurance, banking, DISCs, controlled foreign subsidiary corporations, possessions corporations, corporate farms, construction, credit unions, and low-income housing. Bradley-Gephardt also repeals incentives for research and development, business energy conservation and pollution control investment, finance leasing, collapsible corporations, and tax-exempt private purpose financing. Some of these incentives are more justifiable than others, but none is justifiable in the absolute. They all have flaws in providing windfall gains, complicating the tax law, encouraging tax shelters, and distorting economic activity. The economy will grow faster without these provisions intruding on the economic game.

A final targeted tax incentive, benefitting workers, is the tax exemption for employer-provided fringe benefits. This tax exemption encourages employees to negotiate for compensation in kind—as life insurance, health insurance, legal insurance, and subsidized day care. While all of these forms of compensation may seem desirable, there is no reason why the federal government should intrude between employer and employee to influence how compensation is paid. Workers and employers can decide that for themselves.

Beyond that issue, the tax exemption for fringe benefits causes some serious policy problems. It has become a gaping loophole through which a rapidly increasing proportion of total compensation passes without tax. The more this loophole is used, the smaller the tax base becomes, and the higher tax rates must be; the higher the tax rates, the greater the incentive to pay compensation through fringe benefits. It is a vicious cycle. Further, the tax exemption encourages employees to ask for more of their compensation in the form of insurance than they would otherwise want; some health industry experts say that this is driving up the cost of medical care. And finally, not all workers can get generous fringe benefits; low-wage employees and some of the self-employed are left out. It is unfair that those who don't get fringe benefits have to pay tax on all of their compensation, while those who get fringe benefits don't.

Bradley-Gephardt repeals the exclusion for insurance premium and day-care fringe benefits. Employers and employees will decide on compensation patterns that make more economic sense, tax rates will be significantly lower, and all employees will pay tax on a fairer measure of their income.

Some people argue that the tax subsidies for oil, timber, and banking make the tax system unfair. Economists disagree, explaining that additional resources will flow into the subsidized industries, reducing their rates of return to equal those elsewhere. While this argument is unquestionably theoretically true, it begs some important real-world questions. Unlike in the theoretical models, resources are not perfectly interchangeable, and do not flow instantaneously from one industry to another. Mom and pop cannot fold up their grocery store and whisk it off to Texas to become an oil rig. So despite our theoretical sophistication, we should not dismiss out of hand the alleged unfairness of business tax breaks.

Itemized Deductions

Itemized deductions make the federal government share in selected personal expenses. Those taxpayers who itemize have part of their state and local taxes, medical and interest expenses, casualty losses, and charitable contributions paid for by the federal government. Some of these itemized deductions are more justifiable than others, and some are so embedded in our economy that they would be nearly impossible to remove.

Bradley-Gephardt selects the deductions that are least justifiable and also possible to eliminate; those deductions are repealed. They include the sales and personal property tax deductions, and the deduction of nonbusiness interest expense in excess of investment income. The medical expense deduction is limited to expenses in excess of 10 percent of income (compared to 5 percent under the current law). The objective is to eliminate deductions for routine expenses, so that tax rates can be reduced.

Bradley-Gephardt also limits itemized deductions to the 14 percent basic tax; deductions do not apply to the surtax. (The only exception is that interest expense is deductible from investment income for purposes of the surtax.) This restriction eliminates the "upside-down subsidies" in the current law, whereby up to 50 percent of the medical expenses, mortgage interest, and charitable contributions of high-income taxpayers are reimbursed through the tax system, but as little as 11 percent are reimbursed for low-income households.

The Bradley-Gephardt surtax is thus a tax on adjusted gross income, applying only to the 20 percent of the population with the highest incomes. The surtax thus has an extremely broad base, and its rate can be correspondingly low. This is part of the reason why the highest rate can be as low as 30 percent while collecting current law revenues. If itemized deductions are not limited in this way, tax rates must be higher.

Repealing and limiting itemized deductions helps to get the tax system out of the game. Tax considerations enter into many everyday economic decisions when a taxpayer switches from the standard deduction to itemized deductions. Repealing deductions saves some taxpayers the hassle of itemizing, and reduces the tax intrusion into many itemizers' lives. Reducing tax rates, and limiting the rate to which deductions apply, further dials down tax consciousness. These steps are essential to the ultimate objective.

Restoring Fairness

There is no simple, unambiguous definition of fairness in taxation. No flat rate tax is incontrovertibly fair; there are an infinite variety of definitions of income and levels of exemptions and tax rates for a flat tax, and they can't all be fairest. A more progressive tax is not necessarily fairer; confiscation of the incomes of the rich, or anything near confiscation, would violate many people's conceptions of fairness. In the final analysis, fairness is what the people say it is, and the people's voice on such complex and abstract questions, absent a national referendum, is inevitably unclear.

So no one plan is objectively the fairest; we must decide how the people would judge any given plan. In my judgment, the public would consider the Bradley-Gephardt package to be fairer than both the current tax law and the alternative proposals put forward to date.

Bradley-Gephardt does not redistribute the income tax burden from one income group to another. The amount of income taxes paid in each income group remains the same. Thus, Bradley-Gephardt makes no broad changes in policy toward the distribution of income. Income distribution is a legitimate issue, but it should be considered separately from the tax structure.

While not redistributing the overall tax burden, Bradley-Gephardt removes inequities within each income group. Two people with the same incomes now might pay very different amounts of tax, because one receives untaxed fringe benefits or invests in tax shelters. Bradley-Gephardt broadens the definition of income to include many types of income not now taxed, so people with the same income would pay more nearly the same tax.

Everyone can agree that people with similar incomes should pay generally similar taxes, which they often don't now; and everyone can agree that tax rates should be as low as possible, which they are not now. So everyone should agree to a tax system with a comprehensive definition of income, fewer opportunities for tax manipulation, and a tax burden distribution identical to what we have now. With these structural issues decided, anyone from any persuasion can argue for tax rates that are more or less progressive. That decision, within reasonable bounds, does not affect the basic tax policy imperative of a broad and water-tight tax base.

One aspect of Bradley-Gephardt that seems necessary for reasonable standards of fairness is its increased exemptions and standard deductions. There has been a near-consensus for at least a decade that families in officially defined poverty should pay no income tax, but the exemptions and zero bracket amounts (ZBAs) that protect poor families from paying income tax have been eroded substantially by inflation since last adjusted in 1978. The 1981 tax law included substantial tax rate cuts, but did not increase the exemptions and zero bracket amounts; so the tax burdens of poor families increased substantially, not just from prior inflation, but from inflation from 1981 through 1984. In its neglect of these problems, the 1981 tax law did have a bias toward the wealthy, who received more than enough in tax rate cuts to compensate them for inflation. Every tax proposal will have to redress this neglect to pass muster.

In sum, while there can be no definitive conclusion, Bradley-Gephardt as a package seems to me to be likely to meet with public approval. It eliminates demonstrable inequities in the tax code, but maintains the distribution of the tax burden that was established in 1981 and that the Congress has refused to change since. While no tax system will ever satisfy everyone's subjective opinion of the proper distribution of income, this one eliminates structural imbalances that are objectively unfair.

Feasibility and Transition

An idea like Bradley-Gephardt has no practical value unless it can be enacted and implemented. Bradley-Gephardt, in my opinion, has the overall design most favorable to prospects for enactment and ease of transition. Nonetheless, there should be no illusions that enactment will be painless and transition easy. Despite the obvious need for such a restructuring, quantum change inevitably involves dislocations and sparks resistance.

Bradley-Gephardt may be more politically feasible than many smaller-scale approaches in at least one important sense. By removing many leakages in the tax base simultaneously, Bradley-Gephardt does allow for a reduction of tax rates. This gives taxpayers who lose important tax preferences some compensation in the form of significantly lower tax rates. In contrast, limited approaches to tax base broadening, such as those of this and the preceding two years, raise little revenue and allow no rate reduction; so taxpayers who lose their preferences are singled out to bear the burden of narrowing the deficit. This process has become increasingly painful, and is now perhaps so painful that it cannot be continued. The Bradley-Gephardt approach may be the only way to make further progress on broadening the tax base and reducing the deficit in the long run.

A second plus of Bradley-Gephardt is its building on the current tax system, rather than altering the structure radically. Progressive rates are retained, as are standard deductions and personal exemptions. This means that the pattern of taxpayers' liabilities will remain much the same. In contrast, other proposals that shift to flat rates and different forms of low-income relief redistribute taxes from one income class, or one group otherwise defined (the elderly, the self-employed), to another.

One of the problems with restructuring the tax system without a tax cut to sweeten the deal is that some people have to pay higher taxes. When taxpayers are blindsided in this way, they have painful adjustments to make. By following the patterns of the current law, Bradley-Gephardt minimizes those tax increases and the adjustments that necessarily follow.

Bradley-Gephardt has a long leg up on the pure flat taxes in that it maintains the broadly used tax deductions for mortgage interest, charitable contributions, and state and local income and property taxes. Lower tax rates reduce the value of these deductions, but lower tax rates are a necessary part of any proposal to get the income tax out of the economic game. Going still further and repealing these deductions would leave homeowners, homebuilders, and charitable institutions with the most painful transitions. Retaining these deductions, as Bradley-Gephardt does, makes the necessary restructuring easier.

Proponents of tax bills with no deductions have argued that allowing some deductions makes success less likely. They claim that the first deduction opens the flood gates to a bidding war, and that the end result will be worse than the current law. No one can prove that logic wrong. But many of the same people expect to add mortgage interest and other deductions to their bills at the markup stage to increase their chances of passage. Bradley-Gephardt makes the necessary judgments and compromises about deductions up front. Any additional deductions must be paid for by raising more revenue elsewhere, presumably with higher rates. This "pay-as-you-go" approach should have at least the same chance of success as starting with a "clean bill" as an admitted first offer.

While Bradley-Gephardt makes the necessary changes as easy as possible, change is never painless. Changing the tax system without cutting taxes means that some people have to pay more. The Congress has had to face this reality in its efforts to narrow the deficit over the last three years, and so this is nothing new. But the process of passing Bradley-Gephardt, even with its much lower tax rates, should not be compared with the tax rate cutting in 1981. Leadership will be required to restructure the tax law, much more than just to cut taxes.

Some people argue that no major restructuring can be done now because people have made investments in the last few years in reliance on existing tax preferences. They say that tax reform must wait for five or ten years, when it will be more feasible. This argument ignores the reality that people will continue to act in reliance on existing tax preferences in the next five or ten years. There is no easy time to break with the past. But those same investors knew that several recent presidents, IRS commissioners, and members of Congress, including Bill Bradley and Dick Gephardt, have called for a broader tax base with less opportunity for abuse. These investors knew the risks they were taking, and those risks were built into the returns on their investments. They have reaped their rewards. Their special interests should not stand in the way of the general interest.

Ten years ago, the American people believed that the federal individual income tax was our fairest tax, and "Made in Japan" was the punch line of a joke. Can we afford to wait ten more years for a fairer, more growth-oriented tax law?

Reference is sometimes made to transition rules that will ease the pain for the taxpayers with affected investments. The effectiveness of targeted transition rules should not be exaggerated. An asset whose profit comes mainly from reducing taxes will fall in market value if the tax benefit is taken away. Allowing the current owner to retain his tax benefit for any number of years or until he sells the asset will not prevent this fall in market value. The best that can be done is to enact the restructuring with a prospective effective date, that is, to take effect perhaps two years after enactment. That will give markets time to determine the new values of affected assets, and will give taxpayers notice to reconsider investments in these areas. Some targeted transition rules may help to a limited further degree, but such procedures are no cure-all, and they can complicate the law and create new opportunities for manipulation.

Without any doubt, 1985 will be a year of challenges in economic policy. Tax policy will be one part. The choices will not be easy, but the reward to wisdom and leadership could be great.

Bradley-Gephardt and the Deficit

Bradley-Gephardt is designed to raise revenues equal to the current law's in its first year (in the current version of the bill, 1985). However, it would raise increasingly more revenue in every succeeding year. This is because it would repeal tax loopholes that are growing faster than the economy, including many tax shelter deductions and employer-provided fringe benefits. This means that Bradley-Gephardt can make a substantial contribution to a long-term deficit reduction program.

Bradley-Gephardt contrasts sharply with some of the competing proposals that would not only lose revenue in their initial years, but would lose increasing amounts of revenue every year into the long run.

Conclusions

Not too long ago, the federal income tax was respected by the American public, and had a relatively limited impact on our daily economic life. Today, however, the income tax has become an integral part of the economic game. Some individuals and many businesses plan their every move around the tax law. This tax consciousness leads to massive economic waste, as valuable resources are devoted to complying with the tax law and minimizing tax liabilities. It is divisive and demoralizing, as some taxpayers watch others cut legal corners to reduce their taxes, and wonder whether they should do the same. And above all, it just isn't fair.

The Bradley-Gephardt bill is one attempt to get the tax system out of the game. It cuts tax rates dramatically, to reduce the incentives for tax manipulation; and it repeals many of the tax law provisions that make manipulation possible. It would remove tax considerations from many economic decisions, and restore market forces to their proper role. The economy should work better, and the popular wrath against the tax system would be dissipated.

The deterioration of our tax system has made the last ten years an exciting time for policymakers and tax specialists. A rapid succession of tax acts has been passed to plug the growing leaks in our tax base and stop the growth of noncompliance and abuse. Other legislation has aimed to increase incentives and stimulate growth. The watershed tax law of 1981, while correct in its intention to reduce tax rates, failed to take the additional necessary steps of broadening the tax base and stopping tax manipulation; indeed, the new law made matters worse. So public respect for the tax law has continued to fall, and noncompliance to climb.

Bradley-Gephardt gives us a chance to end that excitement—by stopping all the high stakes tax sheltering, getting the tax system off of businessmen's minds, and ending the distrust and suspicion of one taxpayer for another. The economic game will become more exciting—with more attention to markets, productivity, competition, and profits. But the tax end of the operation, after the usual frenzy of the legislative process, should become rather dull.

For people of the tax persuasion, the last ten years have been kind of fun. But in the interests of the taxpayer and the federal government, we might give Bradley-Gephardt a close look.

Let's make taxes boring again.

5 • Semantics of the Flat Rate Tax and Tax Reform

Two of the most frequently used terms in economics and politics today are "flat rate tax" and "tax reform." Hardly a policy agenda appears that does not include one or both. Yet these terms mean different things to different people. The current imprecision may cause some confusion, and may delay and distract the political debate. An evaluation of the role of these concepts today might not get far beyond a definition of terms. This analysis will try to get at least that far, with a few subjective observations along the way.

What Is the Flat Rate Tax?

For a policy option whose hallmark is simplicity, the flat rate tax has become a surprisingly complex and slippery concept. The federal income tax has had graduated rates since its inception. Until World War II, the upper graduated rates affected only a few people—but so did the lowest rate, for that matter, because only a small minority of the population paid income tax at all. The rates themselves were quite low, except in the period during and immediately after World War I.

World War II brought the income tax to a majority of the population and pushed the highest marginal rates above 90 percent for the first time. The postwar buildup in strategic arms and the Korean conflict kept government spending high and required continuation of high tax rates. It was in the subsequent atmosphere of somewhat reduced tensions that the high and steeply graduated marginal tax rates, previously accepted in the spirit of wartime sacrifice, were first questioned.

Reprinted with permission from *Cato Journal*, Vol. 5, No. 2 (Fall 1985), pp. 437–48. © Cato Institute.

Pure and Practical Flat Taxes

To many, the connotation of a "flat tax" is something that is completely uncompromised; all income is subject to tax and is taxed at a single rate. That was not the form that the most prominent early flat tax proposal took. When Blum and Kalven (1953) raised their objections to "the uneasy case for progressive taxation," they proposed in its place what they called a "degressive tax," that is, a tax at a single rate on all income above some exemption or standard deduction. The exemption or deduction was included to avoid the ethical failing of imposing taxes on the poor (though there was no official definition of poverty at the time).

With the low-income relief of their degressive tax, Blum and Kalven introduced a certain arbitrariness into the flat tax concept. They admit that the appropriate size for the exemption or deduction is necessarily controversial. It is but a short step from the degressive tax to any number of variations that bear little resemblance to the traditional notion of a pure flat tax.

Modified Flat Taxes

In fact, the current tax debate has moved from the flatness of the billiard table to the finely drawn distinctions of a quality relief map. The issue is not flatness in absolute terms, but rather comparative degrees of flatness. Milton Friedman, a long-standing advocate of the flat tax, has himself argued for imposing a maximum marginal rate (usually 25 percent) at the top of the current graduated tax schedule (Friedman 1980). This would put a sizable minority of taxpayers into a single marginal rate bracket, but it would leave little of total income subject to tax in that bracket. Thus, it would be a flat tax at the margin for a few, but by no means a flat tax for the many.

After Friedman's suggestion, numerous analysts have tried other variations on the basic flat tax theme to achieve particular combinations of objectives. Of the prominent tax proposals currently on the table, only one—the Hall-Rabushka package introduced by Senators Dennis DeConcini and Steven Symms—could be described as a flat rate tax by even the very general definition of having a single tax rate. And even that proposal seems somewhat distant from the mainstream of policymakers' thinking at this time.

The object of most policymakers' affection now is the so-called modified flat tax (this term being an improvement of the prototype "progressive flat tax"). The modification, of course, is that the modified flat tax is not flat. Two of the proposals in this category, the Treasury's package of November 1984 and the "Fair Tax" proposed by Senator Bill Bradley and Representative Richard Gephardt, employ only three tax rate brackets (down from the current law's 14 non-zero rate brackets for married couples and 15 for single people), with the lowest bracket extending high enough on the income scale to accommodate upward of 70 percent of all taxpayers (Friedman's suggestion stood on its head). These proposals are flat taxes, therefore, for the majority of the population; but they both specify significant progressivity at the upper end of the income scale (with maximum rates of 35 percent and 30 percent respectively). A third prominent proposal, the Kemp-Kasten "FAST Tax," has a basic tax rate of 24 percent, but allows a 20 percent exclusion of earned income up to the amount of the Social Security payroll tax wage base, phasing the exclusion out over the next roughly $60,000 of earned income. Thus, the Kemp-Kasten bill has what is in effect another three-bracket system, but in this case with the highest rate in the middle (where the earned income exclusion phases out).

The reason for the algebraic gymnastics in the Kemp-Kasten proposal, and the reason why the Hall-Rabushka proposal has not caught on outside of a relatively narrow circle, is simply that a single marginal rate of tax, whatever the low-income allowances, will significantly redistribute the tax burden. In particular, with low-income relief provisions anywhere near the levels of the current law, the single-rate tax will lift a sizable share of the tax burden from upper income groups and increase the tax burden for median income groups. Members of Congress and others have been reluctant to endorse approaches that would increase the tax liabilities of the majority of their constituents.

The only defense against these redistributive effects within the constraint of a single tax rate is to cut the yield of the tax (either by reducing the tax rate or increasing the low-income relief) until middle income taxpayers are held harmless. This leaves the federal government short of revenue, of course; it also gives upper income taxpayers even larger tax cuts.

Both the revenue loss and the upper income tax cuts have been denied by some advocates on the ground that there would be substantial supply-side increases in income and tax revenues on the part of these upper income taxpayers. Regardless of whether these supply-side effects would materialize, several factors must be kept in mind. First, the federal budget is now in substantial deficit. If a flat rate tax with a substantial revenue cost is enacted, and if the supply-side responses do not materialize, the short-term economic costs could be catastrophic, and the long-term costs would certainly be serious. Second, unlike the 1981 across-the-board tax rate cuts, a flat rate tax would reduce the marginal tax rate and thus enhance incentives almost exclusively for the upper income population; thus, the flat rate tax's supply-side leverage on the population as a whole would be less. Although the claims of supply-side responses to the 1981 law focus mainly on these upper income groups, it is clear that the responses, if they have occurred, have not yielded sufficient revenues to control the deficit.

In sum, there are no pure flat rate tax proposals (meaning a single tax rate and no relief to lower income groups) on the market today. This should not be surprising, nor should it be lamented; the tradition of the last 20 years of lifting the tax burden from the poor should be continued. The flat tax mantle, however, can easily be spread over such tax systems as the Hall-Rabushka proposal, but these systems have failed to hold center stage.

Should the modified flat tax, in its many incarnations, be considered part of this flat tax family? The 1984 Treasury proposal (Treasury I) and the Bradley-Gephardt proposal are single-rate taxes for the bulk of the population. On the other hand, there are precedents from traditional tax reform for lower rate income taxes with many fewer brackets (for example, the Treasury's 1977 Blueprints for Basic Tax Reform had three income tax brackets). Thus, the parentage of the modified flat tax is uncertain, though there are apparent family resemblances from both the flat tax and the tax reform clans. If the lineage of the modified flat tax is subject to dispute, how do the two strains embodied in it relate to one another?

What Is Tax Reform?

As noted earlier, there has been an identifiable strain of tax policy analysis known as "tax reform" for some time. But in recent years, this strain has become even more confused than the flat tax concept. This confusion is due mainly to the differing values of various analysts and policymakers. In part, however, the confusion about the identity of tax reform is due to the political appeal of the term. According to one of the tongue-in-cheek "Ten Commandments of Tax Policy," "Whatever you want to do, call it reform." This section examines the subcategories of tax reform to see how the flat tax fits in. What is tax reform, and how does it relate to our recent policy debate?

Economic Income

Perhaps the most traditional strain of the tax reform school calls for the use of an economic measure of income. This strain points out the distinctions between the "true" income of taxpayers, including all accretions to their economic well-being, and the measure of income that is used for tax purposes. The earliest contributions to this school of thought were absolutely fundamental to the development of scholarly thinking on income taxation (Haig 1921; Simons 1938). It was this scholarly literature that led to the understanding of income for tax purposes as consumption plus the increase of net worth over a given accounting period.

Departures from the true measure of income are seen as harmful by this school of tax reform for at least four reasons. First, if some income is categorically excluded from taxation, recipients of that income are unfairly advantaged. Second, those who do not in the first instance receive their income in the preferred forms will be induced to move into the preferred forms of economic activity, thereby distorting the allocation of resources and reducing national income. Third, some taxpayers will try to take advantage of the tax preferences in an artificial way through legal and accounting devices, thereby complicating tax administration and eroding the integrity of the tax system. And finally, tax preferences result in lost revenue, thereby forcing tax rates up, dampening incentives for productive economic activity, and increasing incentives for tax avoidance and evasion.

The recent activity of this school of tax reform has been the measurement of the margin between economic income and income as defined for tax purposes (Pechman 1965; Pechman and Okner 1972; Minarik 1980). These measurements serve to identify the sources of divergence between economic income and income for tax purposes and to show the relative importance of these various sources. A natural outgrowth of these measurements is the ability to predict the growth of the tax base that would result if particular departures from an economic measure of income were eliminated. These results can be used to determine the tax rate reductions that could be allowed if the tax base were broadened in particular ways. The end products are schemes for tax reform in this traditional mold, typically involving substantially reduced marginal tax rates at a constant level and distribution of the tax burden (Pechman and Okner 1972; Minarik 1977). From the traditional tax reform point of view, the reduction in marginal rates is vital; the increase in incentives for productive activity and the decrease of incentives for avoidance and evasion rate almost as high in importance as the greater neutrality of the elimination of tax preferences.

Tax reform defined in this way clearly resembles the flat tax in its purest form. Similarly, with its emphasis on lower marginal tax rates, traditional income tax reform has much in common with the flat tax. Some conflict arises, however, over maintaining the distribution of the tax burden. The single-rate tax necessarily redistributes the tax burden from the most well-to-do to the middle class. This result is not determined theoretically, but rather empirically, from the degree to which elimination of existing income tax preferences increases the size of the tax base at different levels up and down the income scale.

Measuring Income during Inflation

The United States has endured substantial inflation since the genesis of the recent interest in the flat tax and tax reform. Economic research has increasingly emphasized the adverse effect of inflation on the measurement of income from capital. It is well known that inflation erodes the principal amount of fixed-income assets, leaving some of the interest receipts, in effect, to keep the principal value whole. Because all of the interest is taxed, however, taxable income exceeds real income; in fact, depending on the circumstances, the tax due can exceed the real income. Likewise, real capital gains are overstated when measured by nominal gains, because inflation erodes the purchasing power of the originally invested principal. Finally, depreciation deductions based on historical cost fall short of the replacement cost of physical capital assets when there is inflation.

There seems little doubt that inflation neutrality would be desirable in principle. The issue is how to attain it. Within the confines of the income tax, indexing the basis of capital assets is the only way. Owners of fixed-income assets would need to claim negative income each year, equal to the inflation-induced depreciation of the principal amount of their assets. Taxpayers who realize capital gains would claim an adjustment to the basis of their assets. Depreciation deductions would be adjusted for the increase of replacement cost due to inflation.

An alternative route is using an expenditure rather than an income base for the entire tax. Under the expenditure tax all purchases of capital assets would be immediately deductible as saving (as opposed to consumption, which is the base of the tax). Transition to an expenditure tax would be a complicated matter, however, with particular problems in dealing with the consumption of retirees out of prior fully taxed savings.

Some analysts have concluded that tax reform must include an indexation of the income base for inflation. That principle underlies the Treasury I proposal (1984). Other analyses stress the difficulty and complexity of indexing the tax code without leaving distortions greater than those caused by inflation. Moreover, any judgment on indexation involves an implicit forecast of future inflation. If prices are relatively stable, the costs of indexation may well exceed the costs of inflation in an unindexed system; with more rapid inflation, this comparison is certainly reversed (Aaron 1976).

The flat tax may or may not harmonize with indexation. Again, in principle, taxing real income is probably preferable, even though in practice indexation is extraordinarily complex, and may well clash with the simplification aspect of the flat tax. The Treasury plan confirms this problem. Rather than indexing interest income precisely, asset by asset, Treasury I opted for a simpler but imprecise rule-of-thumb approach. The complexity of true indexation was judged simply too great for the average taxpayer to handle. Complexity is a real issue for the average taxpayer, because over half of all tax returns report some interest income.

A further issue in indexation is interest expense. Just as inflation causes interest income to be overstated, it also causes interest expense to be overstated. Indexing interest expense is essential if interest income is indexed; otherwise, taxpayers can design combined borrowing-and-lending transactions wherein they pay tax on only real interest income while they deduct nominal interest expense, enriching themselves at the expense of the Treasury with no economic benefit to society. Indexing interest expense is not only complex; it is also painful. Borrowers, particularly those who borrowed at high, inflation-influenced interest rates, would be indignant at additions to their taxable income because of inflation's erosion of the real value of their debts. To avoid this political firestorm, Treasury I exempted all mortgage debt from indexation, thereby leaving a huge preference, perhaps even greater than the preference in the current law, for owner-occupied housing.

Whether a flat tax should be indexed is thus a multifaceted decision. Purists for taxation of real income would insist on indexation, while others might argue that nominal rates of return can adjust in the marketplace (particularly if variations in marginal tax rates from taxpayer to taxpayer can be significantly reduced) to achieve near-neutral results without the pain and complexity of indexing.

Marginal Rate Reduction

The traditional school of tax reform put great weight on elimination of preferential provisions in the tax law. In contrast, other analysts, most notably Milton Friedman and James Buchanan, have argued much more strongly for marginal rate reduction (Friedman 1980; Buchanan and Brennan 1980). The rate reduction argument centers on the likely behavior of taxpayers with respect to preferences under a regime of substantially lower tax rates. Traditional tax reform holds that taxpayers must be prevented from using tax preferences by repealing them from the law. When this is done, the tax base will be broadened, and marginal rates can be reduced without a loss of revenue. In contrast, the rate reduction school would hold that marginal rate reductions depreciate all preferences in the tax code. At marginal rates below some level, taxpayers would simply cease to use those preferences, because they would cease to be profitable at those lower rates. There would be no need to go through the pain of repealing the preferences in the tax code.

The productivity of the rate reduction strategy depends on the share of income that is now taxed at full rates and the degree of tax subsidy available for preferred investments. The experience of the 1981 tax rate cuts was not encouraging. The Accelerated Cost Recovery System (ACRS) and other tax preferences combined to make tax sheltering more, rather than less, profitable. The 1981 and 1982 Internal Revenue Service statistics showed that the entire partnership sector of the economy ran net losses for the first time in the history of the statistics (Piet 1983 and 1984). Given the rest of the tax code, the 1981 rate cuts were not enough to stop tax sheltering and its resultant waste of vital resources.

Could a deeper rate cut in a flat tax leave tax revenues whole without a rewriting of the details of the tax code? Experience cannot answer this question definitively. So whether the flat tax and this branch of tax reform are in harmony must remain a matter of opinion.

Targeted Subsidies

Another definition of tax reform runs almost directly counter to the traditional school, though it leans somewhat on the real economic income point of view. This definition would hold that tax reform is the provision of subsidies to activities that are important to economic growth. Thus, the enactment of ACRS or the expansion of the capital gains exclusion might be called "reform," even though they push the definition of income for tax purposes even farther away from true economic income (Bloomfield 1983). The rationale for this position in the case of income from capital may be that such income is mismeasured during inflation.

The problem with this definition of reform from the traditional view is that it requires outguessing the market—finding and subsidizing activities that would do more for the economy than those that would be selected by the unconstrained operation of the marketplace. This is a tall order for any individual or committee to achieve. Another problem is that whatever the intent of tax subsidies, they always create opportunities for manipulation and avoidance; some of the intended subsidy leaks into tax sheltering schemes, distorting resource allocation and demeaning the income tax itself.

Targeted subsidies and the flat tax would have a tense marriage. Lower rates would reduce revenue in the first instance, and if repeal of existing tax preferences were compromised by the introduction of new ones (or the retaining of selected old ones), the revenue cost could be prohibitive. If flat tax advocates were not satisfied with low and uniform tax rates on all of income, the entire concept would be open to question.

The Budget

There are two schools of thought concerning the budget. To some observers, the budget deficit is paramount. A tax change would be less than a reform if it failed to raise whatever additional revenue was necessary to reduce the deficit to a manageable size. That amount of revenue would be determined in a multipart political process, in which different categories of spending would be examined for politically acceptable and programmatically desirable cuts, and the tax system would be left to make up the difference. Whatever structural improvement of the tax system that could be had at that point would be welcome, but it would be the frosting on the cake in the larger view of things.

According to another point of view, the real issue is the total amount of government spending. Total spending is the real burden on the public from this viewpoint, and the state of the tax system is at a lower level of concern. This view suggests that tax revenue cuts that force later spending reductions are a real fiscal reform, regardless of the tax policy consequences. Any government deficit that ensues while the public sector is cut down to size is a transitional problem at worst.

How the flat tax fits in this dichotomy is anybody's guess. Proponents of supply-side economics might see a flat tax as a deficit remedy, satisfying the antideficit school. Others might see a modified flat tax as the least distorting and least painful way to raise additional revenues under static economic assumptions. On the opposite side of the street, a low, single-rate tax might be a convenient way to cut federal revenue and force major surgery on the spending side.

Obviously, the deficit is a divisive issue, and when it cross-cuts the tax reform debate it leaves the body politic in a shambles. It is hard to say for certain how the many splinters of these policy positions will come back together, if at all. Public opinion certainly has moved toward a broader tax base and lower tax rates, but the trend is tenuous.

We do not know what the flat tax really is, but we do not know what tax reform is either. The positive connotations of the word "reform" have made it a handy banner for just about any cause. Traditional strains of thought are divided on the appropriate distribution of the tax burden, the proper response to the problem of inflation, and the optimal size of the federal establishment. When the politics of the budget deficit compound these fractures, it is clear that there is no single strong limb to support the flat tax or any other tax policy concept.

Conclusion

This paper should confirm what just about everyone thought already: that the people identified with or supportive of the issues of "tax reform," "the flat tax," or other near-synonyms are far from a coalition, but rather constitute the most loosely knit group of traditionalists, supply-siders, budget cutters, and budget balancers imaginable. They all want economic growth, but they cannot agree on how much they should hope or plan for. They all want a sound fiscal policy, but their conceptions of what that means are all over the lot. They all want low tax rates, but they would cite reasons that are probably mutually inconsistent.

Whenever such a shaky consensus begins to congeal, the members have to ask themselves what really matters, lest the consensus dissipate just as suddenly. In this instance, some policymakers who want a broader tax base as a primary objective, and others who want lower tax rates first and foremost, have found themselves in the same uniforms. There will be the inevitable debates over who got there first and why; but those questions are for after the game. The real issue is where the common ground is and how the unlikely allies can fight together to achieve all of their objectives.

In my opinion, the elemental force behind the recent demand for a new tax policy is fairness—the public's desire for it, and the current tax system's lack of it. The public's complaint is not based on too much or too little rate graduation, though perhaps everyone has a notion of a preferred rate schedule. Rather, the public unrest is based on the current law's lack of integrity and certainty, on its willingness to be bought for the benefit of any group with a lobbyist, a lawyer, and an accountant. The public complains because it perceives that some people need not heed the broad outlines of the law. So long as the tax law does not treat all taxpayers in roughly the same way, it invites noncompliance and abuse, twisting the vicious circle one more turn.

In 1981 the tax legislative process got caught up in a bidding war, with the two sides vying for support by offering a better deal to certain select interest groups. The result was not public satisfaction, but rather a public demand for something different. The same thing could happen again. The groups that had the political power to extract preferences from the current law could continue to press their interests, and the political process could respond to such claims. The result, however, would have the same fundamental flaw that has caused today's drive for change: the preferential treatment of a select few.

It is important that all sides of the flat tax coalition remember that the essential attribute of that tax is a connotation of equal treatment; the "flat" in most people's minds probably characterizes the proverbial playing field more than the rate schedule. A single rate with exceptions for today's favored groups will face the same public hostility as the current law. If the subject of tax shelters remains on the financial page of every daily newspaper, tax reform will have accomplished nothing. A flat tax, modified or otherwise, can reduce tax rates and budget deficits, and it can simplify forms and instructions. But it must command the respect of the taxpayers to be called "reform."

References

Aaron, Henry J., ed. 1976. *Inflation and the Income Tax*. Washington, D.C.: Brookings Institution.

Bloomfield, Mark. 1983. "Capital Gains Tax Cut Increased Treasury Revenue," *Tax Notes 22*, p. 692.

Blum, Walter J., and Kalven, Harry, Jr. 1953. *The Uneasy Case for Progressive Taxation*. Chicago: University of Chicago Press.

Buchanan, James, and Brennan, Geoffrey. 1980. "Tax Reform Without Tears," in *The Economics of Taxation*. Edited by Henry J. Aaron and Michael J. Boskin. Washington, D.C.: Brookings Institution, pp. 33–53.

Friedman, Milton. 1980. "A Simple Tax Reform," *Newsweek* 68, p. 68.

Haig, Robert Murray, ed. 1921. *The Federal Income Tax*. New York: Columbia University Press.

Minarik, Joseph J. 1977. "The Yield of a Comprehensive Income Tax," in *Comprehensive Income Taxation*. Edited by Joseph A. Pechman. Washington, D.C.: Brookings Institution, pp. 227–98.

Minarik, Joseph J. 1980. "Who Doesn't Bear the Tax Burden?" in *The Economics of Taxation*. Edited by Henry J. Aaron and Michael J. Boskin. Washington, D.C.: Brookings Institution, pp. 55–68.

Pechman, Joseph A. 1965. "Individual Income Tax Provisions of the Revenue Act of 1964," *Journal of Finance* 20, pp. 247–72.

Pechman, Joseph A., and Okner, Benjamin A. 1972. "Individual Income Tax Erosion by Income Classes," in U.S. Joint Economic Committee, *The Economics of Federal Subsidy Programs*, Compendium of Papers, Joint Economic Committee Print, 92 Cong., 2d sess. Washington, D.C.: U.S. Government Printing Office, pp. 13–40.

Piet, Patrick. 1983. "Partnership Returns for 1981 Reflect Tax Shelter Activity," *Statistics of Income Bulletin* 3, pp. 29–40.

Piet, Patrick. 1984. "Partnership Returns, 1982," *Statistics of Income Bulletin* 4, pp. 85–95.

Simons, Henry C. 1938. *Personal Income Taxation*. Chicago: University of Chicago Press.

U.S. Department of the Treasury. 1977. *Blueprints for Basic Tax Reform*. Washington, D.C.: U.S. Government Printing Office.

[Treasury I]. U.S. Department of the Treasury. 1984. *Tax Reform for Fairness, Simplicity, and Economic Growth: The Treasury Department Report to the President*. Washington, D.C.: U.S. Government Printing Office.

6 • Tax Reform at the Crossroads

On November 27 of last year [1984], Treasury Secretary Donald T. Regan submitted to President Reagan a detailed report on the state of the tax system. Secretary Regan charges that ". . . the present U.S. income tax is complex, it is inequitable, and it interferes with economic choices of households and businesses." In its place, he offered ". . . a sweeping and comprehensive reform of the entire tax code."

The Treasury report marks a dramatic turn in the tax-policy proposals and pronouncements of the Reagan Administration. It could be a milestone in the making of tax policy itself. Now, for the first time in recent memory, an incumbent administration and members of Congress from both parties are on record in favor of fundamental income tax reform. If these forces have their way, we could have the most significant advance of economic policy in at least a generation.

How We Got Here

Less than four years ago, action on income tax policy appeared to have come to an end. The 1981 tax cuts gave away all of the revenue that Uncle Sam could afford to lose for many years, leaving little or no latitude for policy initiatives of any kind.

In just a few short months, however, the end of tax policy became the beginning of a period of unparalleled activity—for the very same reason. The loss of tax revenue that was thought to prevent tax cuts came to enforce tax increases. The tax bills of 1982 and 1984, and the abortive attempt at tax legislation in 1983, were the result.

Reprinted from *Challenge* 28:1, 4–11.

The 1982 and 1984 bills were good legislation. They narrowed the deficits in election years—a remarkable political feat. At the same time, they eliminated abuses and obsolete subsidies in the law, making the tax system fairer. Nonetheless, these bills did not solve our problems in any dimension. They left the deficit smaller, but still far too large. Further, they left the tax system in its less than satisfactory condition, popularly perceived as unfair and excessively complex. The bills were themselves extraordinarily complex, thousands of pages long, adding restrictions and conditions to existing provisions of the code. So despite all of this legislative activity, we have a full agenda of unfinished business on income-tax policy.

The problems with the income tax have long standing. By all the evidence, the public's prime complaint is that it is unfair. People believe that the clever can avoid tax and the dishonest can evade it, leaving the average citizen to carry the whole load. This perception is fed by press coverage of and advertising for tax shelters. It is impossible to open the financial section of a newspaper nowadays without seeing an offer of real estate, oil-producing property, or anything from a car to a sailboat to some worthless trinket—purely for purposes of saving on income taxes. Tax reduction has become a multi-billion dollar game for fun and profit, but only those with well above average income and wealth can play.

Tax sheltering and manipulation build upon the mass of special exceptions to the fundamental rule of taxing all income "from whatever source derived." These selective exclusions, deductions, and credits lengthen the tax law, forms, and instructions. They also complicate immeasurably economic decisions—not just tax computations—because tax considerations must be factored into those decisions.

The tax law contains numerous provisions that selectively benefit particular industries or forms of activity: real estate, mineral exploration, banking, insurance, timber, and so on. Besides losing revenue and complicating the law, these provisions distort economic choices. Resources are diverted to uses that are less profitable in the market but yield compensating tax benefits. When economic activity is targeted to satisfy the tax law rather than the market, our national income falls, and we are all poorer in the long run. Further, these provisions are the building blocks from which many tax shelters are constructed.

The number of such preferences has been growing. In 1967, the first list of tax expenditures included fifty preferential exceptions to the general tax rules. By 1983, that number had grown to 105. So legislation itself has made the tax system more complex and more discriminatory.

Further, inflation and the explosion of tax preferences have interacted to increase taxpayers' marginal tax rates. Inflation has accelerated substantially over the postwar years, pushing taxpayers into higher tax-rate brackets, increasing both their tax liabilities and the marginal rates they faced. The Congress cut taxes periodically to a roughly constant share of total income in spite of this "bracket creep." For the most part, however, taxes were cut not by reducing tax rates, but rather by increasing personal exemptions and standard deductions and by introducing or increasing tax preferences. The result has been something approximating lump-sum tax cuts with continuing bracket creep, raising the amount of tax due on the last dollar of every taxpayer's income. The median-income family was in the 17 percent bracket in 1965, immediately after the Kennedy tax cuts, but was up to the 24 percent bracket by 1980, just before Reagan tax cuts. By 1984, the median family was still as high as a 22 percent bracket. For the family at twice the median, the increase was even more striking: from 22 percent in 1965 to 43 percent in 1980.

These higher marginal rates aggravate all of the imperfections in the tax law. Higher marginal rates decrease the incentive for all productive activity, including work and investment. Further, higher tax rates make all deductions and exclusions more valuable. This increases the incentive to use tax preferences and to engage in tax shelter activity. The growth in the number of tax expenditures and the increase in marginal tax rates are mutually reinforcing problems; as taxpayers increasingly use and lobby for tax preferences, the tax base becomes narrower, forcing tax rates higher than they need to be and further increasing the incentive to use the preferences. It is a never-ending cycle.

Inflation also causes a mismeasurement of income from capital. Real capital gains and interest income are overstated (as are interest-expense deductions) because our tax system does not take into account inflation's erosion of the originally invested principal. Depreciation allowances tend to be understated, although since 1954 depreciation has been accelerated relative to actual experience, in part to compensate for inflation. These mismeasurements, coupled with the high marginal tax rates, have tended to discourage saving and productive investment and further encourage tax sheltering as an alternative.

The 1981 Tax Cuts
and the Response in Congress

The Reagan Administration proposed to attack part of the tax system's problem directly, by reducing marginal income-tax rates by an average of 23 percent across the board. Unfortunately, the tax bill as passed made the rest of the problem, the preferential drain on the tax base, even worse. The 1981 law added new tax expenditures and greatly liberalized tax depreciation through the Accelerated Cost Recovery System (ACRS).

One manifestation of the 1981 law's problems is the burgeoning federal budget deficit. Another is the tax system itself; even with the reductions in marginal rates, the package as a whole was not a step forward. Largely because of the overgenerosity of ACRS, tax sheltering has boomed. In 1981 and 1982, the entire partnership sector of the economy showed a net loss—a development unprecedented in the compilation of IRS partnership statistics. The large losses generated in the real estate and oil and gas industries were a direct result of the growth of tax sheltering, and are evidence of an increase in tax-induced economic waste. And because of the overwhelmingly negative popular reaction to the abortive safe-harbor leasing provision, it is probably fair to say that the 1981 law left public opinion of the income tax worse, not better.

The Congress, by all appearances, has come to this same opinion of the 1981 law. Legislation in 1982 and 1984 cut back on ACRS, while other provisions of the 1981 law were repealed or postponed; the rate cuts themselves, however, have been retained.

Congressional dissatisfaction with the 1981 law was such that 1982 might have been called "the year of the flat tax." More than a half-dozen bills for single-rate income taxes were introduced. These bills were, for the most part, simplistic, often using language to repeal "all deductions, exclusions, and credits," but the lack of specificity raised questions as to what was really intended. Further, the tax rates chosen in these bills were unrealistically low and would have caused severe losses (absent extreme supply-side increases in growth, such as did not materialize after the 1981 experiment). Finally, their distributional effects would have been extremely skewed, with large tax cuts for the highest-income taxpayers and tax increases for the middle-income groups. So the flat-tax movement was, for the most part, a symbolic expression of dissatisfaction; practical policy would have to come in some other form.

The Bradley-Gephardt
and Kemp-Kasten Bills

That form already was apparent midway through 1982. The "Fair Tax Act" proposed by Senator Bill Bradley and Representative Richard Gephardt attacked the major problems of the income tax head-on. First, it provided explicit legal language to eliminate the most serious leakages in the current income tax while maintaining the politically sensitive itemized deductions for home mortgage interest, real property taxes, and charitable contributions (at a maximum tax savings of 14 percent of the amount of the deduction). And second, it used the revenue gained through tax-base broadening to reduce tax rates significantly. The rate schedule provided roughly three-fourths of the population with a flat 14 percent tax, but avoided the redistributional problems of the flat tax by adding two progressive rate steps for higher-income persons, leading to a maximum rate of 30 percent. Both total tax revenue and the distribution of the tax burden by income groups remained unchanged. The corporate tax, similarly purged of tax-base leakages, would be changed to a flat 30 percent, with no change in total revenue.

Bradley-Gephardt thus goes well beyond either the 1981 tax cuts or the flat tax. It eliminates virtually every opportunity for manipulative tax avoidance and virtually every source of distortions of economic choices. At the same time, it reduces the incentive for manipulation by cutting tax rates. By all past experience, action on both the opportunity and the incentive for manipulation will be necessary to convert the income tax from a high-stakes game to an impartial system of collecting revenue.

Tax reform of this sort is no free lunch. To finance the rate cuts and achieve neutrality among different economic activities, we must give up many of the incentives that have been added to the income tax over the last quarter-century and even before. Virtually all taxpayers would be affected to some degree. Prominent in Bradley-Gephardt are the repeal of the capital-gains exclusion and the investment tax credit and replacement of ACRS with a less generous and more neutral depreciation system.

To some, the repeal of these supposed saving and investment incentives is counterproductive, but these provisions benefit only a narrow range of productive activity. They cost the Treasury considerable revenue, forcing tax rates up and thereby discouraging all productive activity. Further, they create opportunities and incentives for abuse and manipulation, damaging the integrity of the income tax and wasting resources through tax shelters. The tax law and the economy would be better off with a simple, low-rate system that encouraged all productive activity in an even-handed way.

Repeal of these incentive provisions in Bradley-Gephardt is not a "soak the rich" vendetta. The tax rate schedule in the bill holds each income group harmless relative to current law, and so the rich are not soaked. Rather, it is a simple recognition that targeted tax incentives for saving and investment are less efficient economically than simple reductions in tax rates. The logical next step is to repeal the incentives and use the resulting revenue increase to cut tax rates in a distributionally neutral way.

The Bradley-Gephardt approach caught on strongly in the Congress and in public opinion. Several bills following its general outlines were introduced. Ironically, the "look-alike" bill that has attracted the most attention, the "Fair and Simple Tax Act" (FAST) of Representative Jack Kemp and Senator Robert Kasten, is a step backward to the flat-tax approach, with a basic 25 percent rate for individuals.

As a further argument for lower tax rates and a broader tax base, FAST is welcome. As practical tax policy, however, it has serious shortcomings. The first and most important is revenue. Absent a supply-side economic boom, FAST would lose $20 billion compared to current law in its first year, and the annual revenue loss would grow, not shrink, over time. Its sponsors are banking on a supply-side response to forestall disaster, but given the current deficits after the 1981 supply-side experiment, that does not seem the responsible way to go.

Second, FAST's revenue loss would be distributed almost exclusively to upper-income individuals and corporations. Especially after the controversy about fairness that surrounded the 1981 law, there could be sharp debate over this effect of FAST.

The reason for FAST's revenue shortfall and distributional imbalance is its failure to face up to the reality of tax reform. When confronted with the inevitable trade-off between lower tax rates and targeted tax incentives, FAST chooses both. It retains ACRS and a preference for long-term capital gains, even though it reduces tax rates as well. Relying on extraordinary economic growth to bail us out of such a revenue loss is probably too great a risk to run in an already perilous fiscal situation. If supply-side economics is right, the marginal rate reductions in even a revenue-neutral tax reform should increase economic activity and tax revenues substantially, and so there would be plenty of opportunity later on to reduce tax rates further.

A final problem with FAST is complexity. The bill attempts to maintain the appearance of the flat tax while avoiding the worst of the redistributional consequences, by allowing an exclusion equal to 20 percent of earned income up to the amount of the Social Security wage base. The exclusion would then be phased out as earned income increased to about $100,000. Thus, taxpayers with modest amounts of earned income would have to perform a separate computation to determine how much of their income was subject to tax. Taxpayers with earned income above the Social Security wage base, but below $100,000, would have to perform an exceedingly complex computation of the phased-down amount of their exclusions. Two-earner married couples would have to perform these extra computations twice, once for each earner. The only alternative to the taxpayers performing these computations would be additional sets of lookup tables, which could be confused with the ordinary tax tables.

Thus, even in a highly modified form such as the Kemp-Kasten bill, the flat-rate tax is not the way to go. The graduated-rate approach, as proposed in the Bradley-Gephardt bill and others, avoids the flat tax's undesirable redistributional effects and the revenue losses that can follow.

The Treasury's Report

By early 1984, President Reagan acknowledged the appeal of tax reform. In his State of the Union address, he directed Secretary Regan to deliver a report on policy alternatives by year-end. This request itself was a notable event; the 1981 tax cuts had been the cornerstone of the president's economic program. The Treasury wrote in early 1981 "[the] changes are central to restoring incentives and strengthening the growth and productivity of the economy. They will promote each by increasing the after-tax rewards for work, savings, and investment." Yet by November 1984 the Treasury found that the tax system "interferes with the economic choices of households and businesses." This statement represents a considerable change of tone, if not of substance. It is something of a concession for an administration that made such strong claims for the effects of its 1981 tax program.

The Treasury's proposal turned out to be a strong reform of the income tax, with no supply-side overtones. In fact, it followed the outline of the Bradley-Gephardt bill very closely. The Treasury proposed three individual tax-rate brackets, with a large bottom that would be the highest bracket for about three-fourths of the population, along the lines of Bradley-Gephardt. The Treasury rates range from 15 to 35 percent. The proposal would repeal the investment tax credit, replace ACRS with a simpler and more neutral system, and institute a flat-rate, 33 percent corporate tax, again similar to Bradley-Gephardt. The Treasury plan is designed to replace fully the revenues of the current law without relying on forecasts of extraordinary growth, again like Bradley-Gephardt and unlike Kemp-Kasten. That the Treasury would propose such a plan, rather than one following supply-side lines, suggests a strong case for tax reform in the face of what must have been the most strenuous in-house opposition.

There are some significant differences between the Treasury proposal and the Bradley-Gephardt bill, and they follow a general pattern. The latter is a pragmatic piece of legislation, using simple and familiar tools to make some headway against a wide array of tax-policy problems. The former is more theoretically pure. It approaches (though it often does not reach) ideal solutions, even at the cost of greater complexity and heavier computational demands on taxpayers. It is an open question which of the two approaches is superior overall.

Inflation

One major difference between the two proposals is in the definition of the tax base with respect to inflation. Bradley-Gephardt would tax nominal income, but the Treasury plan would index capital income for inflation to eliminate the mismeasurement discussed earlier. In its pure form, such tax-base indexation would be exceedingly complex. Every capital asset and every debt would require a computational adjustment for the effects of inflation, either on a year-by-year basis or on sale.

Under the Treasury plan, the cost basis of capital assets would be adjusted for inflation in computing capital gains, and the basis of depreciable assets would be adjusted each year in calculating tax depreciation. This would involve some complexity for affected taxpayers, but relatively few taxpayers have capital gains or depreciable assets, and those who do generally have the necessary financial sophistication to deal with such complexity.

The barrier to indexing the tax base in the past has not been the handling of capital gains or depreciation, but rather interest income and expense. The potential for manipulation and abuse through borrowing and lending transactions is tremendous, and so it is essential that interest be handled correctly. In particular, interest income and expense must be treated symmetrically, so that taxpayers cannot reap a tax advantage merely by wash borrowing and lending transactions (as would happen, for example, if interest income were indexed but interest expense were not). Likewise, if depreciation and capital gains were indexed, interest expense would have to be indexed as well, to prevent tax-advantaged wash transactions involving borrowing and investing for capital gain or in depreciable assets.

One important constraint on indexing interest is complexity. Unlike the relatively few taxpayers with capital gains or depreciation, more than 60 percent of all taxpayers receive some interest income, and more than 90 percent of all itemizers deduct some interest expense. Many of these taxpayers are not financially sophisticated, and they are unlikely to understand the computations necessary to adjust the principal amount of each individual asset and debt for inflation. Here the Treasury sought a halfway approach in the interests of simplicity. Instead of requiring indexation of every individual asset and debt, it would disallow a percentage of all interest expense and allow the exclusion of the same percentage of all interest income. The percentage would be determined each year based on the inflation rate and some baseline interest rate. For example, if a representative interest rate in a given year were 10 percent and the inflation rate were 4 percent, the IRS would announce that 40 percent (4 percent divided by 10 percent) of all interest income would be tax-free and 40 percent of all interest expense would be nondeductible. Further, the Treasury specified that home mortgage-interest expenses would not be subject to this adjustment.

The Treasury's proposed procedure would be simpler than actual indexation, because taxpayers could adjust the total amount of their interest income and expenses without detailed computations for each individual asset and debt. By the same token, however, this simple adjustment would not be precise. The percentage of interest excluded should vary from loan to loan according to the interest rate charged. The Treasury argues correctly that its proposal is more accurate than no adjustment at all. But the Treasury adjustment adds complexity to the law, and the complexity may or may not be justified if the system yields imperfect results.

Further, the indexation of interest income creates an incentive for taxpayers to have their income in other forms (such as dividends or rent) construed as interest for tax purposes. This may encourage abuse. Likewise, because mortgage-interest expense is not reduced by the inflation adjustment but mortgage-interest income is, there would be an incentive to borrow and lend with owner-occupied homes as security. It is at least possible that these asymmetries in the handling of interest expense and capital income could lead to serious tax avoidance.

Finally, while the Treasury's proposed interest adjustment would unquestionably be a move to define capital income more correctly, it would tend to shift a burden of risk in financial planning from institutions to individuals. At present, when lenders (mostly financial institutions) and household borrowers negotiate a loan, they compromise on an interest rate that takes into account their expectations of future inflation. If the worst occurs and inflation accelerates, the loser is the institution. One might reasonably argue that this risk is on the proper side of the transaction, given that institutions are better able to anticipate and plan for such contingencies. Indexing interest income and expense would shift some of that risk from institutional lenders to individual borrowers; under the Treasury plan, if inflation accelerates and nothing else changes, the borrower's tax will go up (because his interest deduction will be reduced). For all its merits otherwise, this may be an undesirable reallocation of financial risk to the party less able to bear it.

In short, the Treasury seeks a pure system with all capital income adjusted for inflation, at the cost of significant complication; but the proposal stops short of complete indexation for practical reasons. The resulting system may or may not justify the complexity and the potential abuse involved, considering that the simple reduction of marginal tax rates in any tax-reform proposal reduces at least the consequences of any mismeasurement of capital income due to inflation.

Dividends

The second major difference between the Treasury and the Bradley-Gephardt proposals lies in the taxation of corporate-source income. Bradley-Gephardt continues the current approach of a separate tax on corporations. The Treasury, in contrast, provides for partial relief from the double taxation of corporate dividends, whereby corporate income is taxed once when earned at the corporate level and again when distributed as dividends. The Treasury proposal would allow corporations a deduction for half of dividends paid, thereby reducing, but not eliminating, the double tax.

The double taxation of corporate dividends is a real problem; it distorts corporate choices away from paying dividends and toward retaining earnings. When corporate retentions are routine, those earnings are reinvested not by firms that promise the greatest rate of return on new investment, but by those that are earning profits on old investment; so capital is not freely reallocated to its best uses. Again, there is a total solution to the problem, but again, the Treasury had to back off for practical reasons. The double tax can be eliminated by a method called integration: the corporate tax is in effect abolished, and all corporate income, whether distributed or retained, is attributed to shareholders and taxed only on individual income tax returns. The major problems with integration are that it would be extremely difficult, if not impossible, to report complete corporate income tax information to shareholders quickly enough for them to file timely tax returns, and that the revenue loss from eliminating the corporate tax, especially in the current budgetary stringency, would simply be too great.

The problem with the Treasury solution is that no one has a strong reason to support it. Corporate managers, on the face of it, might like to get a tax deduction; but in the final analysis, they fear that shareholders would argue for more dividends because of the deduction. Corporate managers do not want to pay more dividends, because it would increase their cost of raising investment funds. Shareholders have no pressing interest in the deduction either, because they would benefit from it directly only if they could persuade corporate managers to pay more dividends. So it is not surprising that the investment community has responded lukewarmly to the Treasury proposal despite this valuable deduction.

Again, straightforward tax reform relieves the double-tax problem, though not so much as the Treasury's deduction for dividends paid. Simply cutting the individual and corporate tax rates reduces the double tax on dividends. For example, under the current law, corporate income taxed first at the 46 percent corporate rate and then at the highest 50 percent individual rate bears a 73 percent total tax, while corporate income taxed twice at the Bradley-Gephardt 30 percent rates bears only a 51 percent total tax. The Treasury proposal, with its deduction for half of dividends paid, exacts an even smaller total burden at just under 46 percent; but the revenue lost through this special deduction is part of the reason why the Treasury had to impose higher statutory tax rates, at

33 percent for corporations and a 35 percent maximum for individuals, than the Bradley-Gephardt bill. So again, the Treasury achieves a purer system, though not a totally pure one, at the cost of reduced revenue (and thus higher statutory tax rates to achieve revenue neutrality), greater complexity, and some divisiveness. Thus, it is an open question whether the Treasury package is more desirable overall.

The Corporate Tax Burden

The third major difference between the Treasury and Bradley-Gephardt proposals is the distribution of the tax burden between the household and the corporate sectors. Bradley-Gephardt retains the same level of revenues within both the individual and the corporate income taxes. The Treasury, in contrast, reduces the individual burden by about 8.5 percent, increasing the corporate tax take to make up the difference. (This requires a much larger corporate tax increase in percentage terms—about 25 percent, assuming a fairly optimistic baseline corporate-revenue forecast—because corporate revenues under the current law are much smaller than individual revenues.)

This shifting of the tax burden from individuals to corporations has been hailed as a beneficial reversal of the historical trend. Over the entire postwar period, corporate tax revenues have been eroding as a share of the total tax take. In fact, however, the Treasury, rather than making a conscious choice, was somewhat constrained institutionally to reach this result. Even though corporate tax revenues are increased over current law, the corporate rate in the Treasury plan is already two percentage points below the maximum individual rate. If the tax burden were to be shifted back toward the household sector, the top individual rate would have to go up and the corporate rate would have to go down, increasing this gap in the statutory rates. When the top individual and corporate rates differ by too much, abuse and manipulation are encouraged; in particular, it can be lucrative for individuals to incorporate in order to shift taxable income from the higher top individual rate to the lower corporate rate. Although, say, a four-point spread between the two rates would be no higher than that under the current law, at the lower Treasury rates that spread would represent a much greater percentage saving relative to the total tax burden on the individual.

Another constraint on the Treasury is political. To some degree, success in repealing individual income tax preferences requires sharp reductions in statutory tax rates; people would be more willing to give up their preferences if they got larger rate cuts in return. The Treasury's top individual tax rate, at 35 percent, is already five percentage points higher than that of Bradley-Gephardt. There is at least some question of just how much higher the Treasury could afford to go politically and retain some chance of popular support for the package.

So the Treasury's shift of the tax burden to corporations may be less the result of value judgments than of institutional constraints. Even at that, some people might find it a move toward greater fairness. Others would argue that it would cause a serious drain of resources from the corporate sector, leading to reduced investment. One incontrovertible fact is that a ground-breaking reform proposal like Bradley-Gephardt could not have included such a shift of tax burdens and succeeded politically; the whole concept of tax reform could easily have been buried under a debate over the appropriate division of the tax burden between households and corporations.

The differences between the Bradley-Gephardt and Treasury proposals may affect any individual's choice as to which is the preferable approach to tax reform or the one more likely to succeed politically. But from a broader perspective, the differences pale. Both plans would broaden the income tax base and reduce tax rates significantly. Both would eliminate major sources of abuse and economic distortions. Both would make the tax system simpler and fairer, and make the economy function more efficiently. From this perspective, the coincidence between the two proposals is most auspicious.

The issue, then, is not so much which of the two proposals to choose. It is, rather, whether any close relative of either will be enacted into law.

The Prospects for Reform

Since their unveilings, both the Treasury and the Bradley-Gephardt proposals have aroused considerable controversy. Both have been praised for making the tax law simpler and fairer and for removing tax considerations from economic decisions. But both have also been criticized by the interests whose tax preferences would be repealed.

Already, defenses of one or another tax provision are appearing under the subheading, "Not Just Another Loophole." Employer-provided medical insurance, oil exploration, banking, timber, and countless other activities are claiming a special status when it comes to changing the tax law.

The problem is that all of these activities are important to the national interest; but so is every lawful activity that earns a profit. From a public-policy perspective, we have to make a choice. Do we believe in the free market, or do we want to allocate resources by fiat? When one activity is singled out for preferential treatment, every other activity is disadvantaged.

The greatest early resistance to the Treasury proposal has come from advocates of ACRS and the investment tax credit. These interests would prefer the current system, with its high tax rates and large investment subsidies, to a reform that shifts to lower tax rates and minimal (or no) subsidies. The reason, again, is that these interests get the subsidies. They don't want a level playing field, because right now the field is tilted their way.

Even these apparently even-handed investment subsidies can have untoward effects on our economy, however. They bias the tax law against high-technology industries; firms on the technological frontier pay higher than average taxes. Further, they make lucrative but economically wasteful tax shelters possible.

The investment credit and ACRS are defended as necessary; without them, it is argued, investment will trail off and growth and productivity will slow. This argument needs some careful thought. Do we really believe that our nation will not invest, with profit to be made, unless there are tax incentives? Isn't a sharp reduction in statutory tax rates enough to unleash the profit motive? Are corporations somehow different from individuals, such that a reduction in tax rates is not an economic incentive? And can we afford elaborate preferential tax incentives in our current budgetary stress—or will such incentives just drive tax rates higher?

The Treasury proposal was released to the public under unusual circumstances. First, it was an internal document on which final decisions had not yet been made; and second, it was not due to be proposed to the Congress for at least two months, when the regular budget submissions were scheduled. By all accounts, this early release was forced by uncontrollable leaks designed to compromise the program. But the effect was to set up the package as a target for those who would lose their relative advantages.

The question now is what position the Administration will take on the investment subsidies. If it waters down the Treasury proposals on that score, the door will be open for other interests to stake their claims. The tax base will narrow and marginal tax rates will creep up, and the entire package easily could unravel.

If the Administration merely backs away from the Treasury plan, leaving the Congress to legislate on its own, the chances of success will be much reduced. It is difficult for individual members of Congress to resist the approaches of powerful interests. A popular second-term president is in a unique position to take steps that may be painful in the short run but are beneficial in the long run.

So the Administration's position in the tax debate is crucial. With some further impetus, proposals for meaningful reform stand at least a chance of becoming law. The economy and the relationship of our people with their government would both come out ahead. We should not miss this opportunity.

7 • Tax Reform: Up from the Ashes

To great fanfare, tax reform passed the House of Representatives late last year [1985]. It moved on to the Senate amidst uncertain signs from the heavens. The Senate is in the hands of the president's party; the president wants tax reform and, as the most effective Republican campaigner in a crucial election year, he has considerable leverage. But the president himself threatened that he would veto the House bill if it reached his desk unchanged—hardly an auspicious proclamation. And the Senate is a dubious way station for tax reform, with that body's close ties to so many special interests drawn ever tighter by escalating campaign costs.

Any tax reform bill must be a finely balanced instrument. It must weigh the agendas of powerful interests against the burdens of poor and middle-class households and the revenue needs of the federal government. It must win political support for quantum change from groups who find security, and sometimes comfort, in the status quo. In this need for balance is tax reform's greatest vulnerability; it can be destroyed directly, or through a series of seemingly minor amendments that reduce its revenue potential or impose excessively on some important group, and thus send it spinning subtly and slowly out of control.

The strength of sound tax reform lies in its underlying principles: equal treatment, simplicity, and nonintervention in private decisions. This is a prosperous society; the burden of government can be light, if all share it according to their means. Tax reform that enforces that principle can be nearly unassailable; those who

Reprinted from *Challenge* 29:3, pp. 33–39.

would oppose it must ask for special treatment from a people whose instincts are fair. Once the proper balance is struck—with a total burden light enough that no extremes demand relief, and with no exceptions to suggest still further exceptions in a futile and endless pursuit of rough justice—tax reform can demand support from unlikely sources simply because opposition would be political self-destruction. This is, as Senator Bill Bradley put it, "the power of the idea."

Tax reform was brought before the Senate Finance Committee by its chairman, Bob Packwood (R.) of Oregon, in an unbalanced form. The original Packwood bill ostensibly lifted tax burdens from poor families, but then reimposed those burdens through theoretically unsound increases in excise taxes. Even more damaging, it continued special treatment for certain powerful industry groups, including the chairman's own favored timber industry. The bill was attacked, successfully, with the scalpel rather than the ax. In a series of discrete amendments, committee members joined the chairman in restoring favors for their own favorite interests, gradually dropping the revenue yield far below what was needed. The chairman had no alternative but to withdraw the proposal.

Tax reform was saved by a sudden and unexpected return to principle. After several days of flailing about for a solution, Chairman Packwood put forward a new plan, emphasizing fewer exceptions and still lower tax rates. Even the timber industry was touched indirectly. The new plan was not perfect, but it was close enough to the ideal that attacking it became increasingly dangerous. The amendments proposed were more cautious than bold, and some that had succeeded against the first plan failed in more modest form against the second. After notable procedural victories and limited defeats, the plan passed the committee by a unanimous vote. Even those who early in the process had publicly stated their opposition to any tax reform were forced to vote for the bill.

The victory of tax reform in the Finance Committee is by no means the end of the story. Passage on the Senate floor is a daunting task, with unlimited debate and amendments perhaps as much or even more of an obstacle than the committee's long-standing adherence to special interests. Nonetheless, the unanimous approval of the committee is both a strong, tangible endorsement of the bill and a symbol of its sharing in "the power of the idea." Its prospects on the floor are far brighter than was ever hoped.

Whose Gospel Is This?

One puzzle of tax reform—at least to some observers—is the nature of the current bills. By this late stage in its conception, tax reform has passed through many hands: from an original Democratic advocate, to a Republican imitator, to a Republican president, to the Democratic lower house, to the Republican Senate. The ownership of the concept is certainly in doubt.

Ownership is unimportant, however; what matters is lineage. Tax policy has passed from the pursuit of an ideal of fairness, simplicity, and neutrality, through a brief and single-minded fascination with economic growth, and back to its original ideal in less than a decade. Over that time, major tax legislation was an almost annual ritual. Now, on the brink of the most far-reaching law since the enactment of the income tax almost three-quarters of a century ago, our conception and understanding of what we are about to do could determine tax policy for many years to come. If the principle of equal treatment is firmly established, it could begin an era of fundamental policy stability. In contrast, if this legislation is seen as a continuation of the mindless and futile pursuit of dramatically faster growth—which gave us tax preferences for varied forms and facsimiles of saving and investment—the recent rapid swings of tax policy could continue, and erosion of the new, higher standard could be assured.

Thus, there is a real significance—not merely a grasping for glory—in the identity of Chairman Packwood's tax reform bill. The meaning of traditional tax reform has always been subject to dispute, more by its critics than by its advocates. Likewise, the meaning of the supply-side economics of the late 1970s and early 1980s was never clear, mostly because of the lack of a theoretical foundation. Nonetheless, it is important to put the new tax reform legislation in the context of this policy debate. There are several key issues that give some crucial clues.

Lower Statutory Rates

The hallmark of the second Packwood plan is lower statutory tax rates. Its two-bracket individual rate schedule—a 15 percent first rate and 27 percent second rate—is lower than was contemplated by either the administration or the House. (The 27 percent maximum rate is unambiguously lower than the administration's 35 percent and the House's 38 percent; the 15 percent first bracket rate is numerically the same as the administration's and the House's, but significantly more taxpayers would reach beyond the 15 percent bracket into a 25 percent bracket under the House bill.) Thus, the Packwood plan more than meets the president's demand for a maximum individual rate of 35 percent.

It is important to recall, however, that the theme of tax reform for at least the past 30 years has been broadening the tax base and reducing tax rates. So the Packwood plan is unquestionably in the mainstream of a reform current long predating Reagan.

It is true that reducing statutory rates was the original hallmark of supply-side economics; candidate Reagan campaigned in 1980 for a 30 percent across-the-board reduction of individual income tax rates. Thus, supply-side economics, or "Reaganomics," might claim the Packwood plan as its own; clearly, the president himself played a major role in setting this legislative process in motion. But in several respects, the Packwood plan is a *reversal*, not a continuation, of the first Reagan tax policy. In fact, in some respects, the Packwood plan defies the president's expressed demands for this very bill. Specifically:

Individual Retirement Accounts

The Packwood plan pays for its very low marginal tax rates by repealing the deduction for contributions to Individual Retirement Accounts (IRAs) by employees who are covered by pension plans. In fact, the chairman proposed to repeal IRAs for covered employees altogether; only an amendment in the mark-up process restored nondeductible contributions. Apart from the revenue loss, Chairman Packwood and others argued that IRAs have failed in their stated purpose of increasing savings.

This position runs sharply counter to the current policy, and the policy of 1981. An original cosponsor of the 1981 tax-rate-cut legislation, Senator William Roth (R.) of Delaware, is a major supporter of IRAs and tried to restore them in the Finance Committee. The president's proposal would have expanded IRAs by allowing nonworking spouses to contribute. That step would have moved IRAs even farther from their original role as a pension substitute toward the supply-side conception of an unrestricted incentive to save.

The Packwood plan's restriction of IRAs is a significant departure from current tax policy and from the president's plan. It turns from the notion of targeted subsidies towards neutrality. As such, it is much more in the spirit of traditional tax reform than of the incentive-oriented tax policy of the 1980s.

Capital Gains

The Packwood plan eliminates the current law's exclusion of 60 percent of long-term capital gains. This is a complete reversal of one of the key elements of recent incentive-oriented policy. Back in 1978, for example, early advocates of supply-side economics had expanded the exclusion to 60 percent from 50 percent. In the 1981 legislation, the reduction of the maximum capital gains rate from 28 percent to 20 percent was explicitly accelerated to more than six months prior to the other tax rate cuts. The administration's 1985 tax reform proposal would have reduced the maximum capital gains tax rate to 17.5 percent, and the president made lower capital gains taxes part of his ultimatum on the House bill.

Again, this provision of the Packwood plan is a giant step away from current policy, which sees a preference for capital gains as a powerful incentive for growth, and towards traditional tax reform, which sees capital gains as a form of income that should be taxed like any other. It is also a violation of the president's demands for the Senate tax bill, which the president has apparently chosen to ignore.

Taxing Corporations

The Packwood plan follows the administration and the House bill in increasing corporate income taxes. The investment tax credit would be repealed and numerous tax subsidies targeted to specific industries would be curtailed (in the administration proposal, explicitly; in the House and the Finance Committee bills, mostly by subjecting them to a minimum tax). In partial compensation, the maximum statutory corporate tax rate would be sharply reduced (in the administration and the Packwood plans, to 33 percent; in the House bill, to 36 percent, from the current 45 percent).

While there is, therefore, little conflict between the Packwood plan and the administration proposal, both would undertake a significant shift from the current law. The Accelerated Cost Recovery System was one of the keystones of the Reagan administration's 1981 tax policy; in combination with the investment tax credit, it constitutes an enormous subsidy to investments in depreciable capital. Even the administration's reform plan was a significant departure from current policy, and the Finance Committee's bill is even more so (the committee's depreciation proposal, while more generous than the current law, is less generous than the administration's version).

Thus, again, the Finance Committee bill would depart dramatically from the incentive-oriented policy in the current law toward a more neutral system. As with the cutback of IRAs and the elimination of the capital gains exclusion, this marks a significant change in philosophy from the landmark legislation of just five years ago. If this change in philosophy is widely recognized and accepted, future proposals to reintroduce subsidies will have a hurdle to overcome; they will need to change the entire new thrust of policy. Targeted benefit proposals for particular industries or activities will be that much more obvious against the backdrop of a law that has few or none.

Some Problems

As noted earlier, the Packwood plan is not perfect. In at least three respects, it does not aspire to tax reform's ideal of precise measurement of income. We have learned to live with imperfection under the current law; businesses are organized somewhat differently, regulations are somewhat more elaborate, asset values are somewhat higher or lower than what they might be. But adjusting to new imperfections is painful, and takes time. There will be some shocks in adjusting to the Packwood plan if it becomes law without change. Some of the problem areas in the Packwood plan are described below.

Limitation on Passive Losses

An important cause of distortions of economic choices and losses of tax revenues is the use of tax shelters. In recent years, wealthy investors have made increasing use of highly leveraged investments in tax-favored assets and activities (such as real estate, oil and gas properties, and farming) to generate artificial tax losses which offset positive incomes from other sources. Every tax reform plan has sought to limit tax sheltering through repeal of the investment credit and cutbacks of accounting abuses involving the timing of recognition of income and expense.

The Packwood plan was perhaps less far-reaching than others in some of the specific income-measurement issues. It more than made up the difference, however, with a blanket antishelter provision. The new bill simply disallows the deduction of losses from so-called "passive investments"—those in which the investor does not have a management or operating role. Thus, the typical limited partnership tax shelter investment will be allowed no income figure lower than zero on an individual income tax return (though a gradual phase-in over five years is provided).

The seriousness of the tax shelter problem and the effect of the proposed loss limitation are demonstrated by the reaction thus far. Under this rule, investors in real estate or other partnerships will be able to earn income within those partnerships tax free, if tax preferences and accounting devices enable them to show no profit for tax purposes. But mere tax exemption is an enormous tax increase for current tax shelter investments, which now show negative income for tax purposes. The affected industries claim that their existence is threatened, and are lobbying vigorously against the committee bill.

The effect of the loss limitation is greatest on the most recent investments, which will lose several years of anticipated tax losses. Because those losses were built into the prices of the assets, the owners are subject to significant capital losses upon the sale of their assets, as well as higher-than-anticipated taxes in the interim. This has led the affected industries to claim that the "rules of the game" have been changed without fair warning. These complaints, however, have limited merit. If the federal government cannot change its tax policies in any way that affects existing investments, then tax policy can never change. An adverse change toward investment in any particular asset cannot hold current investors harmless; even allowing current investors to continue to use the existing law subjects them to capital loss, because prospective buyers of those assets will offer prices dependent on the tax treatment in the new law. Further, where the tax law is a major determinant of the value of an investment, investors should take into account the risk that the tax law will change.

Nonetheless, the passive loss limitation will have some unintended effects. It will certainly prevent the deduction of tax shelter losses. It will also prevent the deduction of some legitimate losses. New businesses routinely realize losses in their early years. All businesses have some bad years. Passive investors in those businesses will not be able to deduct their losses, which is an undesirable outcome. Also adversely affected will be the low-income housing industry, which is an admitted tax shelter, but is also the sole source of low-cost housing now that direct federal provision is virtually zero.

A further weakness of the loss limitation provision is a last-minute exception for the oil and gas industry introduced by the Finance Committee (which has several members from oil and gas producing states). Under the committee bill, investors in oil and gas shelters can continue to deduct their losses, while investors in real estate, farming, and other shelters cannot. This provision in effect makes oil and gas the only available tax shelter, and thus is highly favorable. The sharp drop in the price of oil has left the industry in poor health, and so some members may be inclined to allow the exception. This sympathy is ill advised, however, because an exception to the tax shelter rules will provide no help now, when the industry needs it, but will be an excessive benefit when oil prices recover.

The passive loss limitation provision will be attacked because of its leniency to oil and gas, on the one hand, and because of its harshness to many legitimate businesses, on the other. Meanwhile, all affected tax shelter industries will be lobbying against it. It is counted on to provide substantial revenue in the Finance Committee bill, and so its defeat would be a serious blow.

Phaseouts of the Bottom Rate Bracket and the Personal Exemption

A major attraction of the Packwood plan, as was noted earlier, is its low level of marginal tax rates. The maximum rate, however, is not as low as it may appear. This could cause political difficulty.

To meet its total revenue needs and to hold the tax cut for upper-income taxpayers to an acceptable level, the Packwood plan phases out two tax benefits in a manner that increases the effective top marginal tax rate. The first such phaseout applies to the tax savings from having paid tax in the lower (15 percent) tax bracket. For married couples, the first $29,300 of taxable income is taxed at the 15 percent rate. Additional income up to $75,000 is taxed at the higher (27 percent) rate. Income between $75,000 and $145,320 is taxed at a 32 percent rate, however, to eliminate the savings that the taxpayer enjoyed by paying only 15 percent on his first $29,300 of income. For taxpayers with $145,320 of income, the amount of tax due is as though all taxable income had been taxed at the 27 percent rate.

At that point, a second phaseout begins. The 27 percent marginal tax rate is reinstated, but between $145,320 and $185,320 of taxable income, the personal exemptions ($2,000 per taxpayer and dependent) are phased out. Thus, a family of four would lose its $8,000 of personal exemptions gradually as its taxable income increased from $145,320 to

$185,320. For that family, the effective marginal tax rate is 32.4 percent (which is 1.2 times the stated marginal tax rate of 27 percent, because the $8,000 of phased out personal exemptions is equal to 0.2 times the $40,000 of taxable income in the $145,320 to $185,320 interval). The most curious effect of this phaseout of the personal exemptions is that the marginal tax rate depends on family size, with the largest families facing the highest marginal tax rates. A childless couple would pay 29.7 percent, while a family of eight would pay 37.8 percent. The 27 percent marginal rate applies to all taxable income above $185,320. (Analogous phaseouts of the benefit of the 15 percent bracket and the personal exemptions apply to single taxpayers and heads of households, at slightly different levels of taxable income.)

These phaseouts certainly cast doubt on the accuracy of the claimed 27 percent maximum marginal tax rate, and they also raise political and economic issues. Eliminating the capital gains exclusion involves increasing the maximum tax rate on capital gains from the current law's 20 percent. It was painful to raise the maximum capital gains rate to the Packwood plan's stated maximum marginal tax rate of 27 percent. It is not at all certain whether elimination of the exclusion will survive politically in the full Senate with a maximum rate on capital gains that would routinely exceed 30 percent. Further, all of the economic benefits of the claimed low marginal tax rates are diminished to the extent that the actual rates exceed the stated levels.

The phaseouts are among the least understood aspects of the Packwood plan. They caused some legislative confusion, and could cause confusion among taxpayers as well. Senate Majority Leader Robert Dole (R. Kans.) has expressed his desire to repeal the phaseouts. This will be difficult, however, because it will require raising revenue from upper-income taxpayers to make up the revenue loss and to compensate for the shifting of the tax burden. Simply increasing the stated maximum 27 percent marginal rate would have this general effect, but it would detract from the appeal of the bill. In addition, it could destroy the shaky consensus for the elimination of the capital gains exclusion.

The Minimum Tax

The ideal of tax reform is to eliminate all preferential tax rules. If that is accomplished, the tax system will be fair and there will be no need for a minimum tax, such as that in the current law, to deal with those who do not pay their share under the basic tax structure. An important subsidiary benefit is that the tax system will be much simpler with only one set of rules.

The administration, the House, and the Senate all despaired of achieving this ideal and restored the corporate and individual minimum taxes. At each stage of the legislative process, the reliance on the minimum taxes became greater. The Packwood plan would increase the revenues raised under the minimum taxes by several orders of magnitude compared to the current law.

The individual minimum tax would apply to more tax preferences than that in the current law, and would be paid by far more taxpayers. This is a significant complication, because many taxpayers will need to compute both the ordinary and the minimum tax to see which applies. It also complicates economic choices, because some taxpayers will find that altering their decisions will avoid the minimum tax and reduce their tax liabilities.

The corporate minimum tax in the Packwood plan is especially controversial. It would require that corporations pay a percentage of their accounting or "book" income if that exceeds the tax computed in the usual way. This is a quantum departure from existing tax principles and will have many unpredictable effects. The accounting profession dislikes this minimum tax because it could make the accounting process less objective and more subject to time pressure; a corporation's books would have to be completed before its tax could be determined. Further, though accounting methods are quite standardized, enough discretion remains to make the amount of the minimum tax somewhat arbitrary; but if it chooses its accounting conventions to reduce its minimum tax, a corporation would also reduce the profit that it reports to its shareholders.

Corporations are also unhappy because, even though the Packwood plan retains many corporate tax preferences, basing the minimum tax on book income can render those preferences virtually worthless. And many more corporations will be subject to the minimum tax, which will greatly complicate corporate tax planning.

Even though these minimum taxes are unpopular with tax reform purists, accountants, and businessmen alike, they will be very difficult to replace. The minimum taxes are politically necessary because without them, given the number of tax preferences retained in the Packwood plan, many high-income individuals and profitable corporations would be able to avoid tax altogether. Voting to impose a minimum tax on those tax preferences is politically easier than cutting back the preferences themselves, because not all users of the preferences are subject to the minimum tax. Both replacing the large amounts of revenue raised by the minimum taxes in the Packwood plan and preventing all prosperous individuals and corporations from avoiding tax will require a number of painful votes on the underlying tax preferences.

Untouched Tax Issues

While the Packwood plan has been hailed as "true tax reform" by many observers, that judgment is, at least to some degree, relative. Some important tax preferences have gone entirely untouched. One is the exclusion for employee fringe benefits, which allows some workers to receive life and health insurance, pension plan contributions, and other forms of noncash compensation tax free. This exclusion has become a major drain on the tax base, as workers have taken advantage by bargaining for increasing shares of their compensation in fringe benefits. It is also an important cause of unfairness, as workers without fringe benefits must pay the same tax as others with equal cash compensation and generous fringe benefits besides.

A second major untouched tax preference is the exclusion of interest on state and local government bonds that are issued for private purposes. The capital raised with these bonds is turned over to private individuals and businesses to build industrial parks, shopping centers, sports stadiums, and other private projects. Because tax-exempt bonds can pay lower interest rates, private-purpose bond financing is advantageous for states and localities that want to attract business investment. As a result, the volume of tax-exempt, private-purpose bonds has exploded over the last decade. This has distorted the allocation of investment funds toward projects that are amenable to tax-exempt funding, and away from others. It has also so expanded the supply of tax-exempt bonds that it has driven up the interest rates that they must offer, greatly reducing the interest advantage of tax-exempt bonds even for such traditional government purposes as building schools and roads. Because no state or local government has any incentive to stop issuing private-purpose bonds, only the federal government can halt this destructive process. While the Packwood plan did not address this issue, both the administration and the House put restrictions on the issuance of private-purpose bonds.

Despite all of these problem areas, the Packwood plan is a significant step forward in tax policy. Senate tax reform advocates have chosen to oppose all amendments in order to prevent a gradual unraveling of the bill; if they are successful, the loss limitation, the phaseouts, and the minimum tax will have to be refined in conference. Of course, the conference must also address the large deficit in the federal budget as well as narrow tax policy issues.

Revenue and Budget Implications

Estimating the revenue effects of far-reaching tax legislation is always difficult. The computational task alone, dealing with tens of interacting and involved legal provisions, is daunting. But these computational issues pale beside questions of taxpayer behavior.

The goal of the Packwood plan was to hold total income tax revenue—and the deficit—constant, by raising $100 billion over five years under the corporate income tax, and cutting the same amount over the same period under the individual income tax. This follows the general outline of the administration and House proposals (though the administration would have shifted about $125 billion, and the House about $140 billion, from the individual to the corporate tax). Thus, in broad outline, the Finance Committee bill would not aggravate the deficit problem.

From a closer viewpoint, however, there is some cause for concern. Early indications are that the Packwood plan would raise more revenue in its first year than the current law, but slightly less in the following years, to achieve an equal five-year total. This raises a fear that the plan might be revenue-neutral over the short run, but lose revenue in the longer term. (This same concern was raised by Treasury Department revenue estimates for the administration proposal.) There are two basic reasons why such an outcome could occur.

First, the Packwood plan raises some revenue in the short term by disallowing postponements of income—for example, most taxpayers could no longer claim deductions for deposits in IRA accounts. Under current law, those IRA deposits are withdrawn later and taxed at that time, increasing future taxable income; under the Packwood plan, without those withdrawals, future taxable income would be lower. Second, changes in the tax law would change taxpayer behavior somewhat. If taxpayers change their decisions in ways that minimize their legal tax due, as we expect they would, taxes might fall somewhat over time in response to changes in the law. For example, taxpayers denied real estate tax shelters might shift their funds into tax-exempt bonds rather than taxable investments.

We should be concerned about long-term revenue implications, but fears in this regard are often exaggerated. Cutting back on postponements in the law does not automatically reduce future taxable income, as some people suggest; the relationships are extremely complicated, and the ultimate changes are likely to be small in any event. Consider the IRA example. Repealing the deductibility of IRA contributions today does reduce taxable withdrawals from IRA accounts tomorrow; but it also reduces deductible contributions to IRA accounts tomorrow. Which will dominate this mathematical relationship is hard to say, but the result is unlikely to be a dramatic decrease in long-run tax revenues. Likewise, taxpayers who are denied one form of tax shelter may choose another one instead of a taxable investment. But it is certain that cutting off the most lucrative shelters, as the Packwood plan does, leaves only less-attractive shelters still standing. In the tax-exempt bond example, a rush of former shelter investors would drive interest rates on tax-exempt bonds down, to the point where some investors would surely be discouraged and move to taxable bonds instead. Further, revenue estimates of the amount of deductions denied when a tax shelter is repealed may well underestimate the taxable income generated when the shelter's invested capital moves to taxable investments. Changes in behavior can cut both ways.

The budget outlook may be brighter, rather than darker, because of tax reform. In one central respect, the Packwood plan leaves the tax system better able to cope with any future budget emergency: It would be both easier and fairer to increase tax rates if need be. It would be easier because with a broader base, a given amount of revenue could be raised with an increase of a smaller number of percentage points in the rates. It would be fairer because an increase in tax rates would apply to all taxpayers, in contrast to the current law where raising tax rates passes over those who successfully avoid tax. (Also, the Packwood plan no longer includes excise tax increases, and so the excise tax tool is left for possible deficit reduction in the short run.)

Up from the Ashes

Just as tax reform appeared doomed in the House after its initial defeat on the floor, so it appeared lost in the Senate Finance Committee after Chairman Packwood withdrew his first plan. The resurrection in the Senate was no less remarkable than that in the House. It was, by all indications, the result of an adherence to principle. The same principle that saved the bill could sustain the policy in the years to come, ending the trauma of over ten years of continuous change in tax policy.

There are problems in the Packwood plan, and they should be addressed. But the plan does achieve a measure of even-handedness that demanded support even from tax reform's early detractors. This power should make it law.

PART IV
TAX REFORM: LEGISLATIVE PROCESS AND OUTCOME

8 • Tax Reform: What Does It Mean?

By all indications the Tax Reform Act of 1986 will be a watershed piece of legislation. The magnitude of this step is so great that it may leave many people a bit disoriented. Some may have unreasonable or inaccurate expectations; others may assume that the policy pendulum will swing back to its old position just as quickly as it moved to the new.

To understand and track the effects of this new law on the taxpayers and the economy, we need to understand the law itself. In particular, we need to know what tax reform can and cannot do to improve the economy; how the new law will affect the federal budget in the short run and the long run; and who will be helped, and who hurt, by the changes in individual income tax rates and deductions. With such an understanding we can assess the merits of the new law, judge its success, and make rational decisions about the future of tax and budget policy.

Tax Reform and the Taxpayers

Who wins and who loses from tax reform? Is the new tax reform bill a repudiation of the progressivity in income taxation to which we have adhered for almost three-quarters of a century? While the outcome of the tax reform process for an individual taxpayer is cut and dried, an assessment of the overall result is far more subjective.

Reprinted with permission from *The Urban Institute Policy and Research Report,* vol. 16, no. 1 (August 1986), pp. 1–6.

The Rich and the Poor

There is no doubt that families at or near the poverty line are among the biggest winners of tax reform. After ten years of virtual constancy in the law, the new act will significantly increase the personal exemptions and standard deductions that shield low-income persons from tax. At least six million poor and near-poor taxpayers will be removed from the tax roll in a policy improvement that is acknowledged from every segment of the political spectrum.

For upper-income taxpayers taken as a group, the result is far more ambiguous. According to tentative estimates provided by the Joint Committee on Taxation of the U.S. Congress, upper-income taxpayers—defined as those with at least $200,000 of income—would receive an average tax cut of about $2,500, or 2 percent of their tax liability—less than the 6 percent average tax cut for the population as a whole. But that small tax cut masks a considerable variation within this upper-income population. Taxpayers who now successfully avoid tax would pay considerably more than under current law. If the similar Senate bill is any guide, over 44 percent of those upper-income taxpayers would face tax increases averaging $50,030. At the same time, those now paying more than average tax would receive substantial tax cuts; 55 percent of upper-income taxpayers would receive tax decreases averaging $52,535.

Some observers have pointed to the large tax cuts for those upper-income taxpayers whose taxes decrease and argued that the bill is a bonanza for the rich. Others have used the wide dispersion between the large tax cuts and the large tax increases doled out by the bill and claimed that tax reform is just a reshuffling of money from the rich with tax shelters to the rich without tax shelters. Both of these arguments miss the point of tax reform.

By eliminating many deductions and exclusions now used by only a part of the taxpaying population, the new bill would impose more equal taxes on people with equal incomes—the ultimate goal of fairness in taxation. The tremendous dispersion of the resultant changes of tax liabilities among upper-income taxpayers is nothing more than a measure of the failure of the current tax law to impose equal taxes on equal incomes.

There remain the questions of whether upper-income taxpayers should receive an average tax cut at all, and whether the maximum statutory tax rate in the new bill, 28 percent, is too low. Indeed, some have argued that the new bill is a repudiation of our tradition of progressive income taxation. Again, this interpretation ignores the reality of our current tax system and the process by which tax reform has evolved.

Our current law does have marginal tax rates as high as 50 percent. Although that highest rate is paid by some taxpayers, it is paid far less frequently than the spirit of the law would suggest. Legal maneuverings allow many taxpayers to pay little or no tax and render the rate schedules virtually meaningless. A fixation with those statutory rate schedules as measures of progressivity honors the form, rather than the substance, of the tax system as it exists today. Despite the lower statutory rates, taxpayers with annual incomes of more than $200,000 would pay a higher percentage of the total tax burden under the new bill than they do under the current law. This is in addition to the substantial proposed increase in corporate income taxes, which would ultimately bear on the most wealthy.

Further, any attempt to restore steeper statutory tax rates, like those we have today, would threaten the structural improvements that the tax reform process has attained. Tax reform evolved not as a campaign to reward or penalize any particular income group (except the poor), but rather as a carefully balanced trade of diminished tax preferences for lower tax rates at all income levels. Raising tax rates would go back on this bargain, and inevitably reopen the negotiations over many tax preferences. One amendment proposed on the Senate floor, for example, would have increased the maximum statutory tax rate to 35 percent and marginally increased taxes on upper-income taxpayers, but in the process would have conceded the restoration of an exclusion for part of long-term capital gains—and thus have lost the equal taxes on equal incomes that are the major goal of tax reform. Still more concessions could have been expected to follow if that amendment had passed.

In sum, the new bill would give the highest-income taxpayers tax cuts on average, but those tax cuts would be smaller, in percentage terms, than the average for the entire population. The range of tax cuts and increases for this top income group would be wide—but only because the dispersion of taxes assessed by the current law is equally wide, and that dispersion should be undone because it is unfair. When coupled with the outright lifting of the tax burden from the poor and the near-poor and the increase in corporate taxes, this assessment of tax burdens—not merely the schedule of pro forma tax rates—is fair and progressive.

The Middle Class

For those between the lowest and the highest income groups, the average tax cuts are intermediate in size. Well over 60 percent of all taxpayers with incomes between $10,000 and $100,000 can expect tax cuts—as large as 20 percent on average for those with incomes of $10,000 to $20,000, but varying from 9 percent to 1 percent for the income groups between $20,000 and $100,000. Still, even at moderate incomes, the principle of equal taxes on people with equal incomes dictates that some people now paying taxes well below others in their income range should pay more. In fact, the new bill would impose higher taxes on about one-fourth of those with incomes between $20,000 and $30,000 per year, and about one-third of those with incomes between $30,000 and $40,000 per year.

Why is it fair to impose higher taxes on those with only moderate incomes? There are several answers. First and most obviously, given the discriminatory rules of the current system, the taxes it assesses should hardly be taken as the paragon of fairness. If after tax reform—with lower tax rates, larger universal personal exemptions and standard deductions, and fewer preferential deductions—some moderate income taxpayers wind up paying more, it is likely for good reason.

There are at least two examples of repeals of tax preferences that could lead to justifiable tax increases on middle income households. The deduction for contributions to Individual Retirement Accounts (IRAs) has had only a minimal impact on saving—its intended goal—and has benefited primarily those who had already accumulated wealth and were merely transferring it into tax-favored accounts. The tax deduction for interest on consumer borrowing has subsidized what may be an excessive buildup of consumer debt. Both of these deductions are repealed in the new bill (although low- and middle-income taxpayers can continue to contribute to IRAs and a five-year phase-out of the consumer interest deduction will cushion the impact on those who have already accumulated consumer debt).

There are some changes in the new bill whose rationale is more subtle. For example, the bill would restrict the deduction for medical expenses to those in excess of 7.5 percent of income, rather than 5 percent as under the current law. Some contend that this restriction is an unfair blow to those with medical bills. One could argue fine points: that the deduction is intended only for extraordinary medical expenses, and with nearly 10 percent of total personal consumption now devoted to medical care, the 5 percent floor is too low; and that the medical deduction is often abused and is excessively complex. But the heart of the answer lies deeper. It is that the income tax is not an efficient instrument, whatever the specification of the deduction, to protect people from extraordinary medical costs. For middle-income taxpayers, the deduction would be worth at most 15 cents on the dollar of expenses, because the tax rate is only 15 percent. To continue the current deduction would complicate the tax law and require higher rates for all taxpayers while providing only inadequate help to those with medical expenses.

There is one clue as to whose taxes will tend to be cut most. In the president's tax plans in 1984 and 1985, increasing the personal exemption to $2,000 as a benefit to families was a major goal; and the House and the Senate bills included this step. The larger the family, the more it benefits from the near-doubling of this exemption. Thus, we can expect that families with several children will tend to benefit most from any tax reform plan; and childless couples and single people will tend to pay about the same, or even more if they now rely heavily on the deductions and exclusions that are restricted or repealed. This change is really a restoration of the relative tax burdens of large and small households that were in force in the late 1940s and 1950s, when the personal exemption was even greater than $2,000 if measured in today's dollars. But the instant reversal of the slow, long-term erosion of the personal exemption by inflation will be a shock to the small households whose taxes will rise.

In sum, the great majority of middle-income taxpayers will get modest tax cuts under the new tax plan. By design, families with several children will tend to benefit most; as a side effect, small households will benefit least. The tax system will be more fair, because tax rates will be lower, because there will be greater nondiscriminatory deductions for all taxpayers, and because preferential deductions will be fewer and smaller. Some middle-income taxpayers will face higher taxes; these instances are regrettable, but necessary to attain worthwhile policy goals.

Tax Reform and the Economy

When the 1981 tax cut was passed, the most enthusiastic of its advocates predicted instant, miraculous improvements in the economy. In contrast, tax reform has never been billed as an economic quick fix.

Nonetheless, the continuing atmosphere of 1981, in which each monthly or quarterly economic statistic is viewed as an indicator of the success of long-run policy, could submit the current tax legislation to an irrelevant test and could even provoke an early attempt to reverse our policy course. It is important that we view the economic consequences of tax reform more realistically and so set a reasonable policy for the long haul.

Objectives for the Long Run

The 1981 tax cut was sold primarily on the ground that it would increase work, savings, and investment. In fact, the merits of tax reform on this ground are similar; by reducing the tax bite out of an additional dollar of income—through lower tax rates—tax reform makes all income-producing activity more attractive. Nonetheless, at least in this country, people tend to work and save about the same regardless of the tax rate; reducing the tax rate elicits only a small, marginal increase in work and saving. Thus, this effect of the 1981 tax cut was muted, and the corresponding effect of the 1986 tax reform will be similar.

The ultimate payoff of greater work effort, savings, and investment comes in faster growth of economic output and productivity. If workers work more and have more and better equipment with which to work, they can produce more goods and services, both in absolute terms and for every hour of labor. Realistically, however, not only is the tax-induced increase in work, savings, and investment relatively small, but the link between increases in investment and increases in productivity is very hard to define and demonstrate and is likely relatively weak. Again, the payoff of the 1981 tax cut has been small, and the payoff of the 1986 tax reform is likely to be small as well.

In some important respects, the 1986 tax reform will constitute a significant economic improvement over the current law. The 1981 tax cut created a hodge-podge of incentives that pushed business investment in many irrational directions. That law made many investments that were totally inefficient and wasteful in a business sense into profitable undertakings after tax advantages were considered—the definition of a tax shelter. For example, some investors were driven into investments in commercial buildings that lost money in the marketplace but turned an after-tax profit by generating disproportionately large tax losses that could reduce the tax liability on the investors' incomes from other sources. The economy has suffered as a result—witness the unfulfilled need for capital in some profit-making sectors, and the simultaneous over-building of commercial real estate. The 1986 tax law will make those tax shelters unprofitable and thus free investment capital to flow in more economically productive directions. As a subsidiary benefit, with lesser demands for credit to finance tax shelter investments (and also consumer spending), interest rates should fall, making financing cheaper for legitimate business investment.

However, both the reallocation of capital and the reduction of interest rates will have their payoff only over the long run. It will take several years for new profit-making investment projects to be planned, constructed, and put into service. And even at that point, the ultimate payoff in terms of faster economic growth and greater productivity will likely be subtle. Thus, tax reform will do everything that we can do—and therefore should do—to improve the operation of our economy through tax policy. We must be realistic, however, and recognize that the ultimate burden of competitiveness lies not with the federal government but with the private sector. Tax reform will reduce government interference in private decisions and thus will increase growth and productivity modestly and over the long run; but those who hold their breath waiting for a spectacular impact will likely run out of air.

Tax Reform and the Short Run

The irony of tax reform—and the danger to its survival beyond enactment—is that in the course of pursuing its long-run goals, it could make the short-run economic indicators look worse.

An example is the use of commercial structures as tax shelters. Under the current law our economy is building commercial structures over and above what the market demands just to provide tax savings to private investors. This is wasteful. It hinders our long-term competitiveness and growth, and it must be stopped. When it is stopped, however, and before the demand for industrial and other structures increases to take up the slack, the construction industry will be slowed. Those who ignore the inevitability and the necessity of this adjustment will argue that tax reform is harmful to the economy.

This same effect will extend to the statistics on total investment, which are viewed by some as a barometer of our economic progress. Even though commercial buildings that lose money before taxes are a decrement, rather than an increment, to our economic capacity, they

are included in the national accounts as investment. If wasteful construction of commercial structures were to decline and nothing else
changed in the economy, the national accounts would register a decline
in investment, and some observers would declare an economic emergency. It will be vital to look beneath the surface of the national
accounts to assess the impact of tax reform.

The investment statistics will be distorted further by the timing
effects of the enactment of tax reform. It has been clear for some time
that any tax reform bill will repeal the investment tax credit, which
reduces the taxes of all businesses that invest in equipment. Any rational businessman with investment plans for the near future would acceler-
ate his investments prior to the enactment of tax reform so that he
would receive the investment credit. After the enactment of tax reform,
those accelerated investments would already have been made. The
investment statistics, therefore, would show artificially inflated investment before the enactment of tax reform, artificially reduced investment after the enactment of tax reform, and thus a spurious decline of
investment at tax reform's enactment. It would be easy to read that
spurious effect as evidence that tax reform is bad for business investment over the long run.

In sum, the exaggerated sales pitch for the 1981 tax cut may have
made us impatient, demanding a quick payoff from any economic
policy. In the case of tax reform, such an impatience may lead us to
miss the point of the policy and judge it on false grounds. Economic
growth and competitiveness are slow-moving objectives and are not
easily amenable to manipulation by policy in any event. The impact of
tax reform will be positive but subtle and long in coming. Further, tax
reform will induce some negative wiggles to our economic indicators
in the short run. If we allow these spurious signals and our impatience
for results to lead us to reverse our course a few years down the road,
we will be casting away long-term benefit for short-term gratification.

Tax Reform and the Budget

Some observers have questioned whether the tax reform bill will in fact
fully replace the revenues collected by the current law, both in the long
and the short run. These questions are well within bounds; the revenue
implications of these dramatic changes in the law are to some degree
uncertain. Upon close analysis, there are reasons for optimism and
pessimism about the new bill. Further questions have been raised as to

whether the bill will ease or complicate any subsequent efforts to reduce the deficit; those questions, too, are worthy of examination.

Revenues in the Short Run

While the new tax bill is unprecedentedly far-reaching and therefore includes many unpredictable revenue provisions, the provisions with the largest revenue effects are for the most part predictable modifications of the current law. Under the corporate income tax, for example, we know how much revenue we now lose through investment tax credits claimed each year, and so we know how much revenue will be gained from the repeal of the credit. On the individual tax side we know how many personal exemptions are claimed each year, and so we know how much revenue will be lost by increasing the exemption to $2,000.

There are some substantial provisions whose implications are less clear and whose revenue impact may well be less attractive than the estimates indicate. A prime example is the revenue projected to be gained by improvements in tax compliance. The bill counts on several billions of dollars in net increased revenue as the result of greater administrative expenditures on tax compliance. Obviously, compliance with the law is a vital objective; many taxpayers may well cease dealing honestly with the revenue authorities if they believe that they are alone in so doing. But counting on large sums of revenue from investments so uncertain is surely risky.

At the same time, there are estimates that may be pessimistic. Investment dollars that would have gone into tax shelters—thereby generating negative taxable income—may go into profit-making investments—thereby generating positive taxable income. Though far below expectations, taxable income in the upper brackets increased somewhat since the 1981 tax cuts, lending some support to this argument.

Revenues in the Long Run

There are fears that the Senate bill, even if it raises current-law revenues over the official five-year measurement period, will lose money beyond that time frame. Here again, there are reasons for pessimism, but there are also other factors pointing toward revenue neutrality in the long run.

It is true that the new bill picks up considerable sums—$50 billion over the first five years—through changes in corporate tax accounting that essentially accelerate tax collections from later years, thereby reducing revenues beyond the measurement period, both under the ordinary tax and the minimum tax. The accounting changes require that corporations recognize income sooner, meaning that taxable income later is reduced by an equivalent amount. Further, corporations may learn over time to arrange their activities to incur less tax than is anticipated.

There are other factors, however, that would tend to increase revenues in the long run. For one, the bill would spend significant sums on transitions rules—exemptions from the new tax provisions for previously undertaken investment projects that rely on the prior law. Because the revenue loss from those transition rules is temporary—once the tax benefits from the ongoing projects are used, the revenue loss declines to zero—they are only a short-term revenue drain, making the long-term revenue picture brighter relative to the official short-term numbers.

Another positive factor is the change in depreciation of business plant and equipment. The bill changes depreciation in ways that raise significant amounts of revenue in the long run, and that long-run pickup is much larger than the short-run gain, making the long-run revenue picture more favorable than the short-run figures would suggest.

Exactly how these positive and negative long-run influences will balance out is impossible to predict. What is clear, however, is that any predictions of a long-run revenue disaster are far too pessimistic; the negative long-term factors are balanced by other positive influences. It is highly probable that any reduction in tax revenues in the long run will be small enough to be manageable through minor adjustments of the revenue system.

Budget Options

Even if the tax reform legislation is ultimately revenue neutral, we will still face the same budget deficit problem we have today. And because most budget analysts agree that some additional revenues will be needed to solve the deficit problem, they naturally wonder how tax reform will affect our options.

Some people fear that tax reform will make deficit reduction more difficult. They argue that once tax loopholes are closed and rates are cut in full compensation, it will be politically impossible to raise tax rates, and there will be no loopholes left to close, taking the income tax off of our menu of policy tools for dealing with the deficit. This concern is probably unfounded.

First, the Congress could now pass a tax reform bill with the same repeals of deductions and exclusions but slightly higher tax rates to take a step toward deficit reduction. The reason why such a path is rejected in favor of revenue-neutral tax reform is that the Congress lacks the will—mostly because the president has made it clear that he will veto any such bill.

The simple fact is that the Congress will have the same option of slightly higher tax rates at any future date when its will is stronger and the president's veto threat is removed. The political obstacles to raising the tax rates to that level are the same as those to setting the rates at that level in the first instance—and if those obstacles are conceivably surmountable now, they will be conceivably surmountable later. The Congress must weigh any popular reaction against such a step against the long-term benefit to the country—the same balancing that it did, correctly, in reversing its field from the huge tax cut of 1981 to the deficit-reducing tax increase of 1982.

A second fact is that, as dramatic an improvement as the 1986 tax reform has the potential to be, it will leave further loopholes that could be closed to raise more revenue later on. The bill makes no significant inroads against the tax exemption for employer-provided fringe benefits, which is a growing drain on the tax base and an unfair advantage to those who receive such benefits against those who do not. The bill narrows only modestly the loophole for private-purpose, tax-exempt bonds. And while closing off most tax shelter avenues, the bill leaves some opportunities for artificial losses in the oil and gas industry. These remaining flaws in the tax base could be mended to accumulate a tidy sum for deficit reduction.

Conclusion

The Tax Reform Act of 1986 has the potential to be a once-in-a-generation legislative achievement. That achievement cannot be measured solely in economic terms. The bill does all that could be expected of tax legislation in providing a more rational market for productive uses of investment capital; but the potential of tax legislation for accelerating economic growth and productivity is strictly limited. The real achievement of the law lies elsewhere: in the attainment of tax fairness, with nearly equal taxes on those with equal incomes. This achievement required a massive reshuffling of the current tax system, and this reshuffling will cause some pain. But if our expectations are reasonable and our goal is progress in the long run, the new law could give the nation a tax system worthy of the public trust—and perhaps a new and better attitude toward government as a whole.

9 • How Tax Reform Came About

The adoption of the Tax Reform Act of 1986 is widely recognized as a legislative landmark, not just in economic policy but in any terms. It is hard to think of an equivalent instance of an economic idea coming from nowhere to become the law of the land. Yet this achievement is full of uniqueness and irony. The new tax law violated all the rules of conventional wisdom built up by the tax policy fraternity. It was passed along through the legislative process by personalities reversing their own past patterns of behavior, and in some cases, it might be argued, the political law of gravity. It is not clear whether tax reform can be a case study for similar efforts in other policy areas, or just a shooting star to savor (or, depending on one's point of view, to curse). The goal of this article is to explain what the Tax Reform Act of 1986 is and how it happened.

This article is an expanded and updated version of a paper prepared for the Middlebury College conference, "The Spread of Economic Ideas," October 24–26, 1986.

The editor would like to express his appreciation to Marcia Aronoff, Livia Bardin, Peter L. Baumbusch, Bill Bradley, Gina Despres, Richard A. Gephardt, Jane G. Gravelle, Charles R. Hulten, Jim Jaffee, Bob Klayman, Lawrence F. O'Brien III, Joseph A. Pechman, Emil M. Sunley, Tom Troyer, James M. Verdier, Fred Wertheimer, and Mike Wessell for helpful comments and conversations. He would also like to thank Richard B. Booth, Timothy A. Cohn, Robin Mary Donaldson, Todd E. Easton, Nancy E. O'Hara, Arthur Morton, Katherine J. Newman, and Laurent R. Ross for research and programming assistance during his work on tax reform. None of the above should be implicated in any errors.

This paper is a product of the *Changing Domestic Priorities* project which is funded by a consortium of foundations and corporations, principally the Ford Foundation and the John D. and Catherine T. MacArthur Foundation. Opinions expressed herein are the author's alone and should not be attributed to The Urban Institute, its officers, trustees, or funders.

I. What Is the 1986 Tax Reform?

There are two important aspects of the Tax Reform Act of 1986 that must be kept in mind. The first is that the new law was by no means a strictly partisan effort. Among the bill's active supporters were such prominent liberals as Senator Bill Bradley (D-NJ), and such undeniable conservatives as President Ronald Reagan. The vocal opponents of the law included such dyed-in-the-wool liberals as Senator Carl Levin (D-MI), and solid conservatives such as Senator Malcolm Wallop (R-WY). General Motors, a massive industrial giant, supported the bill; USX (formerly U.S. Steel), massive in its own right, opposed it.

This bipartisan split was perfectly predictable (though its legislative outcome was hardly so). Each party was torn between conflicting interests. For the Democrats, the bill was a big tax cut for the poor (a significant plus), and a big tax increase for big real estate (a crushing minus). Even big labor wasn't too sure of where it stood on the bill (on final passage, the AFL-CIO took no position), which left the Democrats hanging. For the Republicans, things were no clearer. Individual corporate executives were thrilled, at least at the end of the process, by the prospect of much lower statutory individual income taxes and tax rates; but their corporations, in many instances, faced higher taxes. Capital intensive businesses lost the investment tax credit and much of the benefit of accelerated depreciation, and venture capitalists were horrified that they would have to pay at the same tax rate as everyone else.

This political confusion muddied the waters considerably. The bill was not a simple presidential proposal, passed through the Congress by a strong majority of his party with a smattering of opposition support. Of course, with one House in opposition control, that script would not play in any event. Even after the President climbed on board, there was always the need to count noses on both sides of the aisle in both Houses, and especially within the tax-writing committees.

The second aspect of the new law, especially important in retrospect, is its economic nature. The Tax Reform Act of 1986 is by no means a state-of-the-art academic creation. It is, rather, a "low-tech," low-budget approach to our tax policy problems—which is still, at least in my opinion, the right approach at this particular time.

Much of recent academic thought has centered on taxes on consumption, rather than income. The notion of a tax on personal expenditure has gathered solid support from the economics profession in the United

States as well as in Europe. (Households would compute their expenditure as their income less all money they saved—and plus all money they borrowed—and would file an annual tax return, just as under the current income tax. The roots of this as yet untried concept will be identified later.) This tax was taken up by some "new-ideas" liberals (such as former Senator Gary Hart [D-CO]), as well as by many traditional conservatives. Other conservatives like Senator William V. Roth (R-DE), as well as liberals such as columnist Robert Kuttner, have advocated a national value-added tax (VAT). Other strains of current thought stay within the bounds of the income tax, but emphasize fine tuning of incentives for investment and other economic activities considered meritorious (including, prominently, research and development).

Instead, the new tax law is a fairly long stride toward the old-line economic ideal of a comprehensive income tax. It downgrades, though it does not completely reject, the key consumption tax principle of deferring tax on the income from capital until it is finally consumed. Further, the new bill leans toward the age-old principle of imposing equal taxes on all forms of economic activity, rather than attempting a theoretically optimal selection of varying tax preferences for particular enterprises. This last position of the bill reaches its logical conclusion in an aggregate tax increase on corporations (though the impact on individual firms varies considerably).

II. Crucial Elements of the Issue

Why was tax reform the subject of a once-in-a-generation legislative phenomenon? Why not another economic issue, like the budget or trade, that is arguably more important? There are several aspects of the issue that made it amenable to fundamental legislative reform.

First, the income tax affects just about everybody, directly, and on a regular basis. It was pointed out in the debate over the tax bill that more Americans signed individual income tax returns in 1984 than voted for president. Most of these taxpayers had their taxes withheld from their paychecks at least once a month. This is in sharp contrast to the federal budget deficit, which is hardly the subject of periodic reminder notices to the great bulk of the population. Further, the deficit's effects on the economy are quite distant to most Americans.

Second, the impact of the income tax on the typical citizen is appreciable, using the obvious measure of the number of dollars paid. In contrast, the typical taxpayer's perceived benefit from a spending initiative—say, a retraining program for workers displaced by import competition—is scaled by the probability of an unpleasant contingency which the taxpayer would likely prefer to repress. Thus, tax reform is closer to the top of people's agendas than many other economic issues.

Third—at least from an economist's point of view—the bulk of the population is more likely to be "right" on tax reform than on many other economic issues. When asked about the federal budget, the typical noneconomist will want it balanced year after year, regardless of the state of the economy. When asked about trade, most Americans might well advocate protectionism to save U.S. jobs. On both of these counts, economists would strongly disagree. But on the income tax, our citizens have told pollsters for years that the system enshrouds unfair advantages for powerful interests. Most economists—including many who favor a personal expenditure tax rather than the income tax— would agree, and would expand on the popular argument by pointing out that serious economic distortions are caused by the many tax preferences in the current law. When most members of Congress hear protectionist pleas, understanding the costs and risks of protectionism, they try to find ways to seem supportive while avoiding the worst. Likewise, members seek prudent budgeting without mandatory balanced budgets (and may avoid consummation of Gramm-Rudman on this account). But when confronted with complaints about the tilted tax playing field, members of Congress have had to trade off the arguments of their constituents against the support they could expect from particular interests for preserving tax preferences. There has long been the potential for a strong ground swell for tax reform forcing these members to make an explicit choice, where sticking with the favored interests could be costly indeed.

Tax reform as practiced in 1986 is also a pro-poor policy without stigma. Families near and below the poverty line receive tax cuts that are in some instances substantial, but only if they receive income that is subject to tax—in most instances, wages. This allows members to aid the less well off with no fear of being associated with "giveaways." (Which is not to say that the tax reform bill was a complete anti-poverty policy—just an easy and a meritorious one.)

Despite having all of these entrées to the typical taxpayer, tax reform is still weak on everybody's bottom line on tax policy: what will it do to my taxes? Tax reform per se—the broadening of the tax base and the equal and counteracting reduction of the tax rates—reduces taxes for the vast majority of the population, but not by very much. And given the popular confusion over how the income tax works, many winners in the process fear that they will be losers. Given further that many of the interests that would lose from tax reform make their primary defense the frightening of those who would win, reforming the income tax code is far from politically easy. If it were, it would have been done a long time ago.

III. A History of the Economic Idea

There was a distinct evolution of the economic idea of "tax reform," in its many manifestations (income tax, consumption tax, and so on).

Economists have long argued for comprehensive income tax reform, defined as broadening the definition of income for tax purposes to match more closely the underlying economic concept. Working from the pre-World War II writings of Robert Murray Haig, Henry C. Simons, and others, Joseph A. Pechman put forward some of the earliest arguments in the 1950s and 1960s. Pechman's major contribution was to quantify the effects of departures from a uniform tax base, in terms of the amount of federal revenue lost and its distribution by income class. With this information spread among the economics profession, and popularized by Philip M. Stern, there arose a greater sense of the tradeoffs between selective tax preferences and lower tax rates. Of course, this realization among the economics profession and the attentive public did not prevent lower tax rates from being traded away for selective tax preferences almost continuously over this period.

At about the same time, Stanley S. Surrey, a lawyer, contributed a new view of the selective tax preferences in the law. He likened the tax savings from a preference for a particular purpose, say encouraging business investment, to a government outlay for the same purpose. Thus was coined the term, "tax expenditures." This concept was first quantified in the late 1960s, and then institutionalized in the federal budget in the mid-1970s, and has had a powerful influence on virtually all deliberations on the federal income tax ever since. On the other hand, proposals to operationalize the tax expenditure concept in the congressional budget process, usually by imposing a limit on tax expenditures like the current process's ceiling on outlays, have consistently failed.

An outgrowth of the tax expenditure idea was another Surrey concept, the "upside-down subsidy." Surrey pointed out that tax expenditures that were delivered through deductions from individual taxable income, such as that for medical expenses, reduced tax liabilities for upper-bracket individuals more than for lower-income persons; thus, at late–1960s tax rates, a dollar of medical expense deduction reduced the taxes of a top-bracket taxpayer by 70 cents, but for a bottom-bracket person by only 14 cents. This outcome struck Surrey as inequitable, and motivated him to argue on principle against tax expenditures (at least in the form of deductions) as a means of pursuing public purposes.

The concerns of Surrey and Pechman might well be typecast as 1960s arguments: largely based on the issue of fairness. While elimination of tax preferences would allow reductions in marginal tax rates and thereby could possibly stimulate the supply of factors of production to some degree, this was a secondary argument at most. Likewise, benefit for the economy through equalizing the taxes of different businesses was seen as subsidiary. The reason was, quite simply, that the nation already had robust economic growth, and the major concern was to spread the fruits more equitably. Thus, when researchers computed the reduction of tax rates that was possible through broadening of the tax base, the emphasis was on which taxpayers got the largest tax cuts; and the baseline position was to distribute the taxes as progressively as possible, subject to a constraint that the top marginal tax rate not be too high.

Of course, by the mid–1970s, with stagflation in full non-swing, national concerns were changing. At first, this raised some subsidiary income tax issues. Economists argued that inflation was distorting the measurement of income in the tax base—overstating the income of lenders and understating the income of borrowers (because inflation allowed borrowers to repay their debts with cheaper dollars); eroding the depreciation deductions of investors in business equipment and structures; and creating and inflating phantom capital gains. These effects created all the wrong incentives: borrow to increase consumption, or to finance with debt instead of equity; and consume existing wealth, rather than reinvesting it in overtaxed physical or financial assets. Some economists saw in these effects the seeds of a long-term economic decline through reduced capital formation. The prescription was indexation of the tax base to reflect inflation-adjusted rather than nominal magnitudes of interest income and expense, depreciation, and capital gains.

A second subsidiary income tax issue, reflective of another strain of tax policy, was concern about the double taxation of corporate-source income—profits taxed once at the corporate level, and again at the individual level when distributed as dividends. Again, the fear was that investment (in incorporated enterprises) would suffer, both absolutely and relative to investment in unincorporated businesses.

As is widely known by now, these relatively subtle strains of income tax thought were supplemented in the late 1970s by a school of thought that was rather less subtle. A young (and some might say cavalier) economist ruined a perfectly good dinner napkin in a Washington, D.C. restaurant, and supply-side economics was born.

Other economists were thinking more systematically—hitting the inflation and double taxation issues precisely, and with one blow. Many were taking off from Lord Nicholas Kaldor's proposal that the tax base be converted from income to consumption. Kaldor's concern had been one of capital formation, or perhaps deformation—he saw the wealthy of England consuming their wealth rather than reinvesting it. When viewed again and with the perspective of more recent developments, this personal expenditure tax—allowing a deduction for saving, and taxing borrowing in full—eliminated the inflation problem (because consumption is always in current dollars) and the double taxation problem (corporations would not be taxed, because they do not consume). An American lawyer, William D. Andrews, filled in many important operational details. David F. Bradford put the U.S. Treasury on the case in 1977 with *Blueprints for Basic Tax Reform*, followed closely by a report by the Meade Commission in England, and a similar study in Sweden written by Sven-Olof Lodin.

Still other economists concerned with capital formation were thinking somewhat more conventionally. Rather than instituting the world's only personal expenditure tax (this tax had been enacted but quickly dropped by India and Sri Lanka), they recommended following the mainstream of Europe with a value-added tax (VAT). The major differences between the personal expenditure tax and the VAT, apart from the novelty of the former, were administrative (the VAT would be an additional tax while the personal expenditure tax would replace the income tax) and distributional (the personal expenditure tax could have its own exemptions and deductions to protect the poor, like our income tax, while the VAT would require some outside mechanism to lift its tax burden from those with low incomes).

It is probably fair to say that the personal expenditure tax had captured the imagination of the greater part of the economics profession by the early 1980s. The exactness of this tax's solutions to the inflation and double taxation problems was the key to this appeal, along with, for some, the desire to tax consumption instead of income as a spur to capital formation. The question was whether fundamental tax issues would reach the top of the nation's policy agenda, and if so, whether the personal expenditure tax could translate into politics as neatly as it had into economics.

IV. A History of Tax Reform Legislation

It would be worthwhile to backtrack a few years and review the history of tax reform legislation. This review will be quite brief for the simple reason that, from the perspective of the scale of the 1986 legislation, very little was going on previously.

There was considerable interest in the income tax in the Great Depression, partly as a device to spread the pain. Huey Long talked about taxes as well as chickens in pots, and Franklin Roosevelt coined his memorable phrases about "malefactors of great wealth" and "heedless self interest" as bad economics over tax policy. Changes in the tax law over that period, however, were not so much fundamental reforms as increases in rates (just as the Mellon tax cuts of the 1920s were simply that).

World War II saw the reach of the income tax extended to the majority of the population, along with the extremely high tax rates that only a national emergency can justify. After the war, the tax law faced a long, gradual return to normality; but again, the changes were not fundamental. The landmark 1954 act recodified the entire income tax law, but the reform was legalistic rather than economic. The tax rates were hardly changed, and there was little true revision of the base.

The tax law remained essentially unchanged until 1964 when President John F. Kennedy, with the advice of tax scholars like Surrey, attempted to reform the income tax at the same time as he cut the tax yield to stimulate the economy. A key element of the bill was a blanket cutback of itemized deductions. Unfortunately, the radical fiscal policy proved extremely controversial, and when the entire initiative foundered in the Congress, the reform elements were jettisoned. The final product had marginal tax rates significantly higher than President Kennedy had originally proposed because of the loss of the reform elements.

In the last days of the Johnson administration, the Treasury, under Stanley Surrey, was requested to undertake a broad study of the structure of the income tax. IRS statistics showing that hundreds of taxpayers with considerable incomes were paying no income tax had caused a minor furor. The result of the Treasury inquiry, which came to be known as the "Surrey Papers," was handed over to Russell Long and Wilbur Mills, chairmen of the Congressional tax writing committees, just after the new Congress began in 1969. The Congress made use of this study in the Tax Reform Act of 1969. This legislation had several noteworthy elements, most prominently the creation of the minimum tax, which responded to the public outcry over tax avoidance. The minimum tax closed, at least partially, some of the most important avenues of such tax avoidance. Nonetheless, the scope of the bill was quite narrow by 1986 standards. Further, by adding a minimum tax onto the existing law, and by dealing with isolated provisions of the law rather than the overall structure, the 1969 act tended to complicate the system rather than simplify it.

After emergency tax relief bills in 1974 and 1975 to deal with the recessionary aftermath of the oil shock, the Congress set out to eliminate remaining perceived abuses and make the relief provisions permanent. The Tax Reform Act of 1976 was seen in retrospect as the high water mark of the tax reform movement of the preceding quarter century. Yet in its further tinkering with the tax code provision by provision, and in its restriction and modification of preferential provisions rather than outright repeal, this Act continued the complication of the law and of economic choices. Although there were many worthwhile reforms in the 1976 law, it is probably best remembered today for an abortive attempt to restore to the income tax base the amount of capital gains not realized but passed on to an heir upon death. This provision, known as "carryover basis," was enacted prospectively in 1976, but then postponed and finally repealed before ever taking effect, in what is now a legendary legislative and policy debacle.

After 1976, the incoming Carter administration went off in one tax policy direction, and the rest of the nation went in another. The new president sought to continue to reform the "disgrace to the human race," as he saw the tax system, while virtually everyone else was concerned about stagflation and the newly discovered productivity slowdown.

Before the administration proposed a tax reform bill, a set of options prepared for the President was leaked to the press. These options met with sufficient opposition to seal the fate of income tax reform legislation. A major lightning rod was the proposal to relieve the double taxation of corporate income by providing shareholders with a credit for the corporate tax already paid on their dividends. This proposal, known as "partial integration," split the business and financial community in two. Stockbrokers loved the idea, seeing the tremendous boost in the appeal of corporate stocks if they carried a tax credit with their dividends. Corporate managers, on the other hand, were appalled that they might have to pay out more of their earnings in dividends, given that the tax credit would make dividends much more attractive to shareholders. Some economists argued that greater dividend payments would tend to reduce investment, given that shareholders would reinvest only part of that income, while others anticipated an improvement in the allocation of capital. These squabbles over integration helped to smother the tax reform baby in its cradle. Another controversial element of the proposal was the elimination of the exclusion for long-term capital gains, which destroyed any good will that the integration proposal might have generated among stockbrokers.

With the early options a nonstarter, the administration led with its chin and sent the Congress a different package that came to be identified with an attack on the "three martini lunch" deduction for businessmen. This second debacle drew a chorus of boos from Capitol Hill, and the Congress legislated on its own. In lieu of tax reform, it sought incentives for investment and growth, by which was meant more and larger selective preferences. The keystone of the bill was an expansion of the preference for long-term capital gains from a 50 percent to a 60 percent exclusion. This provision had an ironic twist which was to echo in the 1986 tax reform debate. An important part of the rationale for a tax cut for capital gains was the effect of inflation in creating "phantom" gains that are taxed as though they were real. Because of this argument, there was considerable talk of indexation of capital gains. But when the Senate Finance Committee emerged from a closed room, it had adopted the 60 percent exclusion. The exclusion is only an inexact compensation for inflation; in fact, for assets held for a long time while inflation has been rapid it can be woefully inadequate. But the exclusion is overgenerous for those who accrue large gains over a very short time. So for all the talk about the capital gains law as an inducement to invest for the long haul, the chosen preference was aimed at quick-turnover (though at least one year), big-profit operators. The effect of inflation was not a problem to be solved, but rather a pretext for more general relief.

It was just a hop, skip, and a jump from the Revenue Act of 1978 to

the Economic Recovery Tax Act of 1981. There were perceived benefits from the 1978 law (particularly in the area of venture capital, a tiny
segment of the economy); the economy stalled in 1979–80; and supply-
side economics caught on with the electorate and candidate Ronald
Reagan. The 1981 law was the antithesis of tax reform; it added tax
expenditures to the already burgeoning list (by this time having twice as
many items at six times the revenue cost of the first list of 1967). And
yet in an ironic way, the 1981 law set the stage for the Tax Reform Act
of 1986.

V. The Drive for Tax Reform, 1981–86

There are two reasons why the 1981 tax cuts caused a greater but
opposite reaction in 1986.

All of the evidence available in 1981 indicated that the income tax
was extremely unpopular with the population in general; it was perceived as being the most unfair tax of all (including state and local
taxes). A cynical view might have been that the across-the-board tax
cut of 1981 would have won over the population just by making taxes
lower, without addressing at all the perceived inequities in the underlying structure of the system. Such was not the case; in fact, the response
to one provision of the 1981 law (safe harbor leasing) was violent
enough to cause an almost immediate reversal.

The corporate side of the 1981 law drastically expanded the tax
benefits of accelerated depreciation for business investment (through
the Accelerated Cost Recovery System, or ACRS), and somewhat
increased the value of the investment credit for some business assets.
The combination of the two was so rich that many firms were expected
to be made completely nontaxable, and thus to lose any further incentive effect of these provisions. Another problem was that these incentives would have no effect at all for new firms, and for other firms that
had recently been running losses, because these firms would owe no
taxes in any event. So the bill would be a boon for General Motors,
which was doing well, but would offer nothing to Chrysler, which was
then on the brink. The administration responded by proposing that the
tax benefits in effect be made salable, through "safe harbor leasing."
Given the premise of ACRS, safe harbor leasing followed perfectly
logically—at least to an economist. But to the population at large, safe
harbor leasing was extremely offensive. It combined a negative corporate income tax, the buying and selling of tax breaks, and the subsidiza-

tion of "losers" all into one foul-smelling package. Only one year later, the safe harbor leasing provision was gutted.

The legacy of safe harbor leasing for the 1986 tax bill is not quantifiable, but could well have been enormous. It may have been the marginal influence that so discredited the tax law in people's minds that fundamental reform became feasible. Further, it is extremely suggestive that a popular resentment toward the very low tax liabilities of profitable corporations helped to drive tax reform in the later stages.

The second major influence of the 1981 law relates to the federal budget and the revenue yield of the income tax. The knee-jerk reaction to the 1981 law, based on past experience, was that this tax cut had cost the federal government so much revenue that further changes in the law would be impossible until many years of inflation and real growth could restore the tax base. What this conventional wisdom failed to recognize was that the revenue cost was in fact even greater than that; it was a revenue hemorrhage so serious that several rounds of emergency surgery were essential. Further, the tax rate cuts had become so much a part of the economic policy baseline, not to mention of the President's agenda, that raising revenue required plugging loopholes in the tax base rather than raising rates. This process exposed many obsolete and unjustifiable tax preferences; it provoked a great deal of unseemly dissembling and outrageous forecasting on the part of affected interests; and it convinced many members of Congress that tax preferences could be repealed without causing the sky to fall in. (The banks' successful counterattack on the withholding from interest and dividends enacted in 1982 also wounded the pride and raised the dander of a number of congressional tax writers, who determined to get even.)

The 1981 law's reduction of the revenue baseline had another, subtler effect. Like it or not, tax reform packages have always been graded according to how far they could reduce the top-bracket individual income tax rate with no loss of revenue and with minimal influence on the progressivity of the tax burden. A crucial factor in the determination of that maximum individual rate is the handling of long-term capital gains. It became evident during the debate on the 1981 law that, simply because it cut taxes so much, an equal-yield, equal-progressivity reformed income tax could be designed with a maximum individual income tax rate of 28 percent if there were no preference for long-term gains. The 28 percent rate was a policy plateau, in that the maximum effective tax rate on long-term gains was set at 28 percent by the 1978 law that was so beloved by the capital formation lobby. If a

reformed tax with a 28 percent top rate would silence (though it certainly would not win over) the capital formation crowd, it was reasoned,
the traditional allies of tax reform might be able to form a coalition
with low-rate supply-siders that would be large enough to pass a bill.
This was the foot in the door for tax reform. And as is fairly widely
recognized by now, that foot was wearing a basketball sneaker.

Personalities make a difference in politics, unlike in abstract economic models, and Senator Bill Bradley (D-NJ) was ideally suited for
advancing tax reform. He had a long-term interest in tax reform, dating
back, he relates, to the signing of his first professional basketball
contract at the age of 23. His lawyer said that they needed to make a
decision on how much income tax Bradley wanted to pay, and Bradley,
confused, asked what that could possibly mean. When confronted with
the myriad of options of how he could accept his compensation, and
their widely varying tax consequences, the pro basketball and tax rook-
ie had his interest piqued and his sensibilities offended. He began
looking into tax policy issues, and reports that he had a strange feeling
when he learned that he was a depreciable asset. After two years of
playing the games (both basketball and taxes), he told his lawyer to
change his compensation package to straight salary and pay whatever
tax resulted. His roommate, Dave DeBusschere, wrote that among
Bradley's eccentricities (which included dressing like a Princeton un-
dergraduate and driving a Volkswagen) was traveling the country during the New York Knickerbockers' first championship season reading
the Tax Reform Act of 1969.

As a senator, Bradley was willing to exert even more effort than was
usual in workaholic Washington on mastering details (which the tax
system has in abundance). He also carried with him the willingness to
engage in long-term efforts as a part of a team. The tax reform effort
required a painful campaign of constituency building, including exten-
sive travel and speaking engagements (among them a spot on the Phil
Donahue show) and writing a book on his tax bill.

Bradley postponed his effort at tax reform through the first half of
his first term, partly in deference as the most junior member of the
Finance Committee and partly to examine the options. The passage of
the 1981 tax law accelerated his efforts, however, as he decided that it
was inherently unstable. (Bradley was the only vote against the bill in
committee.)

Bradley rejected the expenditure tax option even while it was near its
peak of popularity among the economics profession. The reasons were

the same as those cited by economists who opposed the expenditure tax. One was the probable public perception of unfairness in a tax on what people spent rather than on their economic capacity, and the extreme of unfairness that would result unless gifts and bequests were included in the tax base as if spent, an unlikely policy outcome. A second was the danger that the expenditure tax base could become even more leaky than the income tax base in the legislative process. A third was the difficulty of transition, especially in providing adequate relief to older persons (who had already paid income tax on their accumulations of wealth) without depleting the tax base. A fourth was doubt over whether and to what degree a complete lifting of the tax burden on capital and a shifting of it to labor would be an economic plus. A fifth was the lack of experience with the expenditure tax, and the non-trivial possibility of extremely difficult or even insurmountable administrative problems.

A final reason, easy to trivialize but impossible to ignore, was the complexity of the expenditure tax concept to a public raised on an income tax. A policy position must be explained to a senator or representative not just so that he can understand it, but so that he can explain it to his constituents. Members of Congress, when confronted with the expenditure tax, tend to go blank for two different reasons. The first is an initial lack of comprehension. The second, which follows even with their own understanding, is a realization that this concept could never be explained in a town meeting to a cross-section of their constituents. Thus, those economists who bank on significant supply-side responses to an expenditure tax must be prepared to argue that such responses will materialize even if the bulk of the taxpayers do not understand the tax.

So Bradley settled on reform of the existing income tax as a journey on familiar territory. The key principles of the Bradley-Gephardt bill (also named after Rep. Richard Gephardt (D-MO) who joined as House cosponsor) were (1) seeking workability ahead of academic purity and (2) isolating the essence of tax reform from subsidiary issues. The first principle led to the rejection of the consumption tax option, and also to the omission of corporate tax integration and the indexation of the tax base from the bill. It was concluded that indexing and integration would cause prohibitive administrative and political difficulties, which later developments proved to be correct. The second principle dictated that the Bradley-Gephardt bill be both revenue and distribution neutral (that is, that it raise the same total revenue as the current law, and that each individual income class, and corporations taken as a group, pay the same tax as under the current law). Thus, Bradley-Gephardt could not be attacked on the ground that it was a redistributionist scheme, or that it would debilitate the corporate sector. The price of this decision was that Bradley-Gephardt could not offer a dramatic tax cut for low-income persons (though it did increase personal exemptions and standard deductions sufficiently to lift the poor from the tax rolls), and that it could not use a corporate tax increase to avoid the last, painful choices to attain revenue neutrality among individuals.

Bradley-Gephardt had three "signature" provisions. It was the first tax reform proposal to combine a large increase in the amount of low-income relief with a very large first tax rate bracket that would be the only marginal rate for the vast majority of the population. (The Treasury's 1977 *Blueprints for Basic Tax Reform* had the same number of tax rate brackets as the final version of Bradley-Gephardt, but had a very small first bracket, with most taxpayers landing in the second bracket.) This meant that between 70 percent and 80 percent of the population could understand Bradley-Gephardt in very simple terms ("a 14 percent tax on your taxable income")—an important advantage, given that a surprising number of taxpayers do not understand how progressive tax rates work. A second advantage of this formulation, almost unwelcomed, was that it associated Bradley-Gephardt with the "flat tax" boomlet that followed in the initial euphoria after the passage of the 1981 law. This provided useful public exposure, but ran the risk that burgeoning budget deficits and the inevitable increased public understanding would bury Bradley-Gephardt along with the flat tax. In fact, the flat tax fad faded within about a year, but Bradley-Gephardt remained on the scene.

Bradley-Gephardt's second "signature" provision was a limit on the value of itemized deductions to 14 cents on the dollar. In other words, if an itemizing taxpayer in the lowest marginal rate bracket made another dollar of charitable contributions (or any other itemizable expense, except for interest), his tax would decline by 14 cents; if the taxpayer were instead in the highest tax rate bracket, his tax would still decline by the same 14 cents. (Deductible interest expense was not subject to this restriction, so that interest expense and interest income would have their effects at the same marginal rate.) This provision was the subject of intense controversy. It was sometimes castigated on the ground that it took tax savings away from upper-bracket taxpayers unfairly; and sometimes praised on the ground that it solved the Stanley Surrey "upside-down subsidy" problem. It certainly raised a significant amount of revenue from the upper-bracket taxpayers, which allowed the substantial reduction in the top marginal rate. This provision resurfaced, albeit to a limited degree, in the Senate version of the Tax Reform Act of 1986; it was removed in conference, however. (Please note that this provision did *not*, as we suggested elsewhere ["How to Cheat At Tax Reform," *Tax Notes*, September 18, 1987, p. 130], have the effect of phasing out deductions and thereby increasing the effective marginal tax rate above the statutory marginal tax rate.)

The third "signature" provision was added to the second and final version of Bradley-Gephardt, introduced in 1983. The first Bradley-Gephardt bill included changes only to the individual income tax; revisions to the corporate income tax were promised later. The second bill included these corporate reforms (as well as further individual revenue raisers equal in yield to those in the Tax Equity and Fiscal Responsibility Act of 1982). The Bradley-Gephardt corporate tax was a U-turn from the changes of 1981; it eliminated numerous subsidies, including the investment tax credit and most of the benefit of accelerated depreciation, and reduced the corporate rate to a flat 30 percent (equal to the highest individual rate in this second version). The depreciation system was designed to tax all business investments equally. This entire approach bespoke a radically different philosophy from the existing corporate tax; it turned away from government intervention in business decisions, and sought the lowest possible uniform tax burden on corporate income from whatever source. Research on depreciation issues, most notably papers by Jane G. Gravelle and Charles R. Hulten, helped to establish that the efficiency gains from a change to more uniform taxation could exceed any losses from reduced investment subsidies.

Senator Bradley and Representative Gephardt saw their bill as expanding the frontier of the tradeoff between fairness and efficiency. It eliminated numerous inequities in the treatment of taxpayers with similar incomes, and it reduced the tax rates on productive economic activity. Further, it added the business neutrality argument to the efficiency motivation for tax reform; it would eliminate virtually all tax shelter activity, and would steer the resources from shelters and other hitherto favored activities into others that earned more profit apart from the tax benefits. Thus, Bradley-Gephardt allowed its sponsors to argue for fairness and growth at the same time—a possible political strategy for a party that seemed to have lost its way.

Beyond the specifics, however, Bradley-Gephardt was the first high-profile comprehensive income tax reform system ever put forward by members of Congress. Other members had argued for tax reform in the past, espousing the closing of one or two egregious loopholes, and usually overemphasizing the reduced tax rates that would result. (The only exception was Rep. James Corman [D-CA], who submitted his own comprehensive reform proposal, called H.R. 1040. Corman's efforts never came close to fruition, probably in part because the time just was not right.) Bradley and Gephardt made the numbers add up, which meant that all of the repeals of deductions and exclusions had to be made explicit—including those that were less than egregious and had come to be taken as matters of right by large segments of the taxpaying population. It was a very risky step; there was no telling what the political fallout might be. (Every tax expert in Washington remembers that the late Al Ullman, while chairman of the House Ways and Means Committee, lost what was thought to be a safe seat in Oregon at least in part because of his espousal of a value-added tax.) The sponsors braced themselves and waited for the bang. The reaction, however, was encouragingly positive. Apart from a howl from the real estate industry and another from labor unions, the complaints were limited to scattered, answerable objections to the repeal of one minor deduction or another. There was enough positive response to keep the enthusiasm flowing.

In their excellent account of the events surrounding the passage of the Tax Reform Act of 1986 (*Showdown at Gucci Gulch*, Random House, 1987), Jeffrey H. Birnbaum and Alan S. Murray suggest that the twenty-one months following the introduction of the Fair Tax Act of 1982 were a fallow period—that the initiative "seemed to be one of the forgotten proposals, a noble but unrealistic idea." I believe that this is something of an understatement of the efforts and the fruits of 1982–83. As was noted earlier, the cosponsors engaged in a back-breaking promotional campaign for their idea. (Bradley, it was said, "would attend the opening of an envelope.") This process exposed Bradley and Gephardt to all of the criticism of the bill, and educated them, through staff backup, in the justification for their proposals. In part because of this support from the cosponsors, and in part because of its inherent soundness, Bradley-Gephardt benefitted from the "flat tax" publicity boomlet, but remained firmly on the beach when the flat tax was washed away with the tide. This building of credibility for the proposal and its backers raised it gradually from the pipe dream to the long shot category, and subsequent events were to demonstrate just how much momentum it had.

The constituency building effort proceeded into 1984, when presidential politics became an obvious element in every policy debate. There were several developments. The first was when President Reagan, in his January 1984 State of the Union message, directed the Treasury to report specific recommendations for the comprehensive reform of the tax system by December of that year. Press analysis subsequently suggested that the administration feared a Democratic nominee's use of the Bradley-Gephardt bill as an issue in the campaign, and was therefore attempting to preempt the issue. The Treasury study would give the President an advantageous position; he would be wedded to no specifics, but could attack Bradley-Gephardt on chapter and verse pulled out of context. Further, the President at least had the option of allowing the Treasury report to gather dust if he chose later not to pursue the issue. Obviously, the President would not have resorted to this transparent ploy had not Bradley and Gephardt built a sound foundation for their issue.

A second development was the announcement by Representative Jack Kemp (R-NY) and Senator Robert Kasten (R-WI) that they were introducing their own comprehensive income tax bill, or what Rep. Kemp called "a Republican Bradley-Gephardt." The Kemp-Kasten bill, which was revised numerous times over the next two years, was never an influence on the tax reform process (apart from a call to raise the personal exemption to $2,000, which was finally enacted for the end of a long phase-in period). Unlike Bradley-Gephardt, which was developed in close consultation with the Congressional Joint Committee on Taxation and was formulated to attain precise revenue neutrality by the committee's official estimates, Kemp-Kasten was never officially costed out—because the cosponsors did not ask for it. The reason was that Kemp and Kasten knew that it would not achieve revenue neutrality by official estimates, and either did not want to know or preferred to trust in supply-side economics to close the gap. (The *Wall Street Journal* reported that the Treasury estimated the revenue effects of Kemp-Kasten late in the process—for the administration's information, not at the request of Kemp or Kasten—and found it tens of billions of dollars short.) What was important in the Kemp-Kasten bill, however, was having a prominent supply-side conservative jump on the bandwagon of tax reform, thus making it possible for others to join and further broaden the coalition. That influence proved crucial.

As the year wore on, the foremost question was whether Walter Mondale would make tax reform a major part of his presidential campaign. Eventually, of course, he did not. Tom Edsall reported in the *Washington Post* that Mondale was persuaded to avoid tax reform because it would offend the real estate industry, a major source of funds for Democratic political campaigns. Other sources have quoted Mondale as saying, after the election, that failing to embrace tax reform was his most serious mistake of the campaign. So died the Democratic hopes of using tax reform to reclaim the political initiative lost to Ronald Reagan in 1980.

The Treasury then pulled a major surprise by releasing its study several weeks early, on November 27, 1984, and with no prior consultation with the President or the White House staff. Secretary Regan's rationale for the early release was that once the plan was finalized, it was subject to debilitating leaks (which had already begun) and could be picked apart in the press. The fear among tax reformers, however, was that the report was being held up as a target for beneficiaries of the current code, and could have been so discredited that the President could safely walk away from the issue. Secretary Regan's answer to questions about controversial provisions that ". . . this report was written on a word processor; it can be changed," did not ease those fears.

The Treasury report itself, however (subsequently referred to as "Treasury I"), was extremely well received. It confirmed the Bradley judgment that the personal expenditure tax concept was not yet ready for serious consideration. It then followed very similar general lines to Bradley-Gephardt, with three individual rate brackets ranging from 15 to 25 and 35 percent, and with a corporate tax rate of 33 percent. It repealed the investment tax credit and eliminated the acceleration from depreciation on the business side, and pruned the itemized deductions and exclusions for individuals. A major difference from Bradley-Gephardt in the basic individual provisions was eliminating all itemized deductions for state and local taxes, which fit in well with the administration's theme of devolution of responsibilities to the state and local levels but proved extremely controversial.

In several respects, however, Treasury I distinguished itself from Bradley-Gephardt by being extremely elegant. It indexed capital gains and depreciation for inflation by methods that were conventional and well known, but went on to index interest income and expense, which was reputed to be extremely complex, by a new and simplified method. (It would have taxpayers compute their net interest—interest income minus interest expense—without indexation, and then index the net interest according to an economy-wide average interest rate, rather than indexing each account and loan according to its actual interest rate.) It would provide a deduction to corporations for half of the dividends they paid, as a partial step towards integration. Rather than taxing all of health insurance fringe benefits like Bradley-Gephardt, it would leave the first dollars of employer-paid premiums tax free, as an inducement to participation in such insurance plans; only the excess of the premiums over the cap would be taxed. It provided an opposite floor for charitable contributions, so that small, routine amounts of contributions would not be deductible, but large contributions would benefit from the incentive. In these respects, Treasury I was the antithesis of Bradley-Gephardt's creed of practicality over purity. Many economists reacted that the Treasury was sending a Lamborghini out to race the Bradley-Gephardt Volkswagen Beetle.

But Lamborghinis often fail to start on cold mornings, and what was picked apart in Treasury I was for the most part the elegant features. The financial community argued against indexation of capital gains for the same reason that they had in 1978: they preferred an exclusion that would reward them for big gains accrued over short times, rather than inflation protection. The investment community railed against non-accelerated indexed depreciation, asking for bigger up-front deductions that were not contingent upon inflation. Banks found that the streamlined indexation of interest income and expense would grossly understate their profit margins. Corporate managers argued that even if they received a tax deduction for their dividends paid, rather than individual shareholders receiving a credit for dividends received as they would have in the 1977 Carter options, the shareholders would see through the ruse and demand more dividends. Labor unions were opposed to any taxation of fringe benefits, but were violently opposed to the Treasury cap, which would single out their very generous plans for taxation. And the charitable sector protested against the floor on the contributions deduction.

But one simple feature of Treasury I probably caused more controversy and contributed more to the ultimate passage of tax reform than any other: a $25 billion per year increase in corporate income taxes, which financed a $25 billion per year cut in individual taxes. Some observers argued that it was a simple sweetener for individuals, who vote, out of the deep pockets of corporations, who do not. But inside sources suggested that the numbers dictated the result; after defining the individual and corporate tax bases as they thought proper, the

Treasury found that the corporate tax simply raised too much revenue. They lowered the corporate rate 2 percentage points below the top individual rate, but hesitated to go further because of a possible inducement to incorporate hitherto unincorporated businesses to cut taxes with the lower corporate rate. (Birnbaum and Murray report that this process was aided by the unaesthetic 16 percent–28 percent–37 percent first draft individual tax rate schedule, which sounded "like a football call" to Secretary Regan.) With the repeal of the prominent tax preferences plus this tax increase on corporations, Treasury I completed the U-turn from the 1981 business tax policy.

It was probably here rather than in any other connection that this particular president, and his particular party affiliation, had the most to do with the ultimate success of tax reform. For one thing, Ronald Reagan's approach to tax policy is rather unidimensional: the level of the top individual tax rate is far and away his most important consideration. Long-time Reagan watchers relate that the President was deeply offended when his acting career took off at the end of World War II, and he discovered that he was paying 91 percent of his last dollars of income to the federal government. As president, the supply-side ideology had reinforced his aversion to high tax rates. The Treasury's proposed 35 percent maximum rate took on a highly symbolic meaning to the President; he realized that he could claim that the maximum individual income tax rate was cut in half during his term of office if the proposal passed intact. This potential achievement compensated for a multitude of sins, not the least of which would be the knifing of virtually every traditional Republican party constituency with not just the repeal of most major tax preferences, but a net $25 billion per year corporate tax increase to boot.

Further, it is unclear just how closely the President focused on this tradeoff. Surprisingly late in the game, the President was reported to have asked Treasury Secretary Regan about the murmuring of a corporate tax increase in the plan. The secretary reportedly reassured the President that only corporations that now paid no taxes would have their taxes increased, and the President was satisfied. It is far from certain whether a more detailed look at the issue in the Oval Office would have yielded the same result.

Thus, the "Nixon visits China" scenario was replayed. The President unquestionably carried a large number of reluctant Republican votes in both Houses of the Congress. Had Walter Mondale been elected in 1984, those votes would have been unattainable. The Democrats would have had to pass the bill on a straight party-line basis, against charges of unrestrained redistributionism and corporation bashing, with no votes to spare, and under the most intense pressure from their own allied interests. It is hard to imagine how tax reform could have succeeded under those circumstances.

Once on the table, the corporate tax increase was impossible to remove. The extra $25 billion of corporate revenue saved the Treasury from having to make those last hard choices on the individual side that a distribution-neutral bill would have required. With the tax cut, the Treasury could give more relief to the near-poor, which did not buy many votes directly, but to some extent wrapped the bill in the flag. With less revenue to raise, the plan could yield more winners and fewer losers. And perhaps most decisively, once such a tax cut was offered to the voters, it would be political folly to step forward and propose to take it away.

So the greatest danger to Treasury I was that the President would reject it; but instead the President bought on, at least in principle. The next question was what kind of a proposal the Treasury could develop that the President himself would sign. This process proceeded under somewhat different circumstances, because James Baker (hitherto White House chief of staff) and Secretary Regan swapped jobs.

Secretary Baker seemed to be somewhat more of a political concilia-tor than his predecessor, and the final administration proposal, called "Treasury II," seemed at least in part an attempt to mend traditional Republican fences. Indexation of capital gains was dropped, and in its place was a capital gains exclusion that reduced the maximum effective rate on long-term gains relative to current law. Depreciation would still be indexed, but it would be accelerated more than in Treasury I. The corporate deduction for dividends paid was cut from 50 percent to 10 percent. The indexation of interest income and expense was dropped, as was the floor on the charitable contributions deduction. The cap on employer paid medical insurance was replaced by a ludicrous floor that had every covered employee, regardless of the generosity of his plan, paying tax on the first $25 per month. With all of these changes, the bill provided tax cuts for the highest measured income group ($200,000 and over) that were larger, even in percentage terms, than those for the middle class.

Reaction to Treasury II was tinged with disappointment; many economists believed that some tough provisions of Treasury I were sacrificed without a fight. Some were also disappointed with the loss of the elegant features of Treasury I, including indexation; others felt that to be inevitable.

But perhaps the most negative development from Treasury II was the emergence of a revenue shortfall. The concessions made on capital gains, charitable contributions, depreciation, and other provisions made the package revenue short in the early years. Treasury responded by including a "recapture" tax on recent investment. The reasoning was investments made since 1980 received a "double dip," because they benefitted from the investment credit and accelerated depreciation in their early years, while they would also benefit from the drastically reduced corporate tax rate after the tax reform plan became effective. This double dip would be prevented by adding a percentage of depreciation claimed in the early 1980s back into taxable income after the bill passed. This recapture tax was greeted by howls of protest from the corporate sector, and few took it seriously. This left a $56 billion revenue hole in Treasury II over its first five years. Nor, despite Treasury's claims, was it strictly a short-term revenue hole; private economists and the Congressional Budget Office agreed that the new, more generous depreciation system would lose revenue in the long run as well.

The positive side of Treasury II, however, was that the President was firmly on board with tax reform. The obstacles to legislation of this sort are well known: a minority of taxpayers, with a lot to lose, lobbies vigorously, while the majority, each with much less to gain, is silent. In this instance, the odds were even worse. As some indication, while 75 percent of the taxpayers will receive a tax cut under the final bill, a poll found that only 25 percent thought they would. Half of the taxpaying population will get a tax cut but does not believe it. And this majority was not just silent over the course of the congressional deliberations; members reported receiving angry calls from constituents who, after rudimentary examination, were found to benefit from the bill. So without a presidential mandate, the chance that tax reform would pass the Congress were exceedingly slim. With that mandate, there was at least a shot.

The first hurdle was having a Democratic chairman of the House Ways and Means committee introduce a bill at the behest of a Republican president. Rep. Dan Rostenkowski (D-IL) chose to proceed. He saw tax reform as a long-time Democratic principle, and felt that he could not refuse even a Republican president's initiative in such a traditional Democratic direction. Further, he had some personal scores to settle, having been widely thought the loser in his 1981 and 1982 tax bill joustings with Finance Committee Chairman Robert Dole (R-KN). And finally, Rostenkowski had his own ambition. He wanted to be Speaker of the House in the next Congress, after the announced retirement of Tip O'Neill (D-MA). Tax reform, with its expected swipes at the tax preferences of the oil and gas industry, would give Rostenkowski a good chance to separate the front runner for the speakership, Rep. Jim Wright (D-TX), from those traditional Democratic principles of tax reform.

Ways and Means began its deliberations with much fanfare but little success. Though it was firmly under Democratic numerical control, there were some serious problems. First of all, many Democrats saw Treasury II as basically unfair, with its top-heavy tax cuts; their expressed goal was to pass a bill that Ronald Reagan would want to veto. To do so, they wanted the highest possible top individual rate; they felt that they, as Democrats, had more to lose than gain from passing a bill for which Ronald Reagan could take credit. For them, the cause of tax reform was secondary to politics. It took much cajoling from Rostenkowski and much persuasion from Bradley (playing an unusually active role for a Senator in House deliberations) to even get the process to begin. Rostenkowski and Bradley managed to convince many of the members that a better tax reform bill, rather than a sham, would be the best political weapon against the President.

Still, Ways and Means had to go through a collective metamorphosis before it could really get down to work. There was enough influence by affected interests that the chairman lost several votes. The last painful defeat came on a bank provision, where the committee chose to liberalize current law and actually lose rather than gain revenue. Anecdotal accounts have it that an indiscreet industry lobbyist cried, "We won! We won!" outside the committee room after the vote, so humiliating and angering the members (in company with some pointed accounts of the vote in the press) that they returned a few days later to reverse the vote and proceed with new resolve. An important procedural assist came when Chairman Rostenkowski enforced a revenue neutrality requirement on all amendments—if a member wanted to restore a tax preference, he had to propose a base broadener or a rate increase to make up the revenue.

On one front, an unusual alliance was formed. Members from high-tax northeastern and midwestern states pledged to vote in favor of the oil industry, in return for votes against state and local tax deduction repeal from members from oil states. When the dust had settled, Ways and Means had left the state and local tax deductions completely untouched, and had worked out some compromises that were acceptable (barely) to key oil state members.

In general, Ways and Means was tougher on business tax provisions, and easier on individual provisions, than the Treasury. Its individual tax base was sufficiently narrower that it required a fourth, 38 percent bracket to raise less revenue than Treasury II. With a 36 percent corporate rate, the Ways and Means bill raised more from the corporate sector—as was necessary to offset the effects of the state and local tax deduction-oil preference coalition.

The bill passed committee with some unexpected vulnerabilities. In the final deliberations, with the last few billion dollars to raise to achieve revenue neutrality, the chairman found it easier to work in caucus with his own party members; and so the Republicans on the committee felt slighted. That problem, coupled with the natural Republican discomfort with the substance of the bill, added up to big trouble. The spark that ignited the ensuing rebellion was unhappiness among selected members on both sides of the aisle with a last-minute provision that removed a tax advantage for retired government employees. Opponents saw an opportunity in a necessary procedural vote (to adopt a rule governing subsequent consideration), which could kill the bill without any overt statement on the merits of tax reform; the defeat of the rule dealt the bill a stunning defeat before it was ever actually considered. Republicans voted overwhelmingly to kill the bill.

The bill was dead without the President's intervention. He chose to go to work to salvage his major domestic initiative, and lobbied many Republican members to change their votes. The device that apparently made the difference was an ironic letter, saying (in appropriately vague language) that the President disliked the bill and would veto it if it reached his desk in its current form, but urging the members to pass it on to the Senate where the Republican majority would surely improve it. The House Republicans were convinced in sufficient numbers, and the bill passed in an improbable reincarnation on the House floor.

This moved tax reform along to the Senate, where some felt it had even bleaker prospects than it had in the House, despite the Republican majority (or perhaps because of it). In fact, it was an open secret that many House members had considered tax reform to be a free vote, believing that there was no realistic chance that the Senate would ever pass a bill. Finance committee Chairman Robert Packwood (R-OR) had proposed many of the employee benefit tax preferences in the law, and was known to be lukewarm at best on tax reform. He set the tone with a frank statement to a journalist that "I kind of like the tax code the way it is." Nonetheless, Packwood had to respond to the call of his party's leader, so he conferred one-on-one with his members and then holed up with staff to write a bill.

When the chairman emerged, the bill was quite a surprise. It did far less base broadening than the House, and plugged the huge resulting revenue hole by denying businesses the deduction for their excise tax liabilities. The chairman said that he and staff had determined that this deduction was a "loophole." The rest of the committee and the economics profession disagreed, and the committee proceeded with that enormous revenue hole implicitly empty.

The Finance Committee proceedings began much as had those of Ways and Means. The early votes went against the chairman, and his bill fell more and more behind on revenue—with the excise tax revenues still to be made up. As the series of defeats grew longer, Chairman Packwood pulled his own bill out of the committee, realizing that any more losses would destroy its credibility.

There followed a surprising transformation of Robert Packwood. The press has reported it as being instantaneous, in a despairing conversation over a couple of beers with his chief of staff, Bill Diefenderfer. From the events at the time, however, it likely took several days. Packwood and Diefenderfer decided to present the committee with a learning device: a "pure" tax reform bill with no deductions, credits, or exclusions. The members would then suggest which tax preferences they would wish to restore to the law; the staff would report back on the spot the effect that restoring those preferences would have on the attainable tax rates, given the constraint of revenue neutrality. The idea was to teach the members through trial and error the nature of the tradeoff between preferences and low rates.

The staff, in anticipation of this exercise, worked out possible end points of the process. They settled on two versions of such an "almost pure" tax reform bill, each having two tax brackets with the first at 15 percent; one had a top rate of 26 percent, and the other 27 percent. Each used highly unorthodox devices to attain these low rates, including the complete phasing out of the personal exemptions, and of the tax savings from having paid tax at the lower bottom rate, once income exceeded certain levels. Chairman Packwood became intrigued with these packages, and cautiously floated the 27 percent version as a "staff option."

(In a most unusual press conference, Packwood introduced the staff director of the hitherto ultra-anonymous Joint Committee on Taxation, David Brockway, as the author of the plan.)

Before too long, the "Brockway plan" had won Packwood over. He told the press that "I came to believe that Bradley was right," that the best approach to tax policy was to clear the decks of preferences and reduce rates to their lowest possible level. There was a sense in the chairman's arguments of lobbying overload, of hearing too many times that one particular tax preference or another is the key to our prosperity. Packwood now responded to questions from the press and from other members by wondering aloud: if tax incentives were so important, how did the nation's economy perform so well before the income tax even existed?

Packwood solidified his plan with a "core group" consisting of Bradley, George Mitchell (D-ME), Daniel Patrick Moynihan (D-NY), John Chafee (R-RI), and John Danforth (R-MO). A key element of the final package, suggested by Moynihan, was an extreme anti-tax shelter provision which came to be known as the "passive loss limitation." It provided that losses from passive investments (those in which the investor played no managerial role, as is the case in most tax shelters) could not be deducted from other income for tax purposes. In an ideal world, where all investments were made to earn a pretax profit, such a provision would be highly undesirable. Its only merit came from choking off intentional tax sheltering activity, and in the process it threatened to harm many economically motivated passive investments. Nonetheless, the revenue gain from the provision was found to be so enormous ($50 billion over 5 years, a measure of the prevalence of tax shelters) that the committee could not resist it. The provision was even more controversial in that it would apply even to investments made before its enactment, though the limitation would be phased in over 5 years. Other important provisions were the elimination of the preference for long-term capital gains and the significant tightening of the universal Individual Retirement Accounts (IRAs) established just five years before.

On the corporate side, the package had an equally bold provision. The widely anticipated effect of ACRS, in combination with other corporate tax preferences, had been to make a large number of profitable corporations nontaxable. Robert McIntyre, from a largely labor-funded organization called Citizens for Tax Justice, had begun to issue periodic press releases that listed prominent profitable corporations that paid no·tax, and those releases had received tremendous publicity. Now, the members were being hammered in their every public appearance about large profitable corporations paying no taxes. Even the most pro-business members had decided that whatever else happened, this pounding had to stop. (Thus, reports of nontaxable corporations became to tax reform in 1986 what reports of nontaxable high-income individuals were to tax reform in 1969.)

If the cause of the problem was firms with book income but paying no taxes, the staff reasoned, why not tax book income? And so they added to an already aggressive minimum tax a provision that would tax half of any excess of book income over income as otherwise measured for minimum tax purposes. Tax specialists and accountants protested that book income was not defined or intended for tax purposes, that many smaller businesses had no formal books, and that numerous anomalies were sure to result. But again, the appeal (and the revenue pickup) of the provision was too strong, and it passed into the bill.

Still, Packwood's proposal enjoyed considerable corporate support. The reason was the unbalanced nature of the 1981 law. While the business community had marched in lockstep behind the first Reagan tax initiative, it quickly became apparent that some firms did not benefit from it; the most intensive users of the big subsidies for physical investment took all the booty. So in 1986, even though the corporate sector faced a net tax increase of over $25 billion per year, many corporations—those that used few tax preferences—could look forward to tax cuts because of the big proposed reduction in the corporate rate. Other corporations that would pay higher taxes still wanted the more straightforward business environment under a neutral tax law. Some corporate executives had gotten on board the House bill, but with the Packwood initiative, the involvement mushroomed. The CEO Tax Group provided vocal support, and the broader Tax Reform Action Coalition (TRAC) provided lobbying and other support for tax reform. Given the obvious business influence in the legislative process in 1981, both the splitting of the business community and the active support of the pro-tax reform business interests was crucial in 1986.

The extremely low maximum rate in the Chairman's proposal won several conservative members over almost immediately, and the bill had a strange coalition consisting of the ideological extremes of the committee. In time, the relative center joined in. Several threatening amendments were defeated through adherence to a revenue neutrality rule identical to that used in Ways and Means. A final, bitter compromise was the exemption of working interests in oil and gas limited partnerships from the passive loss limitation. That provision, though fought vigorously by many of the more reform-oriented members, was supported by others with a sense that the bill stood a much better chance with the support of those from oil and gas states (including the legendary former chairman, Russell Long [D-LA]). The bill then cleared committee with a unanimous vote.

Unlike on the House floor, where a rule restricted the time for debate and limited amendments to one, the Senate's procedures were totally unrestrained. Supporters of the bill determined to protect it by voting "no" on all amendments, and though only one senator (Danforth) fully adhered, the coalition remained tight enough that no amendment of substance passed. Several came painfully close, however, including one to restore deductibility of IRA contributions, and another to restore the special charitable contributions deduction for nonitemizers. In the end, the bill passed by 97-3, with the dissenters, all Democrats, complaining of regional impacts or insufficient progressivity in the distribution of the burden.

Throughout the darkest days in the House and the Senate, some members of the press stated that the bill "had a life of its own," and that somehow the problems would be worked out and the bill would pass. The developments in the Senate most clearly gave meaning to this interpretation. There was a public reservoir of disapproval of the current law, and that was the raw material with which the two committee chairmen could work; but they did their jobs in quite different ways. The House bill was an enormously skillfully crafted product; the chairman worked closely with his members, discovered which particular preferences each member had to have to satisfy his most important constituent interests, and worked out a compromise that saved all of those preferences and used the repeal of the others to finance the bill. The problem with this approach was that the public, far from expert on tax policy, saw this as a brokered bill; they were told that loopholes dear to important members were retained, sensed this as one more special interest tax bill, and remained lukewarm—even though the bill was a significant improvement over the current law.

The Senate bill operated in an entirely different dimension. Though far from perfect, it came close enough to the ideal of tax reform, with rates much lower than senators had anticipated, that it captured the support of even the most reluctant. It repealed some preferences that were "essential" when measured by the scale of the Ways and Means proceedings, but compensated the offended senators with the extremely low rates. Tax reform became a motherhood and apple pie issue. Almost every senator had said at some point, "I'm for tax reform, but . . . " The Senate bill came close enough to the ideal that the response could be, "Well, this is *real* tax reform—are you for it?"

Senate passage sent the bill to conference. Early commentary suggested an easy melding of two good tax reform bills. In fact, the process was extremely painful, for two reasons. The first was the expected Republican reluctance to raise taxes on corporations, even with the President's support. While the House bill had been tough on corporations, the Senate bill was much gentler, and the Republican majority held to that position most vigorously. They saw their role as improving on the House bill as the President had mandated, and they would support a tax increase for business as large as the President had proposed but no larger.

Secondly, changes in the economic forecast subsequent to the passage of both bills (including lower inflation) plus timing differences (the House bill was written to take effect on January 1, 1986, though that was obviously not feasible for a conference meeting in August) meant that the Senate bill was now seen as revenue short, and that the House bill would increase corporate taxes far above what was originally estimated. The debate in conference became so painful—with the House insisting on heavier corporate taxes and bigger tax cuts for the middle class, and the Senate just as vigorously defending the corporate sector—that Russell Long suggested that Rostenkowski and Packwood attempt to settle the differences in private. The two chairmen could make the painful decisions to which their members could not publicly acquiesce, ultimately delivering a package that could spread such sacrifices evenly.

As this process neared a conclusion, the chairmen were dealt another revenue estimating blow, as the Joint Committee staff fine-tuned its methodologies and reported lower-than-expected revenue totals. The time for the Labor Day recess had come, and the chairmen responded to the new revenue totals with a set of painful final deals. They then called the full conference into session in private. Both sides balked, some heretofore supportive members (including notably Danforth) expressed their vocal opposition, and there was a serious risk that the process would break down. Some members had already left town, and others were sure to follow soon; both chairmen threatened to adjourn the conference for the holiday, amidst a general fear that the inevitable intense lobbying pressure would make a subsequent agreement impossible. In this dramatic atmosphere, Bradley presented to the chairmen, Treasury Secretary Baker, and his Deputy, Richard Darman, a formulation that provided the House with the middle-class relief it demanded without offending the majority of the Senate. The conference met in public session and signed a report late on Saturday, August 16.

Against the backdrop of these events, final passage of the conference report was relatively calm. There was initial suspense when the enormously complex legal drafting ran overtime, and there were rumors of growing unrest in the House. With the President's intervention, however, the Republican minority chose to make its one permitted motion to recommit the bill a straightforward one, rather than adding on politically attractive (but budgetarily infeasible) instructions (such as restoring deductibility for all IRAs and for sales taxes). The House soundly defeated the recommittal motion, and the bill passed comfortably. On the Senate side, there was lengthy debate over the politically sensitive transition rules, but ultimate passage was inevitable.

VI. Conclusion and Prospects

The passage of tax reform required the most incredible confluence of circumstances—almost like an alignment of the planets. The Democrats failed to seize the issue in 1984, and so may have missed a major opportunity; still, the bill likely would not have passed without the initiative and influence of Ronald Reagan. Yet in the final analysis, Ronald Reagan almost certainly would not have taken that initiative without a firm shove from Bill Bradley. Chairman Rostenkowski broke new ground when, despite enormous political obstacles, he dragged a bill through the Committee on Ways and Means. Chairman Packwood, after his own conversion, elevated the issue to a plane where many narrow interests could be safely put aside. And the entire membership of the Congress persisted when the voters' fear of the unknown suggested turning back.

The uniquely broad reach of the new law was both a hindrance and a help to its prospects. The long list of tax preferences repealed and curtailed at some stage in the process made tax reform many powerful enemies. Yet the $25 billion transfer from corporations to individuals, approved almost by chance by a pro-business Republican administration, held out the prospect of tax cuts to more than just the most obvious "losers" from the old law—it served the function of the "sweetener" revenue cut in past reform efforts, and in the textbook model. Further, the cleansing of the corporate tax base permitted a big reduction in the corporate tax rate, even with the $25 billion annual revenue increase. This sizeable rate cut gave enough heavily taxed corporations enough relief that they broke ranks from the united business lobbying front, which had played so large a role in the passage of the 1981 law.

Earlier tax reform efforts could offer tax cuts to both corporations *and* individuals, however, and none approached the 1986 law in scale and success. What was different this time, and what does that portend for the future? One factor was certainly the excesses of the 1981 law, especially safe harbor leasing and the other corporate provisions; they pushed the pendulum so far in one direction that it had to return. The non-tax-paying corporations of 1986 did play the role of the non-tax-paying individuals of 1969. But another factor was the apparently long-lived triumph, in the 1981 law, of the ideology of low marginal tax rates. Important also were Ronald Reagan as its most prominent and effective spokesman, and Bill Bradley as the prime mover with an attractive and viable plan.

Also contributing were the successes of the 1982 and 1984 deficit reduction laws, which smoked out the defenders of existing prefer-ences, and demonstrated that tax base broadening does not ipso facto end economic life on this planet. These models are especially important now, because future reform legislation cannot offer nearly the amount of base broadening—and the corresponding rate reduction—that the 1986 law did; there just isn't as much potential base broadening left. In fact, the days of even revenue-neutral tax reform seem over; any tax reform in the foreseeable future will have to raise revenue, by broaden-ing the tax base without corresponding rate cuts. We know that the 1982–1984 model works; but we know that it is painful and divisive, as each interest brought to the chopping blocks points to the others cower-ing in the background and asks, "Why me?" There were tax prefer-ences spared by the 1986 law, but they were those with the best de-fenses, and only intensified budgetary pressures can reopen those debates.

There is a chance of anti-reform legislation as well. Many offended interests will be back in Washington in 1987 to plead their cases all over again. All of those interests will assign every upcoming economic misfortune to the tax reform bill. And to be sure, some groups were hit hard; real estate is a prime example. But the real estate investments (and many others) that lost from the bill would never have been undertaken without the extreme subsidies in the tax law. Those investments represent the height of economic waste, and a diversion from our long-run national interest. The question was not whether those tax subsidies would be repealed, but when.

Most prominent among the interests asking for a retrial are the recipients of capital gains. For the same reason that capital gains was the keystone of the initial plan for comprehensive reform, so it is the first target of those who would revert to the old regime. A capital gains preference would concentrate an enormous amount of tax relief on the wealthiest individuals in the nation, and so it is their highest priority. (Capital gains has a more tenuous linkage to ultimate capital formation than some other preferences, but that does not seem to have influenced the thinking of the lobbyists.) That relief, if granted, would cause a reaction among liberals to raise statutory tax rates, which would draw more lobbyists from the woodwork; the unravelling process would proceed, perhaps quickly, perhaps not. Already economists-for-lease are arguing that capital gains tax rate cuts would raise revenue, tempting policymakers to befriend their best endowed constituents while narrowing the measured deficit (and expanding the real one—but that would be known only later). It remains to be seen whether the Congress will resist this temptation.

And there are questionable provisions in the new law; the passive loss limitation and the minimum tax on corporate book income are two. Only time will tell whether those provisions can be maintained.

But the new law has an internal consistency that may be its greatest defense. Because of its very low rates, it spreads the burden of government thinly, so that no taxpayer's share is excessive. Thus, any taxpayer who wants his tax preference restored must justify special treatment under a system whose burden is already low, and from a people whose instincts are fair; and the burden avoided through such special treatment must be shifted explicitly to someone else. This strength—and potential resistance to change—is what Bill Bradley called "the power of the idea."

It may take a confluence of circumstances as remarkable as those we have just seen to change, fundamentally, this new tax law.

10 • Tax Policy Issues
Raised by Tax Reform

Just about everyone knows the story of the good Samaritan. To refresh your memories, a traveler outside of his own region came upon the victim of a mugging by the side of the road. The victim had been ignored by his neighbors, but the stranger took pity. He treated the victim's wounds, carried him to a nearby inn, and paid for lodgings until the victim could recover.

We might never have learned of these admirable acts. Fortunately, however, the Samaritan paid the innkeeper with his American Express card, and the carbons were found in the inn's trash dumpster by an enterprising reporter. Thereafter, of course, the modest Samaritan received the recognition that he deserved, including most notably the mention in the president's State of the Union address, and the guest spot on "Miami Vice."

My assignment today is to assess the post-tax-reform world, with a particular focus on key individual income tax issues. To some, the analysis might seem to descend from an excessively high level—perhaps the top of a District of Columbia-sized ivory tower—from which detail is hard to distinguish. I confess that from the think tank where I spend my time, the most pressing issue seems to be the very broad topic of the viability of the Tax Reform Act of 1986 (TRA for short). And to

Opinions expressed herein are the author's alone and should not be attributed to The Urban Institute, its officers, trustees, or funders. Gina Despres, Rob Leonard, and several members of the Committee on Ways and Means, U.S. House of Representatives, provided helpful discussions, but should not be implicated in any errors. Ron Sebastian of the Internal Revenue Service kindly provided useful data and discussion. Susan Wiener provided diligent research assistance.

Reprinted with permission from *National Tax Journal*, September 1988, 291–301.

betray my conclusions, it seems to me that, despite its notoriety, tax reform is much the same kind of stealthy public policy as the actions of the Good Samaritan—its benefits for distinct blocks of voters go unnoticed or even misinterpreted because of a lack of information, bad information, or unshakable preconceptions. Yet I see very little chance that tax reform will be reversed in the foreseeable future. My own preferred course, and the one that I consider most likely, would be for the populace to live with tax reform for awhile, and come to understand and appreciate it.

I try to analyze this question from all sides, including the popular reaction to tax reform, the Congressional experience of 1981–86 and the resulting leanings of the Congress today; the internal pressures of the new law; the external pressure from the ongoing budget deficit; and the further pressure of the next recession. (The remainder of this paper will be subdivided according to those headings.) In general, while some of these forces are hostile to tax reform, none of them seems sufficient to topple it; and so, until (and unless) future contingencies are dealt with, I see an uneasy (but decreasingly so) equilibrium at the basic tax policy position where we find ourselves today.

The Reaction to Tax Reform

While every tax filing season breeds popular dismay, this season [for the 1987 tax year] was probably worse than the usual. Some problems certainly arose from the passage of TRA. But the crucial questions now really are: Was the public reaction worse than what was (or could have been) expected, from this particular change or any other conceivable major change in the tax law? And how serious really was the reaction, on a scale from zero up to safe harbor leasing or withholding on interest and dividends? Is the apparent hostility to the law life-threatening, or is it less serious or likely short-lived? Is the hostility well founded, or is it based on misperceptions? And how is the public reaction viewed by the Congress?

The Nature of Tax Reform

Before considering what the public thinks tax reform is, it is worth thinking about what tax reform really is. The distinction could be crucial.

Tax reform as in TRA necessarily involves a redistribution among taxpayers. That redistribution follows the same pattern as would any shift from policies that benefit narrow groups to others that benefit the population at large. In the first instance, before any improvement of aggregate economic performance expands the amount of income to go around, the beneficiaries of repealed narrow interest provisions lose, and the population at large gains an equivalent amount. However, because the beneficiary groups are small, their loss per person is far larger than society's per person gain. This description is borne out by the estimates of the Joint Committee on Taxation (JCT) that in 1988 TRA's winners will outnumber its losers by almost four to one, but will gain less than half as much per tax return.[1] There naturally follows an application of the classic political science theory of the interested minority and the disinterested majority, from which it has been reasoned that special interest programs will expand with little resistance from the general public. Therefore, tax reform could never happen—a logically sound proposition whose falsehood must be explained elsewhere.[2]

But tax reform having happened, it should be no surprise that, even after the fact, the losers squawk and the winners are silent. For many of the winners, the spoils are barely noticeable; for the losers, the pain is intense. And by the nature of the system, the losers are the most sophisticated and the best organized, with ample means of communicating with both the Congress and the public. We should expect to see them express themselves to both groups if they see any chance of regaining their turf.

Perceptions of Tax Reform

Opportunities for tax reform's losers to recover lost ground may well arise from the misperceptions of tax reform's winners. Just as the public's knowledge of the old tax system was notoriously weak, so its understanding of the new tax law is limited. And we should not be surprised to find knowledgeable and interested parties capitalizing on that fact.

There is built-in hostility for the income tax, for the simple reason that it takes people's money with no specific reward in return. Polls taken since the early 1970s document a sharp decline in the percentage of the population considering the income tax as the most fair tax among the taxes levied by all levels of government.[3]

Yet, strong opinions regarding the income tax are often based upon a weak understanding. Taxpayers have increasingly thrown up their hands and consigned their returns to paid preparers, frequently to claim the standard deduction.[4] And when polled on how the income tax affects the very well off, respondents have wildly overestimated the number who pay no tax at all.[5]

Thus, TRA faced entrenched opposition in the forms of popular hostility, limited mechanical understanding, and misperceptions of the overall impact of the income tax. Under the circumstances, one might easily assume that the reception of tax reform would be unfavorable, regardless of the reception that it might deserve on the merits. In fact, this scenario appears to have materialized.

Was It Fair? For an initiative whose hallmark was fairness, TRA has taken a great deal of criticism on the ground that it is unfair. Much of that criticism appears to be based on a departure of perception from reality.

For many taxpayers, the "fairness" of a change in the law is determined by the answer to the question, "Do my taxes go down?" On this ground and with reference to the JCT estimates, TRA would seem to be a clear political winner. The problem is that people's misunderstandings of the tax law, plus the aforementioned tendency of the winners to be silent while the losers object, has likely distorted the reaction.

The current misperceptions are not unlike those during the Congressional debate on TRA, when one senator argued against the bill on the ground that 75 percent of the respondents to a poll said that they expected their taxes to be higher—while JCT, as noted earlier, estimated that 79 percent of those whose taxes would change would receive a tax cut once the law was fully phased in. Presumably, at that time, at least 54 percent of the population would receive a tax cut, but did not believe it. Even now [1988] public understanding is apparently little improved. A poll by the *Washington Post* found that 58 percent of respondents believed that they were paying more in 1987, even though by JCT estimates 81.5 percent should be paying less this year.[6] Thus, after two years of reflection and computation, the stressful ignorance quotient has fallen only to 39.5 percent (unless the taxpayers, rather than the Joint Committee, are right—in which case Uncle Sam is in for a bonanza).

There are two interrelated reasons why so many taxpayers mistakenly expect the worst from TRA. First, and for whatever reason, taxpayers seem to perceive the elimination of deductions, exclusions or credits far more intensely than they perceive reductions in tax rates. When individual taxpayers were confronted with a proposal for fundamental tax reform, they would often react to the prospect of the loss of a deduction or exclusion by insisting that they would be worse off, regardless of the more than offsetting rate cuts and increases in the personal exemption and standard deduction. Perhaps because taxpayers must compute their own deductions, while the tax rates are hidden in the lookup tables, taxpayers seem to notice the former and not the latter. This phenomenon came to be called "loophole illusion."

Loophole illusion was evident in a 1982 Harris poll, in which respondents overwhelmingly approved of a 14 percent "flat tax" with virtually no exclusions or deductions, and then equally overwhelmingly rejected the repeal of the exclusions and deductions necessary to justify the low rate. It surfaced again in the debate over TRA. An incensed constituent called a senator to protest his support of TRA, which the constituent had calculated would increase his tax enormously. The senator's staff recalculated the taxpayer's liability and discovered that he would in fact receive a handsome tax cut; the constituent had apparently considered the loophole closing, but not the lower rates and the higher personal exemption. (The constituent became a supporter of the bill.)

I find it hard to believe that the majority of taxpayers who insist in opinion polls that their taxes have increased have actually checked their liabilities under the old law. More likely, they have merely assumed from the loss of sales tax and consumer interest deductions that their taxes must be higher, more often than not contrary to fact.

A second reason for taxpayer misperceptions seems to be a mistaken identification of the amount of the tax refund as a measure of tax liability; this phenomenon might well be dubbed "refund illusion." Evidence of refund illusion can be seen in any number of press accounts. Thus, particular taxpayers are characterized as losers under the new law if they owe substantial balances, regardless of how much their withholding and their total liability might have decreased.[7]

Ironically, with the simplified rate structure allowing more accurate withholding for taxpayers with one earner on the return and most income from wages, there has been a clash between the "enlightened" desire for precision, on the one hand, and many taxpayers' preference for a large refund, on the other. And while many of these taxpayers are classic winners from tax reform, they show little gratitude. For some, one can only suppose, the reduction in withholding effective January 1, 1987, coincided with the receipt of regular annual pay increases; the increase in take-home pay may have been ascribed to the pay raise, and the decrease in the tax refund at the end of the year to tax reform. Under those circumstances, tax reform would receive blame instead of credit. Such taxpayers could certainly increase their withholding in future years if they prefer forced saving at a zero interest rate, but many are probably sufficiently confused and intimidated by the entire system that they hesitate to take discretionary action.

Dissatisfaction with end-of-year settlements was probably more widespread than that, however. Any taxpayer who did not look after his withholding over the course of the year, and who lost a few significant deductions or exclusions (such as two-earner professional couples who lost the "marriage penalty deduction," two IRA exclusions, and part of their deduction for consumer interest) could easily have been caught with a balance due instead of a refund. Such taxpayers could well have come out ahead on their final liabilities because of the rate reductions, and could have had big reductions in withholding over the course of the year. Their balances due might have been trivial burdens if spread over one year's worth of paychecks through correct withholding. But these taxpayers, and others with complaints about the new law, were the ones who wrote to their representatives and told their stories to the press, in keeping with the classic model of the unhappy minority speaking up.

Internal Revenue Service (IRS) statistics indicate that changes in refund patterns may well have contributed to the public mood on the new law. Returns filed through May 6 were up 3.5 percent over the year before; but the number of returns with refunds was down very slightly, and the average refund was down by 0.2 percent. These declines broke upward trends from previous years. And interestingly enough, up through the last week of the filing season, average refunds were up; returns filed in the last week had sharply lower refunds than those filed in the last week of last year.[8] Thus, there was apparently a distinct group of aggrieved taxpayers filing their returns late in the season.

All of these influences together probably fed the reservoir of public hostility and cynicism. Just as there has long been a presumption that the tax law is unfair and favors special interests and the well-to-do,[9] so polls now indicate that the new law has the same image.[10] How such perceptions could square with the gestation of the law and the opposition that it faced from innumerable forces is hard to see. But shreds of evidence that might have fed these impressions could have been the transition rules,[11] and the deductibility of loans secured by boats construed as second homes. The taxpayers may have been convinced for so long that the system is tilted against them that they will tend to hold to that conviction, regardless of the preponderance of the evidence.

A related important public relations problem of TRA is its outcomes for upper-income taxpayers. The liabilities of the well-to-do were extremely disperse under the pre–1986 law, and so the elimination of the horizontal inequities required disperse changes to the existing liabilities. Some critics of TRA emphasized the large tax cuts for the highly taxed upper-income persons, and argued that those tax cuts were unjustified. But the maximum tax rate chosen in TRA was that required to give the upper-income group as a whole the smallest possible tax cut; one more percentage point and that group would have had a tax increase, rather than a tax cut. There simply was no political consensus for a tax bill that would have increased taxes on any income group. The failure to understand this, and the vain wish for a blanket tax increase for upper-income taxpayers—in the extreme, a surrendering of tax preferences for no decrease in rates—leaves some observers unhappy about the new law.

Is It Too Complex? The second complaint against TRA is that it is more complicated than the old law, and indeed excessively complicated. Here, tax reform certainly fell short of the ideal, particularly in the restriction of tax preferences instead of their outright repeal, and in the resort to individual and corporate minimum taxes instead of airtight ordinary taxes. Still, it is important to put the complexity issue into context.

Tax reform, even as practiced by TRA, simplifies tax filing for those in typical circumstances. The expanded standard deduction minimizes record keeping and computation; the elimination of specific itemized deductions, the two-earner deduction, income averaging, and other features push in the same direction. For some taxpayers, the higher personal exemption and standard deduction eliminate altogether the need to file. (Admittedly, though, the expansion of the rather complex earned income credit does complicate life for many low-income families, who nonetheless receive substantial tax relief.) And while some might downplay its significance, the revised rate schedule does give the typical taxpayer a clearer intuitive sense of his tax liability as 15 percent of his taxable income; a surprising share of the population simply does not understand the operation of graduated tax rates. Indeed, as practiced by TRA, the shift in complexity mirrors the shift in tax liability—relief for the bulk of the population, and additional complexity for the few (such as those with passive losses).

Given that reality, it is again hard to square the apparent public reaction with the actual changes in the law. Most tax returns claim the standard deduction, and even in the 1987 transition year the number of returns claiming the standard deduction should have increased because of the cutback of the itemized deductions. (The number of nonitemizers will increase still further in 1988, when the standard deduction itself will be increased.) In addition, more than 20 million taxpayers were saved computation of the two-earner deduction, and perhaps 5 million were spared the income averaging computation. And yet, in response to polls, 55 percent said the new law has made the system worse rather than better.[12] Perhaps taxpayers fail to appreciate the simplification resulting from the elimination of preferences that would reduce their taxes, even when accompanied by rate cuts.

Few provisions of the new law would increase complexity to any marked degree for typical taxpayers. Upper-income potential IRA investors need to determine their eligibility for the exclusion, but the number so affected was probably only about 15 million. Recent second mortgage borrowers would certainly be subject to some complexity, but their number is surely relatively small. For those taxpayers, however, allocating interest expense among mortgage, personal, medical, educational, and investment categories would be daunting; and all taxpayers with personal interest do have to calculate the percentage allowed until the phase-in period is complete in 1991. Further concerns would be raised by the "kiddie tax," under which the portfolio income of children would be taxed at their parents' highest marginal tax rate; but again, the number of taxpayers involved is probably small. Despite the relatively low numbers of taxpayers whose returns would be complicated in this way, it is certainly true that those affected would likely be the most sophisticated and articulate taxpayers, who would make their voices heard most effectively.

The IRS data again suggest only a modest impact on complexity for the bulk of the population. Of the ten most frequent causes of tax filing errors on this year's returns, only the third (failing to indicate dependent status on Form 1040EZ) and the seventh (incorrectly calculating the standard deduction on Form 1040A) relate at all to the new law.[13] The overall error rate increased only slightly, by less than one and one-half percent, and the frequency of paid preparers increased only from 40 percent last year to 42 percent this year, on returns filed by April 1.[14] While total returns and Form 1040 returns filed by May 6 increased by 3.5 percent, Form 1040EZ returns increased by 8.7 percent, indicating greater potential simplicity for some taxpayers; filings of Form 1040A fell by 1.6 percent from last year, though, suggesting greater complexity for others. And in one ominous sign, extensions of time to file were requested by 5.5 million taxpayers, up 23.4 percent.[15]

Taken all together, though, complexity does seem to be increased for only a minority of taxpayers. The perception of greater complication probably rests on the long-term level of complexity, more than the current change; on the occurrence of any change at all, which always causes some confusion; and on the "herd effect" of opinion cited with such frequency in the press.

What Might Have Succeeded? While we might lament the public reaction to TRA, it could be instructive to undertake a thought exercise: Most tax experts and political scientists would probably agree that the pre–1986 law was indefensible over the long term, on the grounds of public acceptance, fairness, efficiency, simplicity, and revenue sufficiency. Therefore, it is fair to presume that some alternative would have been required; if not in 1986, then shortly thereafter. So it is fair to ask: What alternative to TRA could have evoked an immediate, widespread, positive response from the taxpaying public? Given the long established preferences of the taxpayers, plus what has been revealed by the new law, it seems most likely that no feasible change would fill that bill.

One thing that has been obvious this year is that taxpayers like to get refunds. Should the IRS swallow its principles to build unnecessary excess withholding into the tables to oblige them?

Another apparent preference of the taxpayers this year is that they do not like to yield tax preferences, even if they receive tax rate cuts in compensation. Should some of the sure efficiency and fairness gainers in the new law, such as the elimination of the double exemption for middle- and upper-income students and elderly, be sacrificed on this ground?

If the taxpayers object to the loss of preferences, some might argue that a simple tax cut, without repeal of preferences, is the only way to popular approval. And yet the record of the virtually unvarnished 1981 tax cuts shows that they did not improve the public opinion of the income tax.[16]

Another line of argument is that the nation would prefer a sales tax if a tax increase were necessary to augment federal revenue, as was indicated by a recent poll.[17] Some might extend that argument to contend that a sales tax would be well received as a replacement for the income tax. Begging the question of whether that extension would be valid, the very same poll showed that the population's greatest objection to the current tax law is that the well-to-do pay too little. How would the taxpayers react once they understood that the sales tax aggravated the point of their concern?

Yet another contender for the role of replacement of the income tax is the personal exemption VAT or "X Tax," a modification of the Hall-Rabushka flat tax.[18] The hallmark of this approach is a neutral treatment of business income, attained by taxing it only at the business level and with expensing of all new investment. The individual income tax therefore becomes a tax on wage and salary income only. It was this latter attribute that made the original Hall-Rabushka proposal unpalatable in the legislative and political processes, and it seems unlikely that that will have changed at this time.

My conclusion from this thought exercise is that no available alternative to TRA could have passed muster with the public. Further, we should not be surprised that this is true. The public dislikes taxation as a first principle, for obvious reasons. The public's first wish for the tax system is "reduce my taxes and raise my neighbor's," which obviously could not be made to come true on a national scale. The public wants simplicity, but at the same time it asks for a myriad of tax preferences focused at a large number of individual circumstances, the complexity of which is conveniently ignored. The public wants low withholding and big refunds. The public wants high taxes on today's rich and low taxes on the future rich, which they all plan to be. Reconciling these conflicting wishes is obviously impossible, and the public's apparent misunderstanding of so many basic tax issues makes even trying extremely dangerous—rather like treating a wounded animal.

Therefore, the task of tax policy must be a gentle balancing act among conflicting public demands. Even further, it must involve, at least to some degree, the ignoring of public demands that are inconsistent with sound policy. This is not unique to tax policy. There are surely advocates of zero foreign aid; zero defense spending; double defense spending; internment of all AIDS victims; and any number of other extreme policy positions, who must be finessed in the political process. The problem with taxes in this respect is that it is the only policy area that sends weekly, biweekly, or monthly reminder notices to virtually the entire population, and whose operation affects the entire population so intimately.

Thus, when members of Congress swallow hard and do the right thing, as they arguably did in TRA, they must be prepared for an adverse reaction. Their best hope is for an eventual public understanding of the soundness of their actions—ideally, with the half-life of the public's misunderstanding being less than two years. Because the response of the Congress will largely determine the future of TRA, it is worth considering the potential outcomes.

How Will the Congress Respond? At this early juncture, and from a very limited viewpoint, it appears as though the Congress is looking back on TRA with realism and patience. There have clearly been many bills submitted to change one or another important element of the law, as there have been in every year for decades, but the prospects of these backtracking exercises appear bleak. Members seem to have expected an initial adverse reaction, for the reasons expressed above, and appear to be prepared to weather it. The chairmen of both tax-writing committees, as well as the ranking minority member in the Senate, have made it clear that their preference is for a period of stability. This path has substantive as well as political merit; as taxpayers become more acquainted with the changes in the new law, as the rate reductions are fully phased in and the vanishing deductions are fully phased out, the law should become easier to deal with and marginally simpler.

There is even the chance that, with a long enough respite from major structural change, there could be salutary developments that will engender a positive public response. Just as news stories of non-taxpaying high-income individuals (as well as corporations) helped to generate public distrust, so could more favorable accounts eventually help to reverse it. The 1984 law has already helped to some degree by reducing the number of upper-income nontaxable returns; TRA could benefit, if the legislative process can wait long enough, from its own advances against vertical and horizontal inequity.

Thus, there is no major push to revise TRA, and no sign of one in the immediate future. The remaining question is whether contingencies could arise to change that. The remainder of this paper will address that possibility.

Internal Pressure for Change

One tax authority recently argued, "There are so many fundamental flaws in the 1986 Act, it is likely to unravel."[19] This argument raises the rather basic question of just what TRA is.

The most fundamental provision of TRA, the substantial reduction of tax rates, has a powerful defense in its popularity. The second fundamental pillar, the broadened tax base, has an equal defense in the nation's budgetary shortfall. What remains at issue is exactly how this base broadening was achieved. One view would be that certain of the base broadening steps are indeed vulnerable, but could be altered or replaced without changing the basic nature of TRA. At least one provision, in my judgment, is very nearly essential.

This section will briefly discuss the implications of four prominent provisions of TRA. In several instances, the subject matter would seem to be more on the turf of an accountant or a lawyer, and this paper will attempt only to set up appropriate warning flags and raise the issues.

Limitation on Passive Losses

One of the most widely heralded provisions of TRA was the limitation on passive losses, which was a sledgehammer attempt at stamping out tax shelters. This provision was introduced within the Senate Finance Committee, and filled a potentially fatal revenue hole.

The passive loss provision has received considerable criticism because of the burden it puts on passive investors who intend to earn positive returns but simply have bad luck; and because of its complexity. On the latter ground, the reception accorded to Form 8582 was probably one of the low spots of the tax filing season.

It is probably true that the passive loss rules will become easier to manage with familiarity and time, but pressures for change will remain. One of the contributions of practitioners over the coming years will have to be a sense of the pressure on the passive loss rules, given the other anti-shelter changes in TRA (especially the slowing of depreciation and the interest deductibility limitations), as well as the lower rates. If the passive loss rules could be superseded by other, possibly less radical, measures (such as extension of the at-risk rules, or some form of limitation on artificial losses [LAL]), the law and forms might be made simpler.

Indeed, the other anti-shelter provisions could conceivably be so strong that passive losses will cease to be an issue in several years. If this is true, the passive loss provision is really a kind of transition rule to raise revenue from preexisting shelters, and has no long-term role in the tax law. This interpretation makes enough intuitive sense that the original revenue estimate for the passive loss rules, which rises over five years to $11.9 billion in 1991, seems incongruous. Obviously, the allocation among the relevant provisions of revenues gained from shutting down tax shelters could be problematical, and the transition rule interpretation could still prove to be accurate. If so, we will need to know the true revenue implications of repealing the passive loss rules after a decent interval, considering that they will still trap some losses of non-shelter businesses.

Limitation on Non-Business Interest

A second area of complexity and pressure for change, alluded to earlier, is the treatment of interest expense. To raise revenue and as a disincentive to excessive reliance on credit, the law draws distinctions among mortgage interest above and below the purchase price of and cost of improvements on owner-occupied homes; interest on loans for education; interest on loans for medical care; interest on loans to finance the holding of financial assets; and interest on loans to finance consumption. Some attempts have already been made to simplify this area, but it remains one that could complicate the tax filing of taxpayers with relatively unsophisticated financial affairs.

The interest limitations have a significant revenue impact, rising to $9.6 billion in 1991 by the original estimates; thus, simplifying the rules cannot be undertaken lightly. Perhaps the only way to raise an equivalent amount of revenue in a related fashion would be to impose some kind of overall cap on non-business interest at a level low enough to bind some homeowners. This would be a significant departure from past policy, even the simplifications already considered; it would likely meet with considerable resistance.

Alternative Minimum Tax

The alternative minimum tax has a revenue gain that is smaller than those of the passive loss and interest allocation rules, and its revenue gain is falling, rather than rising, over time. This is probably because of the several accounting changes that TRA made relative to the pre-existing minimum tax. However, this pattern does not indicate that these changes could be costlessly reversed, because there would be a mirror-image pattern of declining revenue losses from the loosening of the accounting provisions. The minimum tax is inherently complicating, in that it imposes on some taxpayers the requirement of calculating two separate taxes; and there is little doubt that TRA's minimum tax so burdens many more taxpayers than did the prior law's.

In a revenue-short world, dispensing with or minimizing the role of the minimum tax would require tightening some of the included preferences under the ordinary tax. Some such steps have been discussed (including long-term contracts and installment sales), but they would be extremely controversial.

Capital Gains

A keystone provision of TRA was its elimination of the exclusion for long-term capital gains; this raised considerable revenue from the upper-income groups, which was important for distributional reasons. Because the great bulk of the income of the well-to-do is realized in the form of capital gains, the exclusion had a built-in army of articulate and influential supporters. When the business community's advocates for the bill spoke up in 1986, the capital gains exclusion repeal was the one provision which caused them to express some hesitation. Now, restoration of the exclusion is the first objective of many of the losers of the battle of 1986.

If the capital gains exclusion is restored, it could easily be the beginning of a rollback of the fundamentals of TRA. The reward for the surrendering of tax preferences, and the only meaningful deterrent against their reintroduction, is the low top-bracket marginal tax rate. If the tax rate for capital gains and that for ordinary income are decoupled, with the best organized and most articulate interests focusing on the capital gains rate, the pressure to hold the ordinary-income rate down (and therefore, the preferences out) will be greatly reduced. In that circumstance, the objectives of TRA will be in real jeopardy.

The capital gains exclusion was a hot topic in 1987 and early 1988, but the flames seem to have cooled somewhat. Capital gains as an issue relies on the supply-side economics argument that cutting the applicable tax rate raises revenue. Despite extravagant claims by some economists, the revenue estimators for the Congress have held to a more conventional tack.[20] The greatest danger to TRA is that the Congress could succumb to the supply-side arguments in a desperate search for paper revenues in the face of some contingency. Two possible scenarios for this and other threats to TRA are described below to close this paper.

The Budget Deficit

The federal budget deficit is thought by some to pose a serious threat to TRA, and indeed to the income tax itself. The theory goes that the income tax has proved itself incapable of producing sufficient revenue to fund the federal government; some would argue that TRA has reinforced this criticism. By this reasoning, either a large supplementary tax is needed, which would demote the income tax from its current role as the major revenue source; or the income tax must be replaced altogether. The presumed replacement or supplement is a tax on consumption, most frequently a value-added tax (VAT).

It is, of course, uncertain exactly how (and even if) the federal government will mount a frontal assault on its deficit. The precise nature of that assault will have a lot to do with the optimal choice of weaponry. Nonetheless, if there is some support from the spending side, it should be apparent that the income tax could bear considerable additional responsibility. This is even more true after TRA than before.

My colleague Rudolph G. Penner and I recently prepared our own analysis of the deficit problem.[21] We concluded that a broad-based consumption tax is unnecessary to deal with the deficit, and indeed that it would be undesirable. We find it too regressive in its basic form, and too complex and costly if the regressivity is remedied through exclusions or (especially) differential rates. Further, we believe that the alleged advantages of consumption taxes in terms of saving behavior and trade are exaggerated. Finally, we believe that the enactment and implementation of such a tax would take too long for any realistic deficit reduction program.

There are remaining leakages in the income tax base that could be closed to make significant progress against the deficit. Some analysts surely would argue that further base broadening would be too politically painful and too administratively complex. Such arguments must be respected, though it is hard to imagine alternatives that would be politically painless and administratively simple; a broad-based consumption tax would certainly fail on both counts. But if worst came to worst, we must recognize that small increases in the tax rates under TRA would have adverse economic effects far less than continuation of budget deficits at current levels. Especially given the enormous progress made by TRA in reducing rates, the notion that any tax rate increase, however small, would entail significant economic costs is simply not credible.

The Next Recession

At some future date, hopefully distant but possibly near, the nation's rate of economic growth will fall to negative levels. At that time, as in every similar period in modern economic history, the deficit will be driven upward. If the deficit has not before then been brought into line, we will face painful choices. The danger is that the natural upward pressure on the deficit will so offset the normal reduction of private credit demands that interest rates will remain high; and indeed that the monetary authorities may have to support interest rates to attract credit from the rest of the world and defend the value of the dollar. With the large federal deficit at the root of this conundrum, fiscal policy will be unavailable to slow the economy's decline.

Some would see this scenario as another threat to TRA and the income tax. The argument is that deficit reduction will be needed, contrary to the normal stance of fiscal policy in a recession. Increases in the income tax, the argument continues, would be counterproductive because they would discourage investment. Instead, the nation will be forced to impose taxes on consumption.

I find this argument unpersuasive. Taxes that discourage consumption would be just as procyclical as taxes that discourage investment. Indeed, in a recession, we would expect that investment would already be discouraged by a lack of final demand. To further reduce consumption would seem to be the best way to hold investment down.

This argument does not suggest that increasing the income tax will be a good strategy in the next recession; it suggests, rather, that there will be no good strategy in the next recession if we have not already put the deficit under control. The message to the wise is to avoid such an unprecedented no-win situation.

Conclusion

I have set out to assess the health of the Tax Reform Act of 1986. Like any two-year-old that I have ever known, it is not yet ready to run a marathon. However, within obvious and realistic limits, the health of the new law is good.

Public reaction to TRA has been less than enthusiastic; but public opinion of the old law was poor, and the public's reaction to any conceivable alternative to TRA would have been worse. The Congress is, by all appearances, cognizant of this reality, and will probably let the baby mature.

TRA has some possible flaws, but those are for the most part remediable or replaceable without changing the basic nature of the law. There are contingencies, such as action against the deficit, that would put added burdens on TRA; but by any reasonable measure it is better able to bear them than its predecessor. There are other contingencies, like a near-term recession, that could strain TRA; but that is not because of its own weakness, but rather because of that of our current overall fiscal policy.

By this interpretation, the new law should continue fundamentally intact, if not unchanged in detail, into the foreseeable future.

Notes

1. *Tax Notes*, October 6, 1986, pp. 73–75; Joseph J. Minarik, "Appendix: The Yield of a Comprehensive Income Tax," in Joseph A. Pechman, editor, *Comprehensive Income Taxation* (Washington, DC: Brookings, 1977), pp. 277–98.

2. An excellent explanation of the logic of this proposition is John F. Witte, *The Politics and Development of the Federal Income Tax* (Madison, WI: University of Wisconsin Press, 1985). Attempts at explanations of its falsehood include Jeffrey H. Birnbaum and Alan S. Murray, *Showdown at Gucci Gulch* (New York: Random House, 1987); and Joseph J. Minarik, "How Tax Reform Came About," Chapter 9 of this volume.

3. Advisory Commission on Intergovernmental Relations (ACIR), *Changing Public Attitudes on Governments and Taxes* (Washington, DC: U.S. Government Printing Office, 1983), appendix tables E and F–2, pp. 39 and 42; and tables 2 and 3, pp. 8–9.

4. Dorothea Riley, "Individual Income Tax Returns: Selected Characteristics from the 1983 Taxpayer Usage Study," U.S. Department of the Treasury, Internal Revenue Service, *Statistics of Income Bulletin*, Summer 1984, pp. 45–64.

5. The Roper Organization, *The American Public and the Income Tax System, Vol. I: Summary Report*, July 1978, p. 42.

6. *Washington Post*, March 29, 1988, p. E1.

7. *Washington Post*, March 20, 1988, p. A1.

8. Telephone conversation with Ron Sebastian of the Internal Revenue Service.

9. ACIR, *Changing Public Attitudes*, table 7, p. 13.

10. *Tax Notes*, April 25, 1988, p. 532.

11. See a series of articles by Donald L. Barlett and James B. Steele, *Philadelphia Inquirer*, April 10–16, 1988, p. A1.

12. *Tax Notes*, April 11, 1988, p. 283.

13. Telephone conversation with Ron Sebastian of the Internal Revenue Service.

14. *Tax Notes*, April 25, 1988, p. 433.

15. Telephone conversation with Ron Sebastian of the Internal Revenue Service.

16. ACIR, *Changing Public Attitudes*, appendix tables E and F–2, pp. 39 and 42; and tables 2 and 3, pp. 8–9.

17. ACIR, *Changing Public Attitudes*, table 7, p. 13.

18. David F. Bradford, "On the Incidence of Consumption Taxes," in Charles E. Walker and Mark A. Bloomfield, editors, *The Consumption Tax: A Better Alternative?* (Cambridge, MA: Ballinger, 1987); Robert E. Hall and Alvin Rabushka, *Low Tax,*

Simple Tax, Flat Tax (New York: McGraw-Hill, 1983); and *The Flat Tax* (Stanford, California: Hoover Institution Press, 1985); Charles E. McLure, Jr., *The Value-Added Tax: Key to Deficit Reduction?* (Washington, DC: American Enterprise Institute, 1987).

19. *Tax Notes*, May 2, 1988, p. 546.

20. Congressional Budget Office, *How Capital Gains Tax Rates Affect Revenues: The Historical Evidence* (Washington, DC: U.S. Government Printing Office, March 1988).

21. Joseph J. Minarik and Rudolph G. Penner, "Fiscal Choices," in Isabel V. Sawhill, editor, *Challenge to Leadership* (Washington, DC: Urban Institute Press, 1988).

PART V
PERSISTENT DEFICITS AND THE IMPLICATIONS FOR THE 1990s

11 • Fiscal Reality and
Exploding Myths

It has become almost a cliché to say that the next president will inherit a budget mess. Cliché suggests calm. We have endured more than seven years of budget strife, and the sense of crisis has evaporated. But the nation is accumulating future liabilities in unprecedented amounts, and may be moving closer to a true economic crisis. It is important that we understand the costs that we are incurring and the risks that we are running before we set our economic strategy for the next four years.

The federal budget is farther from balance than in any economic expansion since World War II. This greatly reduces our economic policy flexibility both domestically and internationally. Meanwhile, we face a demographically induced fiscal crunch early in the next century. In these circumstances, the budget deficit imposes a long-term pressure on our living standards and threatens to interrupt our current economic expansion.

Our budget problem has been both slow-growing and sudden. A gradual erosion began in the 1970s (see Table 11.1). As the Vietnam War ended, defense spending dropped sharply. That change plus an income tax surtax left the federal budget with a small surplus in fiscal 1969—the last surplus we have seen.

In the succeeding years, defense spending continued to recede, reaching a trough at 4.8 percent of GNP in 1979. Net interest remained roughly constant at 1.7 percent of GNP in the same year. But non-defense spending more than filled the gap, increasing to 14.1 percent of GNP. With revenues down slightly at 18.9 percent of GNP, the deficit

---

Reprinted from *Challenge* 31:4, 4–13. Based on Chapter 9, coauthored with Rudolph G. Penner, in *Challenge to Leadership*, Isabel V. Sawhill, ed., The Urban Institute Press, Washington, D.C., 1988.

Table 11.1

The Federal Budget Totals, 1954–88 Fiscal Years
Percentages of GNP

Year	Defense	Non-defense Social Security	Non-defense Other	Non-defense Total	Net interest	Total	Revenue	Deficit
1954	13.3	0.9	3.6	4.5	1.3	19.2	18.9	0.3
1955	11.1	1.1	4.3	5.4	1.3	17.7	16.9	0.8
1956	10.2	1.3	4.2	5.5	1.2	16.9	17.8	−0.9
1957	10.3	1.5	4.3	5.9	1.2	17.4	18.2	−0.8
1958	10.4	1.8	4.8	6.7	1.2	18.3	17.7	0.6
1959	10.2	2.0	5.7	7.8	1.2	19.1	16.5	2.7
1960	9.5	2.3	5.0	7.3	1.4	18.2	18.3	−0.1
1961	9.6	2.4	5.6	8.0	1.3	18.9	18.2	0.6
1962	9.4	2.6	6.0	8.5	1.2	19.2	17.9	1.3
1963	9.1	2.7	5.9	8.5	1.3	18.9	18.1	0.8
1964	8.7	2.6	6.2	8.8	1.3	18.8	17.9	0.9
1965	7.5	2.6	6.2	8.8	1.3	17.6	17.4	0.2
1966	7.9	2.8	6.3	9.1	1.3	18.2	17.7	0.5
1967	9.0	3.1	6.5	9.5	1.3	19.8	18.7	1.1
1968	9.6	3.4	6.7	10.0	1.3	21.0	18.0	3.0
1969	8.9	3.5	6.0	9.5	1.4	19.8	20.1	−0.3
1970	8.3	3.7	6.4	10.1	1.5	19.8	19.5	0.3
1971	7.5	4.0	7.0	11.0	1.4	19.9	17.7	2.2
1972	6.9	4.1	7.7	11.8	1.3	20.0	18.0	2.0
1973	6.0	4.5	7.4	11.8	1.4	19.2	18.0	1.2
1974	5.6	4.6	7.3	11.9	1.5	19.0	18.6	0.4
1975	5.7	5.1	9.5	14.6	1.5	21.8	18.3	3.5
1976	5.3	5.3	9.8	15.0	1.6	21.9	17.6	4.3
1977	5.0	5.4	9.2	14.6	1.5	21.2	18.4	2.8
1978	4.8	5.4	9.3	14.7	1.6	21.1	18.4	2.7
1979	4.8	5.3	8.7	14.1	1.7	20.6	18.9	1.6
1980	5.0	5.6	9.5	15.1	2.0	22.1	19.4	2.8
1981	5.3	6.0	9.1	15.1	2.3	22.7	20.1	2.6
1982	5.9	6.5	8.7	15.1	2.7	23.8	19.7	4.1
1983	6.3	6.7	8.6	15.3	2.7	24.3	18.1	6.3
1984	6.2	6.4	7.5	13.9	3.0	23.1	18.1	5.0
1985	6.4	6.5	7.9	14.3	3.3	24.0	18.6	5.4
1986	6.5	6.4	7.4	13.9	3.2	23.6	18.3	5.3
1987	6.4	6.4	6.8	13.2	3.1	22.8	19.4	3.4
1988	6.1	6.5	6.7	13.2	3.2	22.6	19.2	3.4

Sources: Budget of the United States; Congressional Budget Office.

Notes: Items may not add to totals due to rounding; Social Security total includes Medicare where applicable.

expanded to a now seemingly modest (but then seemingly excessive) 1.6 percent of GNP.

The 1980s took these developments suddenly to their illogical conclusion. By the end of the Carter Administration, there was a nationwide consensus that U.S. defense capabilities had eroded substantially and needed to be rebuilt. President Reagan took President Carter's proposed defense buildup several steps further, however, and by 1986 defense spending had grown to 6.5 percent of GNP. Cutbacks in nondefense spending were not nearly sufficient to make room for this defense explosion, leaving total nondefense spending at 13.9 percent of GNP. The enormous 1981 tax cuts reduced revenues to 18.3 percent of GNP. And all of the red ink caused by these indiscretions built up a huge debt burden, pushing the annual debt service cost to 3.2 percent of GNP. The federal deficit, four years after the beginning of the economic recovery, had soared to 5.3 percent of GNP. This far exceeded the level of any previous peacetime nonrecession year.

From the perspective of budget balance, these developments—the high defense spending of the 1960s, the high domestic spending of the 1970s, and the tax cuts and the growing interest burden of the 1980s—gave us the worst of all possible worlds.

Since 1986, there have been some salutary changes. First, the defense buildup of the 1980s has been slowed, with real spending flat or declining. Second, tax increases legislated in 1982, 1984, and 1987 have begun to take effect, and the Tax Reform Act of 1986 has provided a short-run revenue bonus. Third, restraint on domestic spending has begun to show up in the budget totals. And finally, continuing economic growth has helped to hold spending down and push revenues up. A substantial fly in this ointment, however, is the large accumulated federal debt and its associated interest burden. In the latest budget figures for 1988, defense spending is projected at 6.1 percent of GNP, nondefense spending at 13.2 percent, and debt service at 3.2 percent. With revenues projected at 19.2 percent of GNP, that leaves a deficit of 3.4 percent of GNP. This figure is down from 1986, but still well above the levels in the economic expansions prior to the 1980s.

Where Are We Going?

The budget projections of the Congressional Budget Office (CBO) suggest that these deficit-reduction efforts will continue to bear fruit. CBO's projected deficit rises slightly in dollar terms from 1987 through 1989, in part because of temporary revenue losses caused by the phasing in of tax reform, and in part because of outlays that were postponed, rather than eliminated, by some earlier deficit-control legislation. Because GNP is expected to grow as well, however, the deficit increases only from 3.4 percent of GNP in 1987 to 3.5 percent in 1989. In the latter year, the projected deficit resumed a gradual decline, falling to 2.1 percent of GNP in 1993, the end of the five-year planning horizon.

To some, these projections represent nirvana. As the deficit slowly declines, growth expands the size of the economy relative to our debt and debt-service costs, making our interest burden easier to bear. At some point beyond our customary five-year budget planning horizon, the deficit would recede into its normal historical range, and the economy would be back on the familiar budgetary turf of the 1950s and 60s.

Unfortunately, this comforting scenario is less than a sure thing. Several forces could easily push the economy and the budget off the desired path; and without further deficit reduction, economic misfortune is only more likely. In fact, one might argue figuratively that this apparently safe economic path runs right along the edge of a cliff.

Risks Along the Way

There are several reasons why a standard five-year budget projection, under any circumstances, is inherently optimistic. There are other reasons why the current five-year budget projection is by its nature even more optimistic than usual.

First of all, budget projections almost always assume continuous economic growth at historically average rates. The choice of average historical growth rates is not in and of itself optimistic; obviously, there are precedents for economic growth rates faster than the historical average. What is optimistic, however, is the assumption of continuous economic growth. Five-year uninterrupted expansions are rare in our economic history. And five more years of continuous growth on top of our current economic expansion would be unprecedented. A self-correcting imbalance in the economy (such as between consumer demand and inventories) could easily arise in such a mature expansion.

If a recession should occur, the federal deficit would jump enormously, as revenues decline and transfer payments climb. (CBO estimated last year that a recession of the depth and duration of 1974–75 would increase the deficit by over $100 billion.) Fiscal policy would be well out of balance, probably precluding fiscal stimulus as a counter-cyclical tool; and the Federal Reserve could be forced to support interest rates somewhat to defend the dollar and assist in financing the deficit. Thus, an unexpected downturn would send the deficit skyward and also render macroeconomic management much more difficult.

Second, budget projections assume that discretionary spending increases only in step with inflation. With continuous economic growth and a progressive tax structure, this assumption virtually guarantees a falling projected deficit. Constant real program spending is an optimistic assumption at any time, given the frequent emergence of national needs and government's eagerness to meet them. However, at this time, this assumption is even more optimistic than usual. Pressures are already felt for added spending on welfare reform, including benefit increases; catastrophic and long-term care insurance for the elderly; expansions of education programs; initiatives aimed at poverty, the underclass, and victims of structural economic change; the new burden of fighting AIDS; inadequate FDIC and FSLIC insurance reserves; and deteriorating infrastructure after years of budgetary stringency, among other programs.

The CBO projections also assume zero real growth in defense spending. However, the new hardware ordered during the defense buildup of the early 1980s is now being delivered, requiring additional expenditures for manning, training, and maintenance. And tensions in the Persian Gulf, or any other military contingency, could add still further pressures on defense spending.

In short, the deficit is projected on a razor's edge of control only with an assumption of flat program spending, and with no allowance for any possible contingencies on the spending side. This favorable projection is thus highly tenuous.

There is a third reason why current budget projections may be optimistic: They assume declining real interest rates. Rising interest rates would increase the federal government's debt-service costs significantly; after five years, a one-percentage-point increase in interest rates would raise annual net interest expense by $30 billion. (The large increase in the national debt has made the budget far more sensitive to interest rates; at the beginning of the decade, the comparable interest rate effect was only about $7 billion.) But perhaps more important, higher interest rates would threaten the expansion by discouraging investment and consumption financed by debt.

The economy is now extraordinarily vulnerable to higher interest rates precisely because of the large federal deficit. A brief look at historical data on U.S. incomes and expenditures will indicate why (see Table 11.2). Through virtually all of the post-World War II period, the sum of U.S. expenditures on consumption, investment, and government was less than the GNP; in other words, the United States ran a trade surplus. In the 1980s, however, in large part (though not entirely) because federal spending has exceeded revenues, the total of what we have spent has exceeded what we have produced. This has required the United States to import more than it has exported, and paying for this excess of foreign goods and services has meant borrowing from foreigners. Today, U.S. credit demands from the rest of the world equal $150 billion per year. The federal deficit adds directly to these credit demands; and the federal government is the largest single borrower in line for credit.

These credit needs threaten U.S. financial markets. Should foreign investors refuse credit to the United States, the shortage of financial capital would drive up U.S. interest rates. This increase would continue until some U.S. borrowers ceased seeking credit because of the higher interest rates, thereby relieving the upward pressure. Because the federal government could not withdraw its credit demands—indeed, with interest costs rising, the federal government would need to borrow more—it would necessarily fall to private borrowers (business investors and consumers of household durables) to postpone their spending plans. In other words, there would be a recession. And in fact, because the growing national debt has increased the federal government's irreducible credit demands, the pressure on private spending—and thus, the resulting recession—would necessarily be greater.

An example of the power of this influence arose in 1987. Early in that year, foreign private investors apparently lost interest in lending to the United States. That left the task to foreign central banks, which intervened to support the dollar in the amount of at least $60 billion and possibly substantially more. The resulting increase in U.S. interest rates is said by some to have lured investors from the stock market to the bond market, resulting in last October's stock market crash. Had foreign central banks not picked up the slack and extended credit to the United States—and the substantial losses that the central banks have endured in the process have become important political issues in some countries—the rise in U.S. interest rates could have proceeded farther, possibly choking off economic growth.

Some would argue that foreign investors have nowhere else to go to

Table 11.2

U.S. Production and Spending, 1954–87
Billions of current $

Year	Production (GNP)	Consumption	Investment	Government purchases	Total spending	Production less spending (net exports)
1954	372.5	239.8	54.1	76.0	369.9	2.6
1955	405.9	257.9	69.7	75.3	402.9	3.0
1956	428.2	270.6	72.7	79.7	423.0	5.3
1957	451.0	285.3	71.1	87.3	443.7	7.3
1958	456.8	294.6	63.6	95.4	453.6	3.3
1959	495.8	316.3	80.2	97.9	494.4	1.5
1960	515.3	330.7	78.2	100.6	509.5	5.9
1961	533.8	341.1	77.1	108.4	526.6	7.2
1962	574.6	361.9	87.6	118.2	567.7	6.9
1963	606.9	381.7	93.1	123.8	598.6	8.2
1964	649.8	409.3	99.6	130.0	638.9	10.9
1965	705.1	440.7	116.2	138.6	695.5	9.7
1966	772.0	477.3	128.6	158.6	764.5	7.5
1967	816.4	503.6	125.7	179.7	809.0	7.4
1968	892.7	552.5	137.0	197.7	887.2	5.5
1969	963.9	597.9	153.2	207.3	958.4	5.6
1970	1,015.5	640.0	148.8	218.2	1,007.0	8.5
1971	1,102.7	691.6	172.5	232.4	1,096.5	6.3
1972	1,212.8	757.6	202.0	250.0	1,209.6	3.2
1973	1,359.3	837.2	238.8	266.5	1,342.5	16.8
1974	1,472.8	916.5	240.8	299.1	1,456.4	16.3
1975	1,598.4	1,012.8	219.6	335.0	1,567.4	31.1
1976	1,782.8	1,129.3	277.7	356.9	1,763.9	18.8
1977	1,990.5	1,257.2	344.1	387.3	1,988.6	1.9
1978	2,249.7	1,403.5	416.8	425.2	2,245.5	4.1
1979	2,508.2	1,566.8	454.8	467.8	2,489.4	18.8
1980	2,732.0	1,732.6	437.0	530.3	2,699.9	32.1
1981	3,052.6	1,915.1	515.5	588.1	3,018.7	33.9
1982	3,166.0	2,050.7	447.3	641.7	3,139.7	26.3
1983	3,405.7	2,234.5	502.3	675.0	3,411.8	−6.1
1984	3,772.2	2,430.5	664.8	735.9	3,831.2	−58.9
1985	4,010.3	2,629.4	641.6	818.6	4,089.6	−79.2
1986	4,235.0	2,799.8	671.0	869.7	4,340.5	−105.5
1987	4,486.2	2,966.0	716.4	923.8	4,606.2	−119.9

Source: Economic Report of the President, 1988.
Note: Items may not add to totals due to rounding.

park their money, and that the investments they have already made in the United States commit them to support our economy; thus, the United States need not limit its dependence on foreign credit. While it is impossible to disprove this line of reasoning, it can be relied upon only at enormous risk. If the United States is in fact the borrower of choice because of its reputation for political and economic stability, our recent budgetary behavior must put that status into some question. And if foreign investors should at some point decide to cut their exchange-rate losses on loans to U.S. borrowers, or if they should find preferable alternative investments—and such decisions could be sudden—it will be too late to head off disastrous consequences. Our current economic course is thus much like playing Russian roulette: The next chamber is probably empty; but then again, it may not be.

One reason to push our luck further might be fear that the fiscal restraint of narrowing the deficit could cause a recession. This fear is probably unfounded, however, if the movement toward budget balance is held within reasonable speed limits (1 percent of GNP per year is probably well within bounds), because monetary policy can compensate. And any risk of deficit reduction must be weighed against the far greater risks of facing the next recession before significant deficit reduction is undertaken.

Thus, the question is not really whether the nation should reduce its budget deficit, but rather how. The risks of inaction are enormous, and as the national debt accumulates and the resultant debt service burden grows, those risks only worsen.

Things We Need to Know

Two changes in recent budgets have important implications. First, net interest has increased enormously; in fact, it has been the fastest grow-ing item in the budget. From 1969 to 1979, net interest increased only from 1.4 percent to 1.7 percent of GNP; since 1979, it has mush-roomed to 3.2 percent of GNP. Net interest has thus crowded other spending of all types out of the budget. The federal government neces-sarily must collect in taxes and pay to its creditors 3.2 percent of GNP before it can undertake any other activities; and if federal spending is somehow constrained to some maximum percentage of GNP, other activities must give way. This reality is both a powerful argument against the budgetary excesses of the recent past, and an indication of how painful corrective action will be in the future.

Second, while nondefense, noninterest spending has trended generally upward over the 1970s and the 1980s, that trend has been fueled largely by Social Security and Medicare. In 1969, Social Security and Medicare combined consumed only 3.5 percent of GNP; but by 1988, they had increased to 6.5 percent of GNP. And while the spending restraint of the early 1980s left Social Security and Medicare generally unscathed, it hit hard at the rest of the domestic budget. Thus, nondefense spending other than Social Security and Medicare is now at a level relative to GNP that is comparable to that of the early 1960s, before the Great Society was born. In 1964, non-Social Security, nondefense spending was 6.2 percent of GNP; by 1976, it increased to 9.8 percent; but it fell to 6.7 percent by 1988, and by 1993 it is projected to fall further to 6.1 percent of GNP.

There are two lessons from this perspective on the budget:

1. Administrations have long sought to hold total spending to no more than about 21 percent of GNP; so, because of the defense buildup and the growth of net interest, the continued expansion of Social Security and Medicare necessarily squeezed other domestic spending. Yet there was virtually no discussion or debate of the merits of this path relative to any conceivable alternative.

2. If domestic spending is targeted for a dominant share of deficit reduction in the near future, the politically powerful Social Security and Medicare programs must be cut; after the program cuts of the 1980s and the growth of the social insurance programs over the last two decades, Social Security and Medicare simply comprise a much greater share of domestic spending.

This development is apparent in federal revenues as well as spending (see Table 11.3). Over the post-Korean War period, there has been a gentle upward trend of revenues relative to GNP, with pronounced peaks during the Vietnam War and in 1980–81. However, revenues exclusive of Social Security taxes exhibit a distinct downward trend, falling from about 15 percent of GNP in the 1950s to about 12 percent of GNP in the 1980s. If Social Security is not a part of the budget problem, as some would argue, then the falling share of non-Social Security taxes certainly is.

Social Security will play an increasingly important role in budget policy. As is only now becoming widely understood, the Social Security retirement system is accumulating significant annual surpluses, and will continue to do so into the next century in anticipation of the costs of the retirement of the baby boom generation. The Social Security sur-

Table 11.3

Detail of Federal Revenue Sources, 1954–88 Fiscal Years
Percentages of GNP

Year	Total	Social insurance	Other
1954	18.9	2.0	16.9
1955	16.9	2.0	14.9
1956	17.8	2.2	15.6
1957	18.2	2.3	15.9
1958	17.7	2.5	15.2
1959	16.5	2.4	14.0
1960	18.3	2.9	15.4
1961	18.2	3.2	15.0
1962	17.9	3.1	14.8
1963	18.1	3.4	14.8
1964	17.9	3.5	14.4
1965	17.4	3.3	14.1
1966	17.7	3.5	14.2
1967	18.7	4.1	14.6
1968	18.0	4.0	14.0
1969	20.1	4.2	15.9
1970	19.5	4.5	15.0
1971	17.7	4.5	13.2
1972	18.0	4.6	13.4
1973	18.0	4.9	13.1
1974	18.6	5.3	13.3
1975	18.3	5.6	12.8
1976	17.6	5.3	12.2
1977	18.4	5.5	12.9
1978	18.4	5.6	12.8
1979	18.9	5.7	13.3
1980	19.4	5.9	13.5
1981	20.1	6.1	13.9
1982	19.7	6.4	13.3
1983	18.1	6.3	11.8
1984	18.1	6.5	11.6
1985	18.6	6.7	11.9
1986	18.3	6.8	11.6
1987	19.4	6.9	12.5
1988	19.2	7.1	12.1

Sources: Budget of the United States; Congressional Budget Office.
Note: Items may not add to totals due to rounding.

pluses—$37 billion in 1988, rising to $97 billion in 1993—underscore the imbalance in the non-Social Security part of the budget. Exclusive of Social Security, the deficit is now $195 billion, rising—in contrast to the deficit in the total budget—to $231 billion in 1993.

The accumulation of a Social Security surplus, by itself, will have little effect on the baby boomers' retirement years. When the federal government withdraws those monies from the trust fund, it will be spending more than it takes in, and the fiscal policy implications will be the same as borrowing. The Social Security reserve will have a real effect only if it is additional savings, which will allow the economy to accumulate more capital and generate more income to cover the benefits. If the federal government continues to run large deficits in the non-Social Security budget, and thereby in effect finances current spending with the Social Security surplus, there will be no additional accumulation of capital to support the retirement of the baby boomers, only a stack of meaningless federal government IOUs.

Thus, growing Social Security obligations, plus the larger national debt and its associated interest burden, should motivate us to take even more aggressive action against the deficit. Otherwise, there will be an unavoidable crimp on our standards of living in the long term, even if we avoid the potential serious economic consequences of the deficit in the near future.

Options: Deficit Targets

The first task in deficit reduction is to choose an appropriate target. Any target is bound to be controversial, because economists have taken varying views of the deficit, considering contingent liabilities in future years, inflation's effect on the value of government assets, and other factors. But the controversy is even deeper simply because preferences on the deficit largely represent individual taste. Government borrowing is an allocation of consumption toward the current generation and away from its successors. We might choose to consume less today to leave a greater store of wealth to our children; or we might choose to consume more because future generations will be better off if productivity increases, as expected.

An absolute minimalist deficit target is one that prevents the ratio of the national debt to GNP from rising; any path that fails this basic test leads to disaster. In fact, for all of the fanfare attending the current favorable budget outlook (not to belittle the painful decisions of the past six years that got us this far), the nation is now barely holding the debt-to-GNP ratio constant. This leaves nothing in reserve for any unfavorable contingency that might arise. Thus, more needs to be done, at least to attain a meaningful safety margin. History suggests the maximum deficit-to-GNP ratio of peacetime post-World War II growth years, about 2 percent, as the "why not the worst?" target. The current projected deficit does not quite reach that target, even after five more years of assumed continuous economic growth.

But there are persuasive arguments for going further, based largely on the cost of the baby boomers' retirement. Making the projected Social Security surplus into true national savings would require that the non-Social Security budget be balanced. Even using the optimistic CBO projections, that would require deficit-reduction actions—either lower spending or higher taxes or both—in the amount of $231 billion, annually, by 1993.

Reaching such a target would require enormous effort; more, perhaps, than many people realize. In fiscal 1987, defense accounted for 28 percent of net outlays, Social Security for about 20 percent, other pensions (mainly military, civil service, and Supplemental Security Income [SSI]) about 6 percent, Medicare about 8 percent, and interest on the debt about 13 percent. Allowance for offsetting contributions to pensions leaves more than 70 percent of total spending in these few programs. Cutting the deficit by $231 billion, or more than 20 percent of current outlays, thus must involve these few major programs that dominate the budget. And considering the constituencies behind Social Security, Medicare, and the national defense—plus the mandatory nature of debt service—any conceivable deficit-reduction package will likely have to increase taxes as well.

Following is an item-by-item survey of the budget that puts the most important programs into this perspective. The specific cuts suggested are by no means the only alternatives, or even necessarily the best; they are enumerated here only to give a sense of the magnitude of the task at hand.

Spending

National Defense

Defense spending appears to some observers as a veritable mother lode of deficit-reduction opportunities. Upon close observation, however, many citizens would probably hesitate. A few facts suggest why.

Major strategic weapons systems are probably the first items that come to mind in the context of deficit reduction. And yet the entire strategic function, prominent and controversial though it may be, constitutes less than 10 percent of defense budget authority. Second to mind would probably be other purchases of hardware; but total procurement, strategic and otherwise, is little more than 30 percent of defense spending. The bulk of the defense budget lies in areas of personnel, maintenance, training, and operations—areas that determine readiness and the ability to respond to far-flung crises.

Cutting spending in these areas necessarily involves risk. No amount of spending would guarantee that conflict would never break out, or that the United States would unquestionably prevail if it did; and so any level or allocation of spending must involve comparative degrees of risk. It is conceivable that the present allocation of spending is inefficient, and that funds could be cut without any additional risk. Yet when Pentagon critics suggest apparently radical reductions and reallocations, the savings relative to the CBO baseline—which already assumes only zero real growth—are quite small. Making such a fundamental shift in defense priorities, as proposed by Joshua Epstein (in *The 1988 Defense Budget*, Washington, D.C.: The Brookings Institution, 1987), would save about $10 billion annually by 1993.

There are allegations of very large inefficiencies in defense spending: maintaining redundant bases or production facilities because of the political importance of their locations, for example. There is no doubt that uncovering and eliminating any such waste would be extraordinarily helpful; but it would seem overly optimistic to count on such savings in the near future.

Social Security

The financial status of the elderly has improved dramatically over the last 20 years; but much of that improvement was due to Social Security, and is quite tenuous. While the poverty rate among the elderly is now below that for the population at large, and while the average income of the elderly is above that for all Americans, a disproportionate share of the elderly is clustered just above the poverty line—not surprisingly, in view of the intention of public policy to move as many of the elderly as possible out of poverty. Large medical expenses, especially for long-term care, can exhaust income and wipe out savings. And obviously, most elderly cannot recover from a financial setback through increased work effort.

Still, the affluence of some elderly (and the dire straits of the budget) suggest that some renegotiation of the implicit Social Security contract may be in order, if not inevitable. A postponement of capping of the annual cost-of-living adjustment (COLA) would be an inconspicuous way of reducing outlays. But any COLA reduction would adversely affect even the least well off. A less burdensome approach would be to increase the partial income taxation of benefits that was initiated in 1983. Taxing 85 percent of benefits (instead of half) for all beneficiaries (instead of only those with incomes above $25,000 for single persons and $32,000 for married couples) would raise over $15 billion per year. Those elderly who are poor would pay no tax because of the personal exemptions and standard deductions in the income tax, and any tax would be levied at the new low rates.

Important long-term savings, though with little or no impact on the budget over the next five years, could be obtained by cutting the benefit formulas on a prospective basis for the current working population. Cutting benefits in this fashion would reduce the needed long-term Social Security reserve, and could justify a corresponding reduction of the payroll tax, together with an equal increase in the income tax. Implicitly, this would move the savings into the general fund, as well as make the overall tax system more progressive. Alternatively, savings could be reallocated to the less secure Medicare trust fund.

Medicare

Rapidly rising medical-care costs have taken their toll on the Medicare program, which will face its own funding crisis at some point in the coming years. Unfortunately, failing some systemic control of medical costs, there is no guarantee that any reduction of Medicare spending will not in fact be felt by the elderly (in terms of higher out-of-pocket costs or reduced access to care) rather than by providers. Recent efforts in this regard have met with partial success at best.

CBO has identified policy changes to save $15 billion per year, with $10 billion targeted at providers (subject to the caveat above) and $5 billion at beneficiaries. Included would be a $6 billion cut of hospital fees, a $3 billion cut of physicians' fees, and a $1 billion reduction of subsidies for medical education and capital expenditures by hospitals, and a $5 billion increase in Supplemental Medical Insurance (SMI) premiums.

Other Entitlements

Beyond Social Security and Medicare, entitlements are comprised largely of the welfare and Medicaid programs and farm subsidies. The programs in the welfare area were cut aggressively in the early 1980s, and few additional savings are apparent. Agricultural subsidies have also been cut, but the outlook is notoriously volatile, and there are large inefficiencies caused by mutually offsetting subsidies offered by the United States and its international trading partners. A change of focus from price to income support, along with aggressive bargaining with our allies, might cut outlays by $6 billion.

Nondefense Discretionary Spending

As was noted earlier, domestic spending has been cut substantially. Grants to state and local governments have been especially hard hit, with general revenue sharing repealed outright. There are still some programs that would appear ripe for cutting, such as the Economic Development Administration and urban development action grants and subsidies such as those to Amtrak; but at most, $10 billion on an annual basis might be saved.

If all of these spending cuts were achieved—as politically unattainable as many of them may seem—the savings would total no more than $56 billion per year by 1993. If they phased in fairly rapidly over the intervening five years, as much as $15 billion in additional interest costs might be saved. The total of $71 billion is obviously far short of the target of $231 billion of annual deficit reduction. While there may well be other options for spending cuts, the size of the gap suggests strongly that tax increases will have to be a part of deficit reduction.

Taxation

The size of the deficit gap remaining after even a draconian spending-reduction package might suggest a new and additional tax, such as a national sales tax or a value-added tax (VAT). But a free-standing consumption tax would carry several important disadvantages. For one, it would likely take two years for the first collections of revenue, which would be a serious handicap for a deficit-reduction program. Second, it would require an additional bureaucracy of the size of that for the corporate income tax. Third, a consumption tax would be distinctly regressive, and reducing that regressivity would greatly complicate either the consumption tax itself (by exempting some products from the tax base, or assigning different rates to different products) or other tax credits or transfer programs. Advantages sometimes claimed for a consumption tax in encouraging exports and household saving are almost certainly exaggerated.

Similarly questionable is the emphasis put on improving tax compliance to reduce the deficit. Better compliance is desirable, if only to encourage honest taxpayers to continue to comply voluntarily. However, our knowledge of the "tax gap"—how big it is, and whether and how it can be reduced—is insufficient to allow us to rely on compliance to reduce the deficit. By the time such a program could be evaluated, it could be too late to correct for optimistic expectations. Instead, we might rely on predictable steps using existing taxes. The excise taxes on alcohol and tobacco could justifiably be increased; these taxes have been eroded substantially by inflation since the early 1950s. The excise tax on gasoline could be increased to slow the alarming growth of consumption. These taxes would be regressive, but small, with the cost to low-income households much less than the income tax cuts provided by the 1986 tax law. Excise tax increases could raise $20 billion per year.

Further tax increases could be undertaken through the income tax. While the changes in the 1986 tax act have caused some confusion, suggesting simple rate increases rather than more complex changes in tax rules, there are tax-base-broadening steps that would be preferable from an economic perspective. Some tax preferences that survived the 1986 tax law are employee benefits for life and health insurance (worth as much as $30 billion per year in additional revenue by 1993), upper-income pension plans and salary reduction plans ($11 billion), and the exclusion of capital gains at death ($6 billion). Smaller tax preferences could be added, along with the excise tax increases specified above, to reach a total of $90 billion by 1993.

If eliminating income-tax preferences is too politically painful or too complex, increasing income tax rates is still an option. Raising the bottom tax rate from 15 percent to 16 percent, the top tax rate from 28 percent to 32 percent, and the corporate tax rate from 34 percent to 35 percent would increase revenues by about $60 billion per year. Although this option is less attractive than broadening the tax base, its ill effects should not be exaggerated. Only eight years ago, with a maximum individual income tax rate of 70 percent, the highest-income taxpayers could keep only 30 cents of their last dollars of income. Even with the rate increases discussed above, those taxpayers could keep 68 cents on the dollar, or more than twice as much.

The tax policy menu here is substantially longer than that on the spending side. Choosing only tax increases equal to the spending cuts enumerated earlier, plus the resulting interest savings, would reduce the total deficit by about 2.5 percent of GNP. That would be enough to balance the total federal budget in 1993. However, for all of the pain, it would still fall short of the ultimate goal of balancing the non-Social Security budget. Excluding Social Security, the budget would still run a deficit of about $90 billion, which the Social Security surplus would offset. This contrast of pain and results is perhaps the best indication of the size of our deficit problem.

Conclusion

If eliminating the federal deficit were easy, it would have been done long ago. Pointing out the dangers of our current course can only steel the will; as the review of the issues above richly demonstrates, the difficulty remains.

Still, if this analysis provokes others to present alternatives, it will have served its purpose. Only an approach that can overcome the political barriers can solve the economic problem. The search for such a solution to our deficit dangers must begin.

Index

VAT, 46–49, 155
  administration of, 48
  collection costs, 48
  fairness issue, 34, 48
  impact, 47, 49
  personal exemption, 191
  as revenue supplement, 54, 196, 217
  support, 151, 165
Venture capital, tax reform impact on, 150
Voluntary compliance. *See* Income tax, compliance

Wages and salaries. *See also* Employee

fringe benefits
supplements, 40, 42
withholdings, 27, 186–87
Wealth
  accumulation of, 59–60
  taxes on, 50, 59–60
Welfare, appropriations, 207
Withholdings, 27, 186–87
  excess, 190
  interest and dividends, 31

X Tax, 191

Zero bracket amounts, 88